American School of Prehistoric Research
PEABODY MUSEUM • HARVARD UNIVERSITY
BULLETIN NO. 36

RURAL ECONOMY IN THE EARLY IRON AGE
Excavations at Hascherkeller, 1978–1981

PETER S. WELLS

With contributions by

Helmut Becker, C. Caroline Quillian, Brenda R. Benefit,
John D. Stubbs, Mary L. Hancock, and Michael Geselowitz

Artifact illustrations by Dorcas Brown

PEABODY MUSEUM OF ARCHAEOLOGY AND ETHNOLOGY
HARVARD UNIVERSITY · CAMBRIDGE, MASSACHUSETTS
1983
Distributed by Harvard University Press

The author and publisher would like to acknowledge the following people for contributing photographs to this bulletin. The numbers refer to the figure numbers in the text.

Rainer Christlein, 4, 5
C. Caroline Quillian, 6, 7, 8, 9, 11, 12, 13, 14, 15, 17, 31, 32, 40, 46, 50, 63a, 73, 74, 75
Hillel Burger, cover photo, 52, 62b, 63b, 66, 67, 70b, 70c, 88
Hillel Burger and C. Caroline Quillian, 76, 77
Karen Huang, 59, 62a, 63c, 64, 65, 68, 70a, 80
John D. Stubbs, 81, 82
Mary L. Hancock, 84, 85, 86, 87

This volume is dedicated to the memory of

Rainer Christlein
(1940–1983)

who provided constant and invaluable support
to the Hascherkeller excavations

Contents

Figures

Tables

Preface

The Hascherkeller excavation project was designed to fill a specific need in prehistoric European studies — systematic investigation of a settlement site of the early final millennium B.C., with the aim of collecting information concerning all aspects of the community's economy. Research on later European prehistory has emphasized cemetery evidence. Graves and whole cemeteries have been extensively excavated, analyzed, and published. The thousands of known bronze hoards of the period have also been widely studied. Settlement research for these centuries has lagged far behind the investigation of these other categories of sites. In the third and fourth decades of the twentieth century, some excellent research was carried out on settlements of the Late Bronze and Early Iron Ages — for example, that conducted by Bersu at the Goldberg in Württemberg (bibliography in Schröter 1975) and at Little Woodbury in Wiltshire, England (Bersu 1940), and that by Reinerth at the Wasserburg Buchau in Württemberg (1928, 1936). Unfortunately, none of these extensive early excavations have been fully published, and in the case of the Goldberg most of the material evidence was lost during World War II. Some exceptional projects carried out since 1950 have also yielded important information about settlement and economy, particularly the investigations at the Heuneburg in southern Württemberg (Kimmig 1975). Still, few settlement excavation projects have produced extensive information about the economic activities of communities.

The economy of settlements during the centuries between 1000 and 800 B.C. is of great importance for an understanding of developments in metallurgy and trade and the formation of the first central European towns during the Early Iron Age (chapter 13). The Hascherkeller project is an attempt to investigate this connection between characteristic settlements of the period and the broader changes in economy. The project has undertaken the total excavation of a typical settlement of the period — not a center of metallurgy or trade — with special emphasis on the recovery of information pertaining to the economic activities of the community living there. About half of the settlement has been excavated so far, and the rest will be investigated in coming field seasons. The Hascherkeller excavations are part of a broader project of excavation and analysis of settlement materials from the beginning of the final millennium B.C. in central Europe, the goal of which is a better understanding of the economic and social changes during the final phases of European prehistory.

Chapters 3 to 10 present the data recovered through excavation and analysis of the remains of the prehistoric settlement, along with interpretation of that data. Chapter 11 presents an interpretation of the depositional history of the site, based on the information collected through excavation. Chapters 12 and 13 offer interpretations of the excavation results and attempt to place the findings from Hascherkeller in the context of the living community and in the context of patterns of change in late prehistoric Europe. These final two chapters are somewhat speculative in attempting to fill out the picture of life in Late Bronze and Early Iron Age Europe to an extent greater than is presently possible from the archaeological data alone.

The principal information about the economy of the community at Hascherkeller is contained in the 11 largest pits on the prehistoric settlement. Since these are much discussed in the text, they are designated with the following abbreviations (see fig. 10 for trench designations):

Long pit in west side of Trench B, Cutting V = BV
Long pit in Trench C = C
Pit in Trench D, Cutting III = DIII
Pit in Trench L = L
Pit in western extension of Trench N = N west extension
Pit in north end of Trench N = N north end
Pit in south end of Trench S = S south end
Pit in Trench S with red fill = S red pit
Pit in north end of Trench S = S north end

Pit in Trench W = W
Pit on south side of Trench AA, Cutting I = AAI

All of the drawings of objects in the text are at a scale of 1:2 unless otherwise noted.

Acknowledgments

The National Science Foundation supported the excavation work at Hascherkeller (BNS78-07349) and provided the funding for this publication of the results (BNS82-09930). Earthwatch and the Center for Field Research of Belmont, Massachusetts, supplied both funds and volunteers, which contributed to the success of the field seasons. The National Geographic Society also provided financial support for the research. A grant from the Clark Fund, administered by the Faculty of Arts and Sciences of Harvard University, helped in the preparation of the illustrations that appear in this report. I thank all of these institutions and the individuals in them for their generous support of the Hascherkeller project.

Dr. Rainer Christlein of Munich and Landshut has generously made the Hascherkeller project possible. In 1977 he offered the settlement as a subject for research and has been generous and helpful in lending his support to all aspects of the work. Dr. Bernd Engelhardt (Landshut) has also provided constant support and valuable advice.

In the initial stages of planning and organizing the project, Prof. C.C. Lamberg-Karlovsky (Cambridge, Mass.), Prof. David Gordon Mitten (Cambridge, Mass.), Prof. Ruth Tringham (Berkeley, Calif.), and Dr. Peter Bogucki (Boston), offered much valuable advice. Dr. Peter Schröter (Munich) helped to assure the success of the venture.

Many individuals in Landshut were extremely kind and hospitable during the field seasons. Mrs. Maria Lindner provided many different kinds of assistance to the excavation team and its members, for which I thank her greatly. Mrs. Ilsebet-Maria Duswald, Dr. Helge Grebe, Mr. and Mrs. Wilfried Böhmer, and Mr. and Mrs. Wittmann all offered generous hospitality to us. Mr. Hans Emslander, the Eichbichler automobile dealership, the Rotary Club of Landshut, and Mr. Hans Brandstetter provided valuable logistical assistance. Mr. Josef Aiden kindly allowed us to carry out fieldwork in the fields that he farms, and Mr. Eduard Ebel constructed many vital pieces of excavation equipment in his shop.

The greatest contribution to the research effort was made by the students who worked on the excavations, doing the digging and mapping, processing finds in the field laboratory, and cheerfully carrying out their kitchen and cleaning chores. Rather than attempting to describe their individual contributions, I list them here alphabetically; those who participated for more than one field season are so marked by the number of seasons in parentheses after their names. Steven Anthony (3), Brenda Benefit (4), Ann Bristol, Julian Chang (2), Martha Davis, Linda Ellis, Steven Erwin (3), Annette Ghee, Mary Hancock (2), Adeline Hofer, Karen Huang, Katherine Kvam, Bettina Martin, Robert McCall (2), Kathryn Nickel (2), Caroline Quillian (3), Sarah Randolph, Karen Rochlin, Harold Rose, Deborah Shepherd, Barbara Smith, Simon Stoddart, John Stubbs (3), Steven Tresser, Keith Ulrich (2).

My wife Joan and stepson Nathaniel lent their assistance to the excavation efforts in 1978, 1979, and 1981, and my son Christopher provided enthusiastic moral support in 1981.

The many Earthwatch volunteers who participated in the excavation and laboratory work also contributed greatly to the success of the project, and I thank them collectively.

Prof. Joachim Boessneck (Munich) generously provided much valuable information about the animal bones recovered from the settlement. Dr. Helmut Schlichtherle (Stuttgart) helped with the collection, processing, and identification of the plant remains. Gary D. Shaffer (Binghamton, N.Y.) provided helpful advice about the daub. Dr. Gregory Houseman (Cambridge, Mass.) helped with technical terms in my translation into English of Dr. Helmut Becker's contribution about his magnetometer survey (chapter 5).

Helpful advice in the analysis and interpretation of the excavation results was provided by the following individuals: Dr. Bernd Becker (Hohenheim), Prof. Rainer Berger (Los Angeles), Dr. Peter Bogucki (Boston), Dr. Richard Bradley (Reading), Dr. Richard Meadow (Cambridge, Mass.), Prof. P. J. R. Modderman (Leiden), Mr. Steven Pendery (Cam-

xvi

bridge, Mass.), Prof. Radomir Pleiner (Prague), Dr. Peter Schröter (Munich), Dr. Susanne Sievers (Tübingen).

Dr. Ulrich Schaaff (Mainz) kindly granted permission for the inclusion of the translation of Dr. Becker's report (chapter 5), which first appeared in German in *Archäologisches Korrespondenzblatt* (vol. 9, 1979), and for the reproduction of several illustrations that first appeared in that journal (see concordance). Prof. James Wiseman (Boston) generously permitted the reproduction of many illustrations that first appeared in the preliminary reports in the *Journal of Field Archaeology*, volumes 6 (1979), 7 (1980), and 8 (1981) (see concordance).

Dorcas Brown drew most of the plans and all of the artifact drawings except figures 36a; 37e; 38j, k, and m; and 39a, which were drawn by Aaron Paul. Nancy Lambert-Brown did the final preparation of the illustrations for publication. Lorna Condon, Donna Dickerson, and Robyn Sweesy of the Publications Department, Peabody Museum, provided much valuable advice throughout the final stages of the preparation of the manuscript. Victoria Harding helped greatly with the workings of the word processor on which the manuscript was typed and edited, and Miriam Palmerola provided much advice about the coding and transmission of the manuscript to the typesetter.

1

Economic Change in Complex Societies: The Case of Central Europe

Europe north of the Mediterranean during the final millennium B.C. is an important context that has received little attention in recent anthropological discussions of the development of complex societies and urbanism. The societies living on that continent were fully metal-using, engaged in long-distance trade, and showed substantial differences in the distribution of wealth and status among their members, yet prehistoric Europeans had no cities comparable to those in the Near East, China, or Mesoamerica (Redman 1978; Lamberg-Karlovsky and Sabloff 1979). Not until around 150 B.C. did the first large-scale settlements begin to form in central Europe. Even with urban centers close by to the south in Greece, Italy, and the Mediterranean coastal lands of France and Spain, central and northern European societies remained nonurban until only decades before Roman armies overran much of the continent.

The case of European societies of the final millennium B.C. is of special interest for a number of reasons, of which two will be noted here. First, European societies were exceptional in the complexity of technology and commerce and in the maintenance of small-scale, diffuse settlement patterns until around 150 B.C. Thus Europe provides an important counter example to the regions in which such aspects of cultural complexity were directly associated with the development of urbanism. Why did the societies of Europe follow a course of cultural development different from the other regions?

Second, the patterns of change in Europe in the final thousand years before Christ are important for understanding the later development of European society and economy. Areas such as the Near East and the Mediterranean Basin were characterized by urban centers throughout the final millennium B.C. Urbanism never faltered in those lands, and many cities such as Athens and Rome have been continuously inhabited from the beginning of that millennium to the present day. In central Europe only a few of the oppida of the period 150 to 10 B.C. could be

considered cities (Cunliffe and Rowley 1976), and the pattern of settlement organization remained nonurban until after A.D. 800 (Hodges 1982), except for Roman cities and towns, which were of Mediterranean cultural origin and character, not central European. Roman cities such as Trier, Cologne, Mainz, and Augsburg declined greatly in size and in commercial activity at the end of Roman administration in the fifth century A.D., and diffuse, rural settlement patterns again came to dominate the countryside (Böhner 1958; Janssen 1976). Investigation of the economic and social developments during the final millennium B.C. can help shed light on the particular characteristics of European society that lay at the basis of the formation of the modern states that emerged during the High Middle Ages.

CHANGES IN THE FINAL MILLENNIUM B.C.

The centuries around the start of the final millennium B.C., roughly 1200 to 800 B.C., were a time of vast cultural change in Europe. During this time the great increases in technological development and scale of manufacturing began that were to characterize the economy of the entire millennium. This period marked a distinct break between the Neolithic and Bronze Age patterns of small-scale industrial productivity and the much more dynamic and larger-scale enterprises of the Iron Age.

The two centuries before 1000 B.C. are believed, on the basis of evidence from pollen samples and settlement locations, to have been warmer and dryer than the preceding period (Steensberg 1936, p. 251; Courtain et al. 1976, p. 176; Coles and Harding 1979, p. 5). Numerous settlements were established on the lakeshores of the time, which were abandoned during the eighth century B.C. and are today underwater. Others were established in high mountainous regions where no settlements had been located before. The total number of settlements in existence also increased at this time (Peroni 1979, pp. 7, 8), and much clearing of forested land was undertaken in order to gain new settlement areas. An increase in population is suggested by this evidence as well as by larger cemeteries than had previously existed. The evidence provided by both settlement and cemetery sites also suggests that settlements were for the first time regularly occupied for several centuries rather than for only a couple of generations (Bouzek et al. 1966; Peroni 1979, p. 9). This new permanence of occupation implies the application of new technical knowledge about conserving the fertility of the agricultural soils, probably through fallowing, use of manure, and perhaps crop rotation.

The changes that are clearest in the archaeological record are in the areas of bronze and pottery production. Much larger quantities of bronze have been recovered from Late Bronze and Early Iron Age sites than from those of the preceding Early and Middle Bronze Ages. The differences are difficult to quantify because comparable assemblages cannot easily be established, but inspection of the metal finds from settlements, graves, and hoards of the different phases of the Bronze Age makes the much greater amounts of metal of the Late Bronze Age readily apparent. Not only were the numbers of objects greater in the later period, but the quantity of metal comprising individual objects was much greater in the Late Bronze Age. Swords, axes, and pins of the Late Bronze Age were much larger on the average than comparable items from earlier times (cf. the objects in the catalogue sections of Müller-Karpe 1959a and Pirling 1980). Since more bronze metal was deposited in hoards, graves, and settlements in the later period, more must have been mined, traded, and cast.

Whole new categories of bronze objects appeared during the Late Bronze Age, particularly elaborate luxury goods, which are found mainly in the richest graves of the period and in some hoards. New forms of swords with thick blades for use with a slashing-and-hacking motion replaced the thin rapiers of the Middle Bronze Age, which were used for thrusting (Müller-Karpe 1962; Schauer 1971). Helmets, cuirasses, and shields made of hammered sheet bronze were produced for some of the wealthiest individuals (Hencken 1971; von Merhart 1954). Vessels of beaten sheet bronze also became common in the wealthy graves of this period (von Merhart 1952) and remained one of the hallmarks of the special material culture of wealthy persons to the birth of Christ. The manufacture of all of these special objects implies the availability of large quantities of bronze metal and the existence of specialized craftsmen skilled in new techniques of working the metal and wealthy individuals with the means to support specialists and acquire large amounts of bronze.

The material culture of communities throughout central Europe was much more uniform around 1000 B.C. than ever before. Regional styles and ornamental motifs in pottery and bronze were less marked than in the Middle Bronze Age, and forms were standardized over large regions of the continent. This new uniformity of material culture implies increased communication among communities and especially among individuals involved in manufacturing. The similarities in elite goods (swords, helmets, bronze vessels) over wide areas of Europe are especially striking, indicating particularly strong connections between wealthy individuals and the craftsmen working for them.

Personal Wealth and Settlement, 1000 to 800 B.C.

The development of new bronze crafts for the production of ornate weaponry and vessels implies the existence of persons with greater than average access to the material resources available. The increase in quantities of gold ornaments also points to the greater acquisition of wealth by some individuals (Drack 1980; Eogan 1981). The evidence from the burials suggests that patterns of the distribution of wealth were continuous from the traditions of the Middle Bronze Age (Stary 1980). Like the richer graves of the preceding period, those of the Late Bronze and earliest Iron Ages contain swords, other weapons, gold ornaments, and pottery; a few contain new features such as bronze vessels and four-wheeled wagons. The great majority of graves do not contain any such goods, but simply one or several ceramic vessels and often one or two bronze items such as pins, bracelets, razors, knives, or pendants (fig. 89). The graves in most cemeteries show a continuum of wealth from poor burials, with no grave goods or a single one, to rich burials, often with as many as 25 objects. Wealth was apparently differentially distributed, but no great gaps existed between the wealth possessed by different parts of the communities. Nor were the wealthiest persons buried in cemeteries separate from the other people, as was sometimes the case later (e.g., Christlein 1973).

Settlements of the period around 1000 B.C. were small compared to those of recent times in Europe. Calculations based upon cemetery evidence suggest that most communities had fewer than 50 individuals, and only very rarely did the number of inhabitants reach 100, possibly in some of the larger of the Swiss and southwest German lakeshore settlements. The evidence from the settlements fully corroborates that from the cemeteries. Distributions of known settlements and cemeteries (e.g., Wagner 1949–1950, p. 196, fig.1; Herrmann 1966, p. 7, fig. 1; Dehn 1972, p. 132, fig. 27) suggest that communities were spread widely over the countryside of central Europe, with denser concentrations in some areas such as broad river valleys than in others. The settlement landscape consisted exclusively of farmsteads and hamlets, without any larger agglomerations.

During this period, for the first time in European prehistory great numbers of fortified hilltop settlements were constructed throughout the continent (Herrmann 1969). In the majority of cases, these hillforts were not empty places for refuge in time of attack but were permanently occupied settlements. Results of excavations show them to have been very similar to the lowland settlements in structure and economy.

The new need for defense implied by the proliferation of the hillforts can best be understood in terms of the increasing quantities of wealth being produced, traded, and accumulated. Never before had Europeans possessed such large quantities of easily portable wealth, especially in the form of bronze but also in gold and other luxury substances such as amber and glass. The tens of thousands of hoards of bronze objects that have been found in central Europe, often containing 50 kilograms and more of metal, are the clearest examples of such accumulated and stored wealth. As individuals and communities acquired greater amounts of wealth it became increasingly necessary to protect it. Bronze and gold objects as well as other luxury goods provided ready targets for bands of raiders intent on seizing booty, a state of affairs well documented in the historical tradition of the early Middle Ages (Grierson 1959; Bloch 1961) and probably characteristic of later prehistoric times as well. The greater quantities of weapons represented in the archaeological record and their increasing effectiveness probably related directly to both the need to defend and the desire to seize such wealth. Keys also appeared in Europe for the first time, indicating a new need to lock valuables up (Pauli 1978, pp. 262–264).

Growth of New Productive Industries

Besides increased production of various categories of bronze objects, both iron and salt were first being extracted from the earth on a substantial scale in the period 1000 to 800 B.C. Though iron did not begin to replace bronze as the principal metal for tools and weapons until well after 600 B.C., from 1000 B.C. on iron was in regular use, as indicated by objects of the

metal recovered from graves and settlements (Kimmig 1964; Pleiner 1980; Pleiner, ed. 1981). Iron was first used especially as ornamental inlay in bronze objects and for blades in composite weapons and tools. The new metal was being smelted and forged in many different parts of central Europe by this time, and some of the smiths early mastered the techniques of producing high-quality products with hardened edges (Pleiner 1968). The development and expansion of ironworking was the principal technological change that affected all aspects of economic life in late prehistoric Europe.

Along with iron and the copper and tin needed for bronze, the other principal mineral to be exploited industrially in this period was salt. The saltmining carried out at Hallstatt in Upper Austria, one of the largest industrial operations in prehistoric Europe, was begun during the tenth and ninth centuries B.C., as demonstrated by a recent series of radiocarbon determinations (Barth et al. 1975). Mining equipment recovered in the galleries worked in this period shows that the operation was already highly organized and systematically executed; though with no graves found from this early period of activity at Hallstatt, we know little about the trade connections and distribution of wealth that are so well documented after 800 B.C. at the site.

The growing industries that generated iron and salt for trade in the period from 1000 to 800 B.C. and the developing commercial systems associated with them led to the formation of the first large and economically specialized communities in prehistoric Europe, the first settlements that can be designated towns (Neustupný 1969; Hensel 1970).

THE EXCAVATIONS AT HASCHERKELLER

These changes at the beginning of the final millennium B.C. are now relatively clear in rough outline. The evidence from cemeteries and hoards is abundant, but that from settlements, the most important for any understanding of economic change, is still scanty. Many settlements of the period 1000 to 800 B.C. have been partly excavated, and a very few have been substantially exposed, the best example being the Wasserburg Buchau (Reinerth 1928, 1936). Yet not one has been extensively studied with the aim of obtaining and examining evidence pertaining to the economy of the people who inhabited it. Some excellent data has been produced from the settlement at Buchau, but it has never been fully published. Many other sites have provided useful information about settlement location, size, structure, and associated material culture. Among the best examples from central Europe are Künzing (Herrmann 1974–1975), Lovčičky (Říhovský 1972), Pliening and Kirchheim (Dannheimer 1976), Dornholzhausen (Janke 1971), Berlin-Lichterfelde (von Müller 1964), Zug-Sumpf (Speck 1955), Auvernier-Nord (Arnold 1981), Zürich Grosser Hafner (Primas and Ruoff 1981), Dampierre (Pétrequin et al. 1969), and the Hohlandsberg (Bonnet 1973, 1974; Jehl and Bonnet 1968, 1971) (see map in fig. 90). But from all of these, little detailed information is available about subsistence economy, organization of production, or trade.

The aim of the excavation project at Hascherkeller has been to study, through areal exposure of the surface of a settlement, the economic organization of a typical community of the beginning of the final millennium B.C. in central Europe. In particular, evidence was sought and collected pertaining to the subsistence economy of the community, manufacturing done at the site, and trade with other communities for the acquisition of raw materials and finished products not available locally. The goal has been to better understand the background of the principal economic changes that were taking place during this period, including the growing production of bronze, the manufacture of the various new elite objects, and the start of larger industries in salt and iron extraction that played a major role in the growth of larger communities during the Early Iron Age. The principal question behind the research carried out at Hascherkeller has been the connection between the typical farming communities in Europe and the ongoing changes in industrial production and commerce.

2

Hascherkeller and Environs

GEOLOGY

Hascherkeller is located close to the center of the Tertiary Hills of Bavaria in the northern region of the Alpine Foreland between the Lech, Danube, and Inn rivers (figs. 1–3). The Tertiary Hills are divided by the Isar River, flowing from southwest to northeast; Hascherkeller is situated on the Isar, at the edge of the lowest terrace on the north bank.

The basal rocks of the Alpine Foreland were deposited during the Permian (280 to 230 million years B.P.) and especially during the Triassic Period (230 to 180 million years B.P.) in three massive series: sandstones, then limestones, and finally marls. Marine transgressions of the Cretaceous Period (135 to 63 million years B.P.) deposited on top of this sequence soft sandstones and clays. At the time of the crustal folding that created the Alps, a geosyncline, or trough, formed to the north of the new mountains in what is now the Alpine Foreland (and also to the south in what is today the Po Plain) and was gradually filled with gravels and sands carried down by mountain streams. These materials constitute the sandstones and conglomerates forming the bases of the Swiss and Bavarian plateaus. Since the Pliocene Epoch of the Tertiary Period (13 to 2 million years B.P.), this thick sedimentary sequence has been cut by rivers and streams during its slow tectonic rise, giving the landscape the characteristic form of gently rolling hills and a wide network of valleys.

The recent geological history of the region was determined by the Alpine glaciers of the Pleistocene Ice Ages. The moraines from the Alpine glaciers extend only as far north as Munich and Mühldorf an der Inn. The Tertiary Hill country was not itself glaciated, but it was much affected by fluvial outwash from the Alpine glaciers. During phases of melting, gravels and sands were carried from the glaciated regions by rivers of meltwater and laid down in thick sheets well ahead of the glaciers in the northern part of the Alpine Foreland. These sediments, deposited when the rivers were at flood level carrying glacial outwash, formed gravel and sand terraces above the present beds of the rivers. The set-

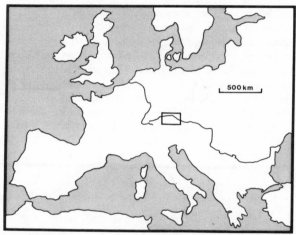

Figure 1. Map of Europe showing the location of the more detailed map in figure 2.

tlement of Hascherkeller is situated on such a terrace.

During the cold phases of the glaciations, fine sediments in the periglacial regions devoid of vegetation were picked up by winds and blown considerable distances before being deposited. These sediments, known as loess, once covered substantial portions of central Europe but have been eroded away from most regions. Loess survives in some important deposits in the Alpine Foreland, especially along the Danube between Kelheim and Passau. Smaller patches of loess are preserved elsewhere, including the narrow zones along the north bank of the Isar. The terrace on which Hascherkeller is located is covered by one such limited zone of surviving loess. Loess forms one of the best agricultural soils of central Europe; it is light, easily worked, and drains well, and hence has been a preferred soil for agriculture since the development of farming in Europe at the start of the Neolithic.

(For further discussion of the geology of the region, see Dickinson 1953, pp. 18–22; Mutton 1961, pp. 304–306; Rutte 1981, p. 238; and Kollmann n.d.)

TOPOGRAPHY

The Tertiary Hill region consists of low, gently sloping hills and a complex network of stream valleys,
and the whole landscape is bisected by the Isar River.
The basal rocks are bedded horizontally, and soft
stones predominate near the surface. Hence, there
are few rock outcrops. The landscape as a whole is
quite uniform, the principal diverging feature being
a valley four to six kilometers wide cut by the Isar
River through the undulating countryside.

   The settlement of Hascherkeller is situated on
the lowest terrace above the north bank of the Isar,
about 15 meters above the level of the river. The
terrace is broad and flat, extending about a thousand
meters to the northwest away from the river valley
before the land rises further. This stretch of terrace
between Altdorf and Essenbach represents some of
the oldest settled land in the region and has yielded
abundant archaeological material of Neolithic, Bronze
Age, Iron Age, Roman, and medieval dates (Christlein 1974, 1975, 1976; Drexler n.d.).

SOILS

The soils of the Tertiary Hill lands are for the most
part developed brown earths and constitute fertile,
easily worked humus. The river valley of the Isar
contains principally gravelly soil. The terrace on
which Hascherkeller is situated, which consists of
gravels and sands, is covered by a thick surface layer
of loess (Drexler n.d.; Gradmann 1964, pp. 381, 382).

VEGETATION

The original vegetation cover of the Tertiary Hill
region was beech-oak forest along with other trees
such as hornbeam, lime, elm, maple, Scotch pine,
and spruce, and probably with a rich ground flora of
such species as hazel, hawthorn, spindle, elder,
bracken, and bramble (Dickinson 1953, pp. 72–76;
Drexler n.d., p. 34). A somewhat different vegetation
population may have inhabited the Isar Valley. The
abundant archaeological evidence of settlement
activity from Neolithic times along the terrace on

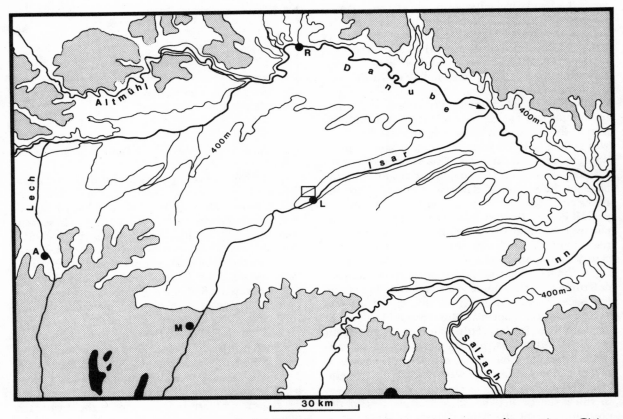

Figure 2. Map showing the situation of Hascherkeller in Lower Bavaria and surrounding regions. Cities
indicated by capital letters are Landshut, Munich, Augsburg, and Regensburg. The contour of 400 m above
sea level is labeled; all land above 500 m above sea level is indicated by screening.

which Hascherkeller is located, along the valley of the Pfettrach, and in other locations around Landshut suggests that much or most of the forest had been cleared early, during Neolithic and Bronze Age times, and remained cleared ever since.

MODERN ECONOMY

Lower Bavaria, the region in which Hascherkeller is situated, is a major agricultural region of modern West Germany. The area around the city of Landshut has a population density of 50 to 75 persons per square kilometer, low for West Germany. Landshut itself has about 80,000 inhabitants and is the largest city in Lower Bavaria.

The lands around the city, including the field on which Hascherkeller is situated, are used principally for the cultivation of cereal grains, including wheat, barley, and corn. Vegetable gardening is also carried out extensively, along with cultivation of sugar beets.

THE SITE

The settlement of Hascherkeller was discovered by Rainer Christlein, then director of the Landshut office of the Bayerisches Landesamt für Denkmalpflege, in the course of taking aerial photographs in the vicinity of Landshut in 1977. He identified the dark lines visible in portions of the field as ditches associated with a prehistoric settlement (figs. 4, 5).

Hascherkeller is the name of a hamlet on the northern outskirts of the city of Landshut. The prehistoric settlement is located on the edge of the lowest terrace of the Isar, overlooking the flat valley which is 3.5 km wide at this point. At its closest, the Isar now flows about 2.5 km from the site; but before the course of the river was brought under control during the Middle Ages, the entire valley was probably divided by meanders of the river, stagnant pools, and marshland. Since the Isar originates in the Alps, the volume of the river varies greatly during different seasons of the year. In late spring when melting in the mountains proceeds the fastest, the flow is greatest. Before it was brought under control, the Isar regularly flooded the valley. Since the prehistoric settlement lies about 15 meters above the level of the river, it would have been safe from such periodic floods. The medieval and modern city of Landshut occupies the part of the valley along the present course of the river. To the north and northwest of Hascherkeller the terrace extends about 1,000 meters back from the edge of the valley as a broad, level expanse before the land rises at the edge of the Tertiary Hills. Like Hascherkeller, the medieval and

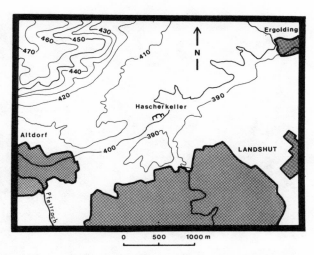

Figure 3. Map showing the location of the three enclosures of the Hascherkeller settlement along the edge of the terrace at the 400 m contour. Densely settled areas are indicated by screening. The Isar River flows from southwest to northeast just south of the area shown here.

modern towns of Altdorf and Essenbach are situated on the edge of the terrace.

The prehistoric settlement is now located in the northern half of a roughly triangular area about 230 m by 170 m that is defined by a straight path on the north, a small, unpaved road on the east, and the two-lane highway between Landshut and Altdorf on the southwest. This triangular field has long been used for farmland; during the summers from 1977 to 1981 it carried crops of corn, wheat, and barley.

When excavation began in the summer of 1978, the entire field was farmland. Since then construction on both the eastern and western sides of the field has greatly changed the landscape. Along the unpaved road forming the eastern boundary of the field next to the houses of modern Hascherkeller, cellars were dug for two new houses in 1978. Archaeologists from the Landshut office of the Bayerisches Landesamt für Denkmalpflege, under the direction of Rainer Christlein, carried out rescue excavations on that part of the site. The plan of the results of that excavation is shown in figure 72.

Upon completion of the Peabody Museum's investigations of the western extremity of the field (from Trench A west to the small road next to the modern cemetery), the city of Landshut built a parking lot on that part of the field to serve the modern cemetery just west of the site.

Figure 4. Aerial photograph of Hascherkeller, looking slightly west of north. The prehistoric settlement is located in the triangular field in the center, bounded by the long, straight path on the north, the gravel road on the east, and the two-lane highway on the southwest. The dark fillings of the two ditches of the western enclosure are visible in the light patch of soil in the western corner of the field. It was the identification of these ditches that resulted in the discovery of the site by Rainer Christlein in 1977. The road intersection at the bottom of the photograph is at the edge of the Isar Valley. The highway cuts diagonally through the terrace, and at the top of the terrace the highway turns toward the west. Just northwest of the prehistoric settlement, across the small road, is the modern cemetery complex. East of the site is the modern hamlet of Hascherkeller. North of the site are the fertile agricultural fields on the terrace. Photograph courtesy of Rainer Christlein.

Figure 5. Aerial photograph of Hascherkeller, looking west. Here the situation of modern settlement in relation to the terrace is well represented. The highway runs along the top of the terrace from the cemetery westward to the town of Altdorf, which is also situated on the edge of the terrace. The buildings to the south of the highway (left of it here) are at the edge of the terrace, as is the prehistoric settlement of Hascherkeller. Modern Hascherkeller is in the right foreground. The broad level expanse of fertile farmland extending back from the terrace edge is clearly shown here. Photograph courtesy of Rainer Christlein.

Figure 6. View from the fourth floor of a building in the northern part of Landshut, looking northwest toward Hascherkeller. The land on which the prehistoric settlement is situated is indicated by a broken line in the center. This view shows the situation of the settlement on the flat top of the terrace. Note also the upward-sloping topography of the Tertiary Hills beyond the terrace.

Figure 7. Composite of two photographs of the settlement area, looking southeast from the northwest corner of the field. On the right is the two-lane highway cutting through the terrace down to the Isar Valley. In the right background is the city of Landshut, and behind it the Tertiary Hills south of the Isar. On the left are houses of the modern hamlet of Hascherkeller.

Figure 8. View from the edge of the terrace, looking southeast down the slope to the Isar Valley. The houses are in the valley.

Figure 9. View from the eastern edge of the field on which the site is located, looking west toward the modern cemetery complex. The prehistoric settlement is situated principally in the left half of the photograph. The bend in the highway at the top of the terrace is visible at the extreme left edge of the photograph.

3

The Excavations at Hascherkeller from 1978 to 1981:
Techniques, Progress, and Results

At the beginning of fieldwork in 1978, a base line was established along the straight path north of the site, and it was surveyed into a bench-mark point at the base of the concrete wall around the modern cemetery. Sections of steel pipe were sunk into the ground along the base line at 20-m intervals to aid in the rapid relocation of base-line points at the start of each subsequent field season. All mapping and laying out of trenches were done from these fixed points with the use of an alidade and plane table and measuring tapes. Frequent checks made at different points on the field showed the measuring system to be consistently accurate to within a few centimeters over the site.

EXCAVATION TECHNIQUES

The excavation techniques employed at Hascherkeller were designed to meet the aims of the project and to accommodate the environmental conditions of the site. The principal aims were (1) large-scale exposure and study of the surface of the prehistoric settlement and (2) collection of all possible data relating to economy.

The surface soil at Hascherkeller is humus developed on loess, and it extends between 0.30 and 1.15 m below the surface on the different parts of the site investigated so far. The subsoil is pure loess, light yellow in color and very fine in consistency, so fine that individual grains cannot be distinguished when it is rubbed between thumb and forefinger. The depth of the loess is unknown. A test pit extending three meters below the top of the loess on the western part of the site did not reach the bottom of the loess.

The modern humus, which is regularly mixed by plowing, extends down 30 to 35 cm below the surface. It is made up of loess and an admixture of organic materials and is very rich and of dark brown color. On much of the site an old humus layer also occurs between the modern humus and the loess subsoil. This layer is not reached by modern plowing

and is much more densely packed and harder than the modern humus.

Generally, the climate of Lower Bavaria in the summer is fairly wet. Much of the weather is hot and sunny, but a substantial amount of rain falls. The best weather conditions for working in the loess soils at Hascherkeller were cool and overcast. In even light rain, the loess turned to slimy mud, making excavation very difficult in the humus layer and impossible once the surface of the subsoil had been reached, at which point the features of the prehistoric settlement became apparent. In hot and dry conditions, usually at midday during periods without rain, the loess soil became extremely hard and could not be cut with a trowel, but only broken in small chunks with a spade or pick. Work on settlement features was virtually impossible once they had hardened under a midday sun.

Because of the high susceptibility of loess to the vagaries of the weather, it was necessary to employ excavation techniques that did not involve leaving large surfaces open, though some surface exposure was necessary in order to study the relationship of settlement features to one another. The compromise solution adopted at Hascherkeller was to work in trenches measuring 5 by 10 m. Leaving a half meter on all four sides for balks, profiles, and measuring lines, the actual area opened initially in each unit was 4 by 9 m. A cutting of this size provided a reasonably large surface area in which to examine settlement features, yet it was small enough so that each layer of soil could be removed relatively quickly and features planned before the soil dried out too much and lost color distinctions.

The humus was removed from each cutting down to the loess subsoil, the surface of the loess was cleaned off, settlement features were photographed and mapped, the four wall profiles were mapped, and the features were then excavated. As soon as a cutting was finished, backfilling began. It was thus possible to excavate each cutting in relatively fresh condition. When rain began to fall, it was necessary to cover the open cuttings with plastic sheets to prevent damage to exposed features.

As at most prehistoric settlements in central Europe situated on flat, open land, the original settlement surface at Hascherkeller does not survive. Relative to most parts of the world, central Europe has been densely occupied since at least the Late Bronze Age, and most land has been plowed hundreds or thousands of times over the past 3,000 years. Recently deeper plows drawn by stronger tractors have been introduced, and as a result prehistoric settlements on agricultural land have been severely damaged. The result at Hascherkeller, as at most settlements, is that the original surface of occupation has been totally destroyed, along with house floors, wall foundations, hearths, shallow postholes and pits, and any other settlement features that were situated on or close to the surface. All that survive are those structures that were located well below the surface, such as deep postholes, ditches, and pits. Only in very rare instances where, for particular local environmental reasons, intensive agriculture has not been practiced subsequent to the prehistoric occupation do surface features of prehistoric settlements survive. This is the case at many of the lakeshore settlements of southwest Germany and Switzerland, such as Wasserburg Buchau (Reinerth 1928, 1936) and Zug-Sumpf (Speck 1955).

Even though modern plows continually stir up and turn over the humus layer, the materials that are thus mixed and moved in that layer have importance for archaeological study. It was noted in the first cuttings that concentrations of pottery and daub on the surface and in the modern humus were always situated directly above prehistoric pits and ditches containing more of the same materials. Apparently, although the plow disturbed and moved such debris, regular plowing had the effect of transporting individual sherds, daub fragments, and bones back and forth, but not carrying the majority of them far from their places of origin. It was thus possible to tentatively associate cultural materials recovered in the modern humus with prehistoric features below. In many cases, sherds found on the surface fit together with others recovered in the subsurface pits. In the analysis and interpretation presented here, however, such materials from the surface and from the humus are excluded from consideration. Only objects recovered below the level of disturbance are treated.

In each 4-by-9-m cutting the humus was excavated by a team of four persons, two with spades and two with shovels, in levels of 20-cm depth until the top of the loess was reached. On some parts of the site, particularly the western portion from which much of the humus had eroded away (fig. 4), the undisturbed loess subsoil was reached after the removal of two layers of humus. Elsewhere, particularly in the middle of the field (Trench D, Cutting III and Trench AA, Cutting III), as many as six 20-cm layers of humus had to be removed before the subsoil was reached.

All cultural material was collected from the surface and from each 20-cm level, with the exception of modern brick, which occurred in fragments over much of the site, and clearly modern rubbish such as bottle caps, beer bottle fragments, jars with screw caps, and metal cans. (Trench H yielded a trash deposit of such modern debris.) Considerable quantities of prehistoric pottery, daub, animal bone, and other materials were recovered in the humus layers, particularly directly above rich settlement pits.

The humus was excavated with spades and shovels rather than with finer implements because much of the humus did not contain any prehistoric material, and no material in the humus was in situ. The two spaders and two shovelers began work at one end of a cutting. Rows of chunks of earth were spaded loose across the cutting. The spaders loosened, lifted, and dropped each clump of humus, then shovelers gently broke each one into small fragments, frequently turning them before shoveling the soil out of the cutting onto the backdirt piles forming along the edges of the cuttings. Practically all objects greater than one centimeter in maximum diameter were recovered using this technique; very few items were ever found on backdirt piles, despite frequent checking. The team of spaders and shovelers worked down the length of the cutting, completing one row at a time. All artifactual materials were collected by 20-cm level.

Once the cutting was brought down to the loess subsoil, hoes and trowels were used to clean the surface of the loess to produce an even and smooth surface. At this stage features dug into the loess, such as ditches and pits, showed up as dark patches in the light yellow loess (fig. 11). The surface of each cutting was photographed and mapped, and the four profiles were drawn.

Because of regular disturbance by plowing, no natural stratigraphy survived in the humus, hence the excavation in 20-cm levels. Most of the pits and ditches also showed no natural stratigraphy, but instead homogeneous fill of light brown to dark brown color and humic character. The exception was the pit in Trench W which contained two stratigraphically distinct, though materially and chronologically similar, layers of rich cultural deposit. Because of the general absence of natural stratigraphy, excavation of ditches and pits was also done in arbitrary levels — 20 cm for ditches, which contained some but not much cultural material, and 10 cm for pits, which contained the most cultural material. All pits were bisected, and each half was excavated separately. The cultural material from each 10-cm level of each half was collected and bagged as a unit. A full profile was obtained through the middle of each pit and was photographed and drawn. All of the soil from each pit was screened through hardware cloth of one-quarter-inch mesh. Soil samples for wet-sieving and flotation were taken from each pit for recovery of floral remains (see chapter 6).

THE COURSE OF EXCAVATION

1978

The first cuttings to be opened in 1978 were those of Trench A. It was thought desirable to begin excavation of the settlement at the location where aerial photography showed settlement remains. Following the identification and investigation of the two ditches in Cuttings I and II of Trench A, excavation was extended to Cutting III to check for possible outer structures, and at the same time to Cuttings II through VI of Trench B, which were believed to be at the center of the settlement. These cuttings produced several rich pits and a ditch very much like the two in Trench A. Trench C also produced a very large and rich pit. The three cuttings of Trench D enabled the investigation of an important pit in the southern part of the settlement, of the remains of a house of the Roman period and of the continuation of the ditch that had been found in Trench B, Cutting IV. The western end of Trench D, Cutting I produced the remains of a brick air shaft associated with a beer cellar that once existed beneath the settlement area and concrete remains of a World War II bunker that had been built into the beer cellar. Cuttings I and II of Trench E located the inner of the two ditches encountered in Trench A, and the connecting trench between EI and BIV enabled the investigation of the intersection of the different portions of the ditch system.

During the summer of 1978 the Bayerisches Landesamt für Denkmalpflege carried out rescue excavations at the eastern edge of the field, where cellar holes for two new houses were being dug. These excavations produced a number of important settlement features (fig. 72). Double ditches similar to those in the western part of the field were found, running east-west and curving in a right-angle bend toward the south. Foundations of five typical Late Bronze Age (Urnfield) houses were found, four of

them marked by six large postholes in two rows of three and the fifth by eight postholes in two rows of four. A long palisade ditch with a right-angle bend in the middle of it was uncovered northeast of the double-ditch enclosure, apparently not aligned with the enclosure. Since one house overlies the double ditches of the one enclosure and another overlies the palisade trench, it is apparent that the houses were not contemporaneous with either of the enclosures.

In the fall of 1978 Dr. Helmut Becker of the Institut für Allgemeine und Angewandte Geophysik of the University of Munich carried out a magnetometer survey over the central portion of the field, between the areas excavated by the Peabody Museum and those by the Bayerisches Landesamt für Denkmalpflege (see chapter 5). The results of this survey played a major role in the planning of the three field seasons of excavation after 1978. The results indicated that the settlement consisted of three contiguous enclosures along the edge of the terrace, each surrounded by double ditches. The magnetometer survey results matched perfectly the excavation results on either side and made it much easier to grasp the overall structure of the site than would have been possible with excavation results alone.

1979

In 1979, the longest field season (13 weeks), it was necessary to complete investigation of the western portion of the site because the city of Landshut planned to construct a parking lot to be used by visitors to the modern cemetery. Cuttings I and II of Trench F picked up the two parallel ditches at a point where they made right-angle bends to the south. A straight ditch containing medieval debris was also encountered in these cuttings and is indicated by a fine line on the plan (fig. 10). At the southern end of Cutting II was an area of modern disturbance. Trench H, just south of F, produced only modern rubbish; all of the ground in this area had been severely disturbed in modern times. Trench G, five meters west of Trench F, also contained principally disturbed soil. The two narrow soundings 1 and 2 and the small Trench J also indicated extensive recent disturbance. A dotted line on the plan of the site indicates the boundary of this zone of disturbance, which probably resulted from activities associated with building and maintaining the highway. Trench R, just north of the line of disturbance, contained undisturbed materials, including the continuation of the southward curve of the outer ditch.

Two important results were established through this investigation of the western edge of the field. First, it was clear that the settlement did not extend beyond the westernmost of the three known enclosures. The magnetometer survey results show that the three enclosures were joined by their boundary ditches at their northern edges; and the excavation of Trenches F and R made clear that there were no further connecting ditches extending to the west. Second, it became apparent that there was a boundary between undisturbed and disturbed soil some 15 m in from the edge of the sidewalk next to the highway. A portion of the settlement along the road had been destroyed before archaeological exploration of the site.

Besides completing the investigation of the western extremity of the site in 1979, seven new cuttings were made in the interior areas of the western and central enclosures and were designated Trenches K, L, M, N, P, Q, and S. Trenches K and M yielded no settlement features and only very small quantities of cultural material in the humus layer. In Trench L was found a large shallow pit containing an abundance of pottery, animal bone, and daub. Trench N contained two rich pits of the main occupation period. Trench P contained in its south wall a single rich pit of Early or Middle Bronze Age date. Trench Q was opened in order to investigate the feature indicated as a strong anomaly on the magnetometer map (fig. 72). It contained a large pit filled with rich, dark soil, but without any prehistoric artifacts in it. The shape of the pit and the character of its fill were very different from those of any of the prehistoric features. It is unclear when this pit was dug and what purpose it served, but most likely it was dug in connection with the beer cellar, the road, or the bunker. Trench S was partially excavated in 1979, and it yielded part of the ditch and two rich pits.

1980

In 1980 the first task was to complete work on Trench S, in the northern end of which a settlement pit was encountered that had been cut by the ditch — the first case of stratigraphic superposition on the site. In the interior of the central enclosure, Trenches T and V were excavated. Trench T yielded two concentrations of cultural material from the main period of occupation, both of which were located within the humus layer and did not extend into the loess subsoil. Since these concentrations of material were within the rich brown humus, they were not recognizable as pits, and it was not possible to define their limits. They are indicated by dotted lines on the site plan (fig. 10) to mark them differently from the clearly defined pits that extended down into the loess. These two features were probably the lower portions

of shallow pits, the upper parts of which had been destroyed by plowing.

Trench V yielded in its west wall a rich pit of the Early or Middle Bronze Age and in its southeast corner several very small pits containing river pebbles and sherds of the main period of occupation.

Trench DIV was opened to check for any further large pits in the vicinity of those in Trenches C and L. In it were found only massive concrete and steel remains of the World War II bunker. Any cultural materials from the prehistoric occupation had been thoroughly destroyed. Trench X completed the investigation of a broad rectangle in the western and central enclosures. It produced no features dug into the loess subsoil.

In 1980 the strong anomaly just north of the northwest corner of the central enclosure was excavated. Dr. Becker had predicted on the basis of his magnetometer survey results that the anomaly indicated the presence of a furnace or oven. Trench W was laid out above the anomaly. In it was an enormous pit containing about half of all the pottery recovered at Hascherkeller and including the remains of a pottery kiln. The pit was bisected north-south, and the western half of it was excavated during the 1980 field season.

1981

In 1981 the eastern half of Trench W was excavated. Trench Z was opened to check for other pits in the northwest corner of the central enclosure, north of the very rich and important pit in Trench BV. Trench Z also served to check the results of the magnetometer survey, to see whether the inner ditch ran where the magnetometer suggested and whether there might be any pits in that area that the magnetometer did not pick up. On both counts the magnetometer proved precisely accurate.

Trench AA was opened south of Trench D, to follow the apparent concentration of settlement pits southward from the center of the main excavation area out toward the edge of the terrace, where the field dips steeply down toward the Isar Valley (fig. 8). Cutting I yielded a large and rich settlement pit of the principal period of occupation, while Cuttings II and III produced pits of Early or Middle Bronze Age date, that in III situated in the old humus above the loess subsoil and thus not precisely definable. Several very small pits of the main period of occupation were also found in these three cuttings.

THE RESULTS OF EXCAVATION

The features of the prehistoric settlement that were

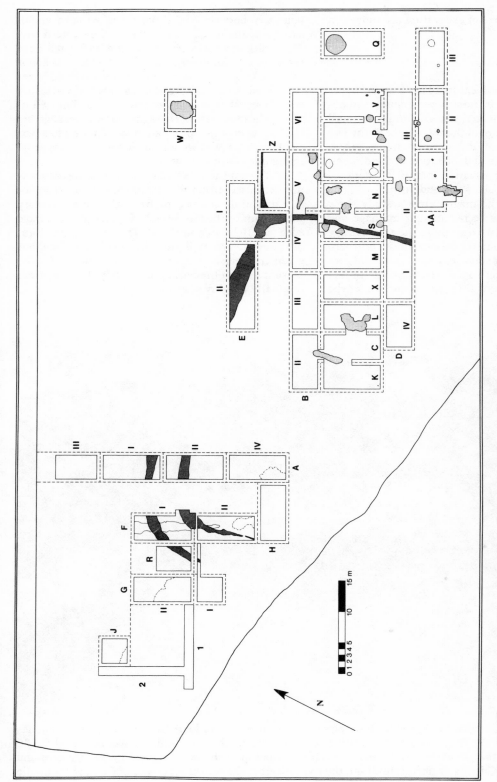

Figure 10. Plan of the settlement of Hascherkeller excavated by the Peabody Museum from 1978 to 1981. Trenches are designated with capital letters, cuttings within trenches (when there is more than one) with roman numerals, and soundings (narrow test trenches) with arabic numerals. The ditches are indicated by wavy-line shading, the pits by dotted shading. The features in Trenches T and AAIII outlined by dotted lines are pits that did not extend down into the loess subsoil; hence, their exact boundaries could not be ascertained. The broken line in Trenches J, GII, FII, and AIV marks the boundary of intensive disturbance in connection with the highway southwest of the site. The feature outlined by a fine solid line in Trench F is a ditch of medieval date.

uncovered in the course of excavation are shown on the site plan, figure 10.

Ditches

The principal structural feature of the Hascherkeller settlement as a whole is the system of double ditches that defines the three rectangular enclosures arranged contiguously at the edge of the terrace above the Isar Valley. The results of the magnetometer survey (chapter 5) provide a good delineation of the ditches, and archaeological excavation permitted detailed investigation of their character and form.

The results of the magnetometer study show that the enclosures were rectangular in shape and extended in a line east-west along the terrace edge (fig. 72). The magnetometer delineated the northern edge of all three enclosures and the side boundaries of the central and eastern ones. Excavation delimited the eastern boundary of the eastern enclosure, the boundary between the central and western enclosures, and the western boundary of the western one. The width of the western enclosure, measured from the center of the inner ditch on each side, was about 54 m. Measurements taken on the magnetometer map of the site indicate that the central enclosure was about 54 m wide, the eastern one about 56 m wide. The closeness of these measurements suggests that the enclosures were laid out according to a particular pattern and were intended to closely approximate one another in size.

The southern boundary of the enclosures was not delimited either by the magnetometer study or by excavation, and it is probable that this boundary was victim to the erosion taking place at the terrace edge (see light area in fig. 4). Thus the precise form of the enclosures will probably never be known, but given the known extent of the enclosures and the present form of the terrace, it is likely that they were originally roughly square.

Figure 11. Trench B, Cuttings IV, V, and VI, looking east. This photograph illustrates the form of the trenches used in excavation, with the exposed area measuring 4 x 9 m. The depth of the humus cover here is about 40 cm. Two features of the prehistoric settlement are visible, the top of the ditch separating the western and central enclosures in Cutting IV (foreground) and the shallow pit at the southeast corner of Cutting V (middle ground). The ranging rod is marked in half-meter intervals.

The form and structure of the ditches were similar throughout the areas excavated so far by the Peabody Museum in the western part of the site and by the Bayerisches Landesamt für Denkmalpflege in the eastern part. The ditches were V-shaped in section. At the widest, they were about 3 m across at the top (that is, at the top of the loess subsoil where they could first be discerned), and they extended a maximum of about 1.5 m down into the loess subsoil. The original depth was greater, since the tops of the ditches were cut off by ancient and modern plowing. The ditch fill consisted of humus of brown and dark brown color, and there was generally no stratification apparent in color, grain size, or soil consistency within the ditch fill. In many cases, just above the bottom of the ditch was a layer of loess (fig. 12), probably material that fell back into the ditch shortly after it had been dug. In several locations there was clear evidence for the redigging of the ditch slightly off-center so that the two profiles were apparent, one cutting into the other (fig. 13; also Christlein 1979, pl. 47,2).

The fill of the ditches contained cultural materials similar to those in the pits but in much smaller quantities and in smaller fragments. Most of the cultural objects were situated in the top 50 cm of the ditch fill, and only infrequently below that depth.

In order to study the ditches, 1-to-2-m-wide sections were cut through them at many locations. The ditch fill was removed in 20-cm layers until the loess subsoil was reached beneath the bottom of the ditch. Both profile faces were cleaned with trowels (fig. 14), photographed in black-and-white and color, and drawn. On the basis of the results of many such cuttings, it was decided not to excavate all of the ditch fill from all parts of the ditches, since very little new information was likely to emerge from such work. The form of the ditches was consistent throughout (Wells 1979, p. 23, fig. 6), as was the character of the fill and the nature of the cultural material in it.

Postholes were found at the bottom of the inner ditch in Trench FII (figs. 15 and 16). The presence of postholes suggests that at least this inner ditch, and perhaps the outer one as well, was dug to hold a palisade of small logs similar to the palisades that survive on lakeshore settlements of the same period, as at Buchau in southern Württemberg (Reinerth 1928, 1936) and at Auvernier (Arnold 1981) and other sites (Egloff 1981) on Lake Neuchâtel in Switzerland. The distance betweeen the centers of the postholes in Trench FII averages 13.7 cm (fig. 16), which may have been the average diameter of the logs implanted in the bottoms of the ditches. The

Figure 12. Profile of the outer ditch in Trench A, west wall of Cutting I.

Figure 13. Profile of the ditch in Trench E, Cutting II, showing the older phase on the left and the newer phase on the right.

Figure 14. Cleaning of the profile face of the outer ditch of the western enclosure in Trench A, Cutting I, in preparation for photographing and drawing.

logs forming the palisades at the other sites mentioned were of similar size. Although postholes were encountered in the bottom of the ditch only at this one location, it is likely that posts stood in all of the inner ditches at the site, and perhaps also in the outer ones, since all of them are of the same size, shape, and character. It is possible that at this one location the posts were sunk farther down into the loess subsoil than elsewhere. If posts had been merely set into the bottom of the ditches, and not hammered farther down into the underlying loess, and topsoil thrown back into the ditches around the posts to support them, no archaeological trace of the posts would survive in the climatic and soil conditions at Hascherkeller.

The use of such log palisades around small settlements is well documented throughout Europe from Neolithic times (e.g., Ihmig 1971; Vermeersch

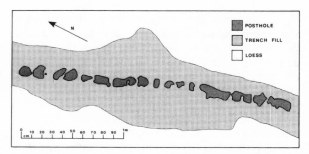

Figure 16. Postholes at the bottom of the inner ditch on the west side of the western enclosure, in Trench FII.

and Walter 1978) through the Late Iron Age (e.g., Bulleid 1924, p. 26). At the Neolithic settlements cited, ditches similar to those at Hascherkeller were dug in which to implant posts. It is likely that many of the ditches around prehistoric settlements were dug to hold such palisades.

In the environment of central Europe, logs probably last 25 to 50 years on the average (Bakker et al. 1977, p. 223; Pauli 1980, p. 311, n. 51). The repair of the palisades, or parts of them at a time, would account for the redigging of the ditches that is apparent in several locations at Hascherkeller. (The great proliferation of post bases at such lakeshore settlements as Buchau probably reflects not the existence of a thick wall of posts, as Reinerth thought [1936, p. 125], but rather the fact that individual posts lasted only a few decades before their tops rotted away and they needed to be replaced.)

Such palisades as that which surrounded the settlement of Hascherkeller cannot be regarded as military defenses; they would not have been substantial enough to have deterred even a couple of determined attackers. Their purpose was probably for keeping wild animals such as wolves away from the settlement and domestic animals in (see Bocquet 1979, p. 59; Percival 1980, p. 80).

The Pits

The settlement pits at Hascherkeller are the most important features of the prehistoric occupation. As at Hascherkeller, at many other settlements of this period and of preceding and succeeding ones neither the actual occupational surface nor remains of buildings are preserved, but only pits and ditches dug well into the underlying subsoil (Coles and Harding 1979, p. 358; Joachim 1980, p. 355). At Hascherkeller the pits contained the principal evidence of the structures that stood on the site, in the form of wall plaster. They also contained food debris in the form of

Figure 15. Part of the row of postholes at the bottom of the inner ditch on the west side of the western enclosure, in Trench FII. The ruler is marked off in centimeters.

carbonized plant seeds and animal bones and most of the cultural material left by the inhabitants of the settlement. The interpretation of the community that lived at Hascherkeller depends primarily on the character and contents of the pits.

Most of the pits at Hascherkeller became apparent during the initial removal of the humus layer on the site. In some cases, pottery, daub, and animal bone on the surface of the field indicated the presence of a pit below. Other times, such cultural materials were first encountered in the top or second 20-cm layer of the humus. In such cases, all of the materials from a concentration in a part of a cutting were bagged together, separate from the scattered cultural materials from other parts of the cutting.

Once the humus was removed and the surface of the loess subsoil cleaned with hoes and trowels, the form of the pit became clear (fig. 17). The pits appeared at this stage as dark, humus-filled intrusions in the light yellow loess subsoil. In general the fill of the pits was considerably darker than that of the ditches, suggesting a denser concentration of organic material in them.

The form of the pits at the level of the top of the loess (which was not the original top of the pits, but was the highest stage at which the form could be recognized) varied from nearly round, to nearly rectangular, to extended rectangular, to irregularly bloblike (figs. 18–22). The size of the pits, the form of their vertical sections, and their contents also varied greatly, and in this variation lies the principal information pertaining to the structure and economy of the prehistoric settlement.

A total of 21 pits were encountered and investigated in the four field seasons from 1978 to 1981. Other smaller, humus-filled intrusions into the loess subsoil (less than 0.75 m in maximum dimension) were studied that contained only a few sherds or fragments of other cultural materials. Their significance was in every case unclear, and they are not considered among the pits here. Some may have been the bottom ends of postholes, though no patterns were apparent to suggest buildings or fences. It was sometimes difficult to distinguish possible very small postholes from mole holes, which are abundant on the site. In any case, these smaller features

Figure 17. Pit at the north end of Trench N, at the level of the top of the loess subsoil. This photograph shows the typical appearance of a pit dug into the subsoil.

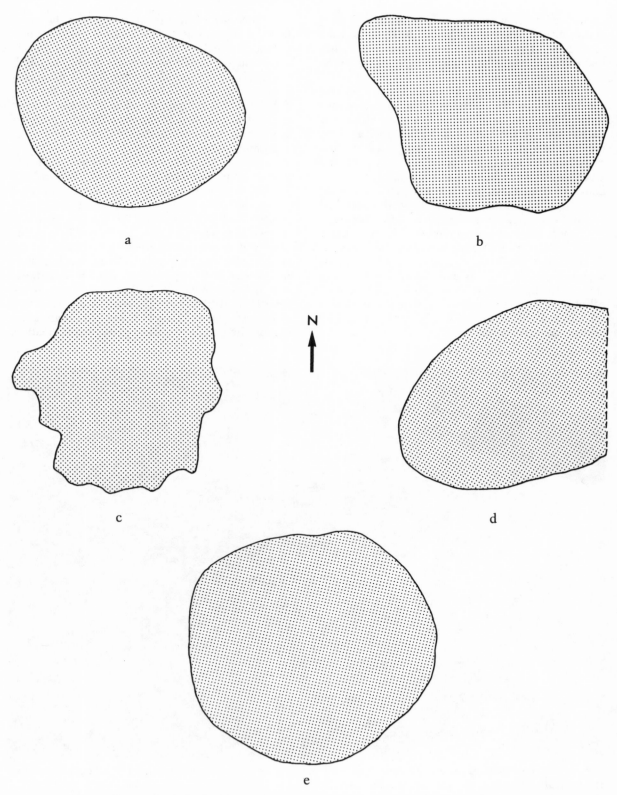

Figure 18. Plans of tops of pits (at the level of the top of the loess subsoil). a. S south end. b. S red pit. c. N west extension. d. S north end. e. DIII. Scale 1:20.

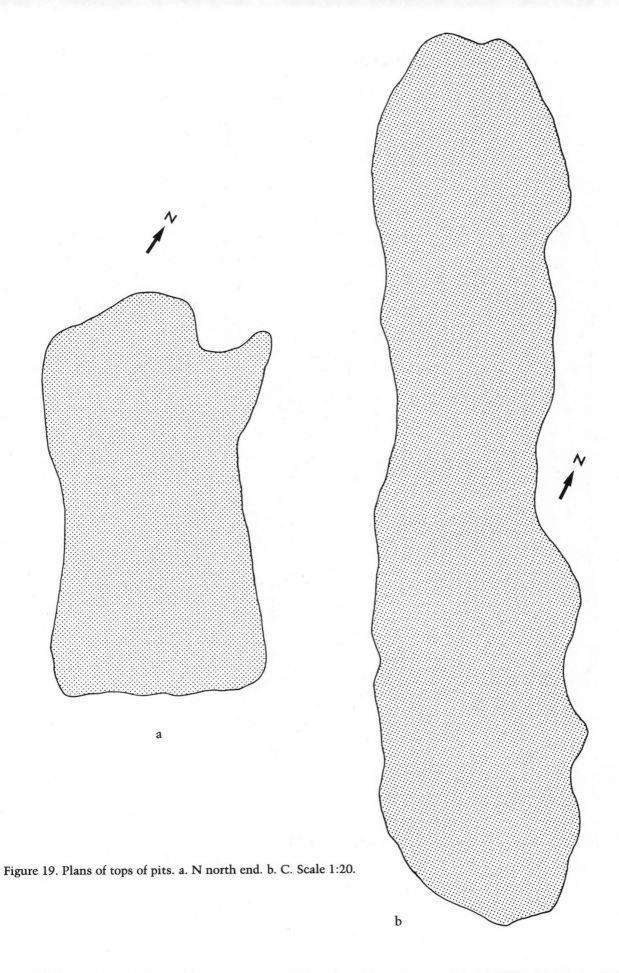

Figure 19. Plans of tops of pits. a. N north end. b. C. Scale 1:20.

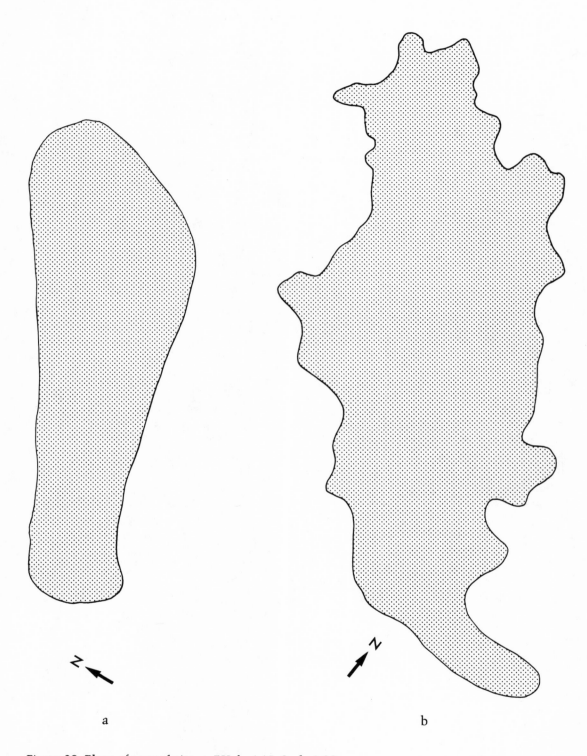

a   b

Figure 20. Plans of tops of pits. a. BV. b. AAI. Scale 1:20.

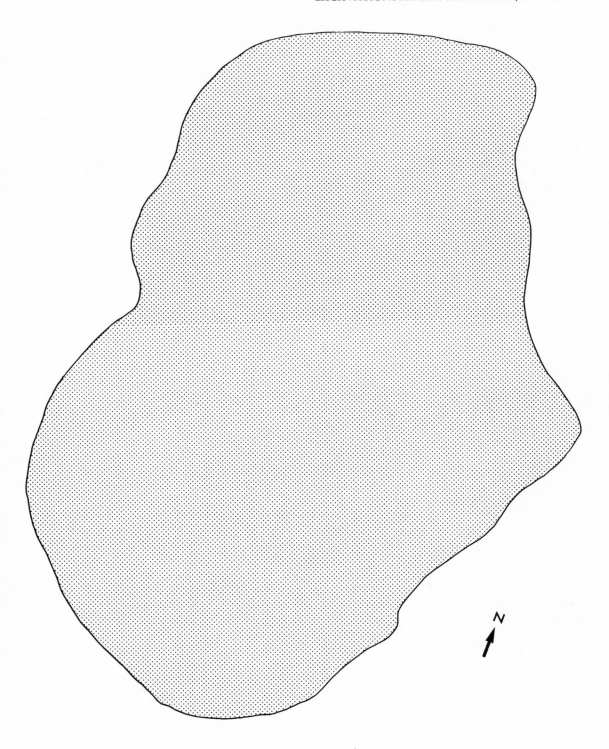

Figure 21. Plan of top of pit. Trench W. Scale 1:20.

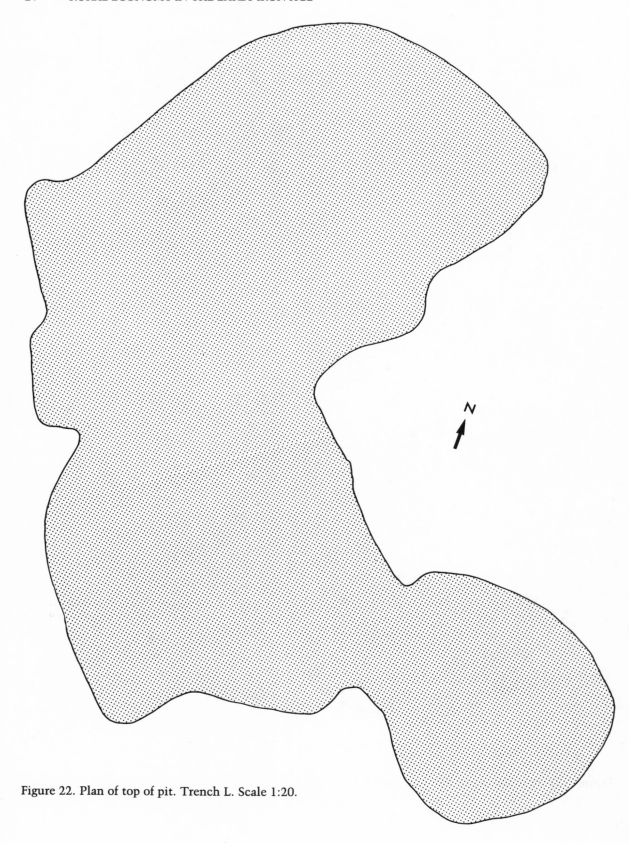

Figure 22. Plan of top of pit. Trench L. Scale 1:20.

did not contain appreciable quantities of cultural material and are best regarded as the remains of various indeterminate structures and activities of the living community. The profusion of structural remains of the beer cellar and World War II bunker, which were concentrated in Cuttings DI and DIV, are also omitted from discussion here.

Of the 21 substantial pits on the settlement surface, the large one filled with sticky dark brown fill in Trench Q was probably a recent feature. It differed in form and in the character of its fill from all of the prehistoric pits, and it contained none of the prehistoric cultural materials of the other pits.

Of the 20 remaining pits, 13 belonged to the principal period of occupation (1000 to 800 B.C.). Of the other 7, the pit in the east wall of Cutting BV was of indeterminate date. It was shallow and contained only 21 sherds that are probably of the main period of occupation, but the ascription cannot be made with certainty. Five pits were of Early or Middle Bronze Age date: one in the south wall of Trench BV, one in the south wall of Trench P, one in the balk on the west side of Trench V, one in Trench AAII, and one in the deep humus of Trench AAIII. One pit was of Roman date and contained the daub remains of a hut (the pit in the east end of Trench DII).

This study will concern itself only with the remains of the principal period of occupation; the cultural materials of Early and Middle Bronze Age and Roman date will be presented in another context.

Of the 13 pits belonging to the main period of occupation, two, those in Trench T, were very shallow and were found only as concentrations of sherds, daub, and animal bones within the humus. These two pits did not extend down into the loess subsoil. Because they were situated in the humus, some mixing and loss of pit contents is possible through the agency of the plow; hence, for the detailed analysis of materials from the site only the 11 pits that extended well below the top of the loess subsoil will be considered here. These 11, all of which contained rich concentrations of cultural material, can be regarded as closed find-associations, insofar as archaeological units are ever closed. (To judge from the only slight overall displacement of cultural materials through rodent activity and worm action on the site, it is very unlikely that such agencies would have caused any appreciable disruption of the cultural context of the pit contents.)

Figures 23 through 25 show sections cut through each of the pits in order to indicate their vertical forms. Here again there is considerable variation in shape and size, which bears directly on the use to which the pits were put. The pit in Trench W can be left out of the interpretive discussion here since it is very different from all others in form, contents, and function, as it contained the remains of a kiln and the associated debris.

The three pits of long, thin shape, those in Trenches BV, C, and AAI, all have similar sections — cup-shaped and symmetrical. All three contained notable concentrations of daub (fig. 29).

The large pit in Trench L, the rectangular pit in Trench N, and the round pit in the west wall of Trench N all have shallow, saucer-shaped sections with gently sloping sides.

The four remaining pits, DIII, S north end, S red pit, and S south end, are all deep relative to their top surface areas and have steep sides. Depth and steepness are particularly marked in the case of the pits DIII and S south wall, where the walls are nearly vertical and even undercut.

As at Hascherkeller, the majority of settlements of this period are characterized principally by their pits. Pits very similar to those at Hascherkeller are common on settlements throughout central Europe and in other parts of the continent (e.g., Bouzek and Koutecký 1964; Pétrequin et al. 1969; Schwellnus and Hermanns 1979; Bradley et al. 1980). They form the principal context of archaeological material on dry-land settlements of this period. The case of the lakeshore settlements is different. Pits have not been much discussed in connection with these settlements, probably because in the boggy environments pits would have had no use as storage spaces or as sources of clay. Foodstuffs were most likely stored in wooden structures above the ground, as Reinerth's reconstructed granary at Buchau suggests (1936, p. 136, fig. 62).

The character of the fill from all of the pits is similar; it is of light brown to dark brown color, in contrast to the surrounding light yellow loess subsoil, it is homogeneous and fine-grained like the loess, and it is relatively hard-packed. The form, shape, and contents of the pits vary, however, and in this variation lies the evidence upon which interpretations of the different features can be made. Four principal criteria are especially important:

1. Size and shape both of the top (i.e., at the level of the top of the loess subsoil) and of the vertical section.
2. Quantities and character of daub and pottery. Both the amounts and degrees of fragmentation and rounding of daub pieces in the different pits suggest differences in the locational relationships between pits and aboveground structures that stood on the site. Different proportions of differ-

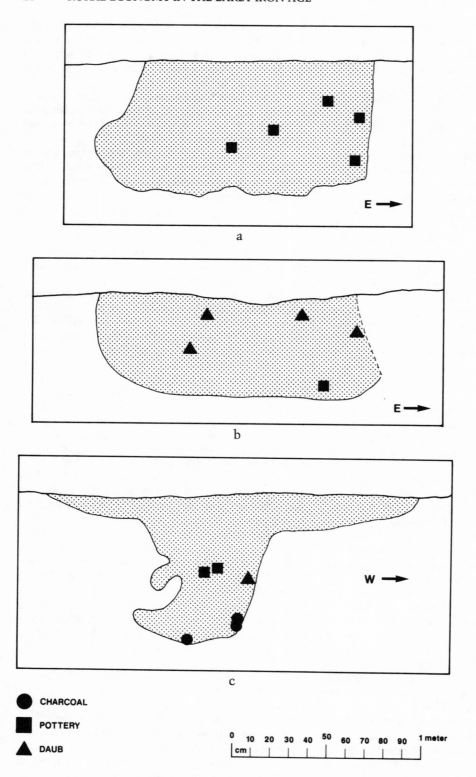

Figure 23. Vertical profiles through pits. a. DIII. b. S north end. c. S south end.

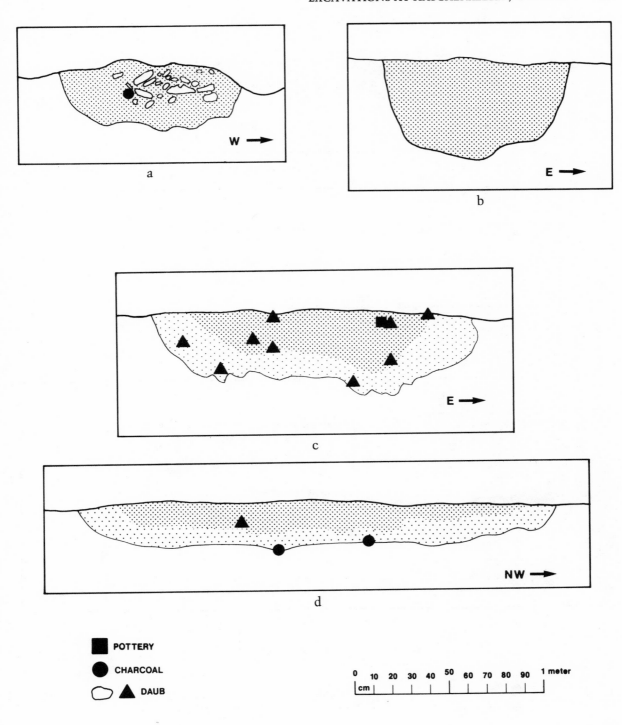

Figure 24. Vertical profiles through pits. a. AAI. b. C. c. L. d. N north end.

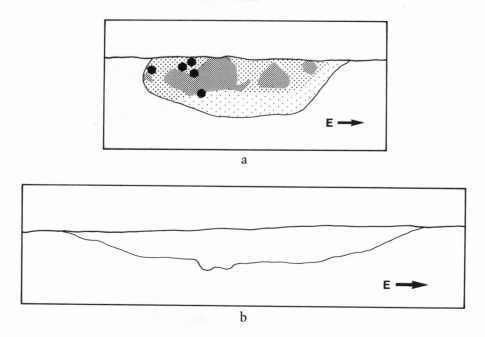

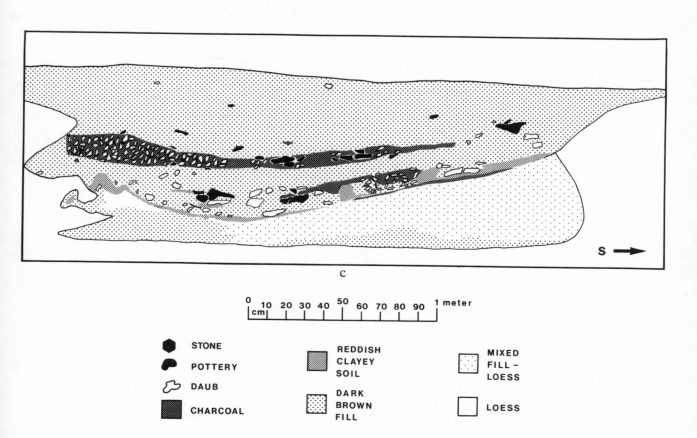

Figure 25. Vertical profiles through pits. a. S red pit. b. N west extension. c. W.

ent kinds of pottery in the pits suggest much about the purpose and location of the pits, and the degree of fragmentation of sherds contributes additional information. Bone fragmentation yields similar evidence (chapter 7).

3. The presence in some pits of special objects used in manufacturing provides information about the pits, for example, the mold from the pit in the west extension of Trench N and the waster sherds from Trench W.

4. Special structures such as the remains of the kiln in Trench W provide information about the uses of pits.

Much has been written about the function of round-topped, straight-sided, and flat-bottomed pits such as those in Trenches DIII, S north end, and S south end. Since Bersu's detailed treatment of the pits at Little Woodbury (1940), virtually all investigators, working both with the available archaeological data and with ethnographic and historical examples, have agreed that pits of this form were most likely storage pits for foodstuffs, in particular cereal grains (e.g., Bouzek and Koutecký 1964; Bouzek et al. 1966, pp. 80-82; Bowen and Wood 1967; Ellison and Drewett 1971; Reynolds 1974, 1979a, 1979b; Bradley et al. 1980). Experiments have shown how grain, including seed grain, can be stored for a year and more provided that a proper airtight covering is constructed over the pit (Bowen and Wood 1967; Reynolds 1974, 1979a, 1979b). Linings for pits, deemed likely by many investigators, were found to be unnecessary by Reynolds (1974, p. 130) provided that the pit was properly prepared before receiving its contents. At the settlement of Aldermaston Wharf in southern Britain, pit 68 of this form contained some 500 g of carbonized grain at its base, and pit 62 contained a 3-cm-thick clay lining suggestive of a grain storage structure (Bradley et al. 1980, p. 223, fig. 5,62.68; p. 224).

Generally, pits were probably not dug on prehistoric settlements expressly for the purpose of rubbish disposal (Bersu 1940, p. 60; Bouzek and Koutecký 1964, p. 43). In the small-scale settlements of the Late Bronze and Early Iron Ages, it is unlikely that people would have gone to the trouble to dig pits in which to throw broken pottery and animal bones. More likely, they simply tossed broken pots aside to be trampled into the earth and threw the bones to the pigs and dogs. The rubbish that occurs in pits at these settlements is part of the general debris from the surface of the settlements that was kicked or washed into pits unintentionally. This reasoning makes good sense of the character of the fill of the pits at Hascherkeller. Rarely did they contain dense concentrations of pottery or bone as would be expected if handfuls of trash had been thrown in at a time. The cultural debris in the pits was scattered throughout the fill in most instances.

The distinction between primary versus secondary deposition of cultural materials is important here. Primary deposition can be understood as deposition of materials in the same locations where they served their intended purposes. The storage vessels in the supposed cellar holes in Trenches BV and AAI were in primary contexts since they were still in the cellars where they had been used during the life of the community. The structural remains of the kiln and at least some of the waster sherds in Trench W were also in their primary locations.

Secondary deposition is the deposition of materials outside of the locations in which they served their intended purposes. All trash — broken pottery, animal bones, and daub, as well as fragmentary bronze, iron, and stone objects — was in secondary contexts in the pits. These materials were used elsewhere than in the pits.

Since secondarily deposited materials can be expected to have traveled farther than those in primary deposits, we would expect such materials to be more fragmented than those in primary deposits (Bradley and Fulford 1980). In fact the sherds in the primary deposits of the cellar holes in Trenches BV and AAI have substantially larger average weights than sherds in the secondary deposits of storage pits and borrow pits (table 1). This pattern is also recognizable in the fragmentation of bone in the different contexts of the settlement (chapter 7).

All of the cultural material in the ditches had been secondarily deposited. This secondary deposition was reflected in the diffuse, scattered character of that material and in the generally higher degree of fragmentation of pottery, daub, and animal bone recovered in the ditch fill than in the pits. As Brenda Benefit notes in connection with the animal bones (chapter 7), the materials from the ditches closely resemble those that were probably trampled and crushed on the settlement surface before deposition, such as those recovered in the Trench L borrow pit.

Pottery from the Pits. A total of 14,853 sherds from the principal period of occupation at Hascherkeller were recovered in the first four field seasons. No complete vessels were found, nor were more than a handful of vessels that could be completely restored on the basis of the sherds. It is thus clear that much of the pottery that was used at the settlement is now missing. Some was probably washed away down the edge of the terrace over the millennia, to be eroded or carried away by the branches of the Isar.

All of the pottery falls into the general category of "settlement pottery" and is plainer, less fine, and less ornate than the contemporaneous pottery placed in burials. Decoration is minimal. Between 1 and 4 percent of the sherds from each of the 11 principal pits bore some kind of decoration. No painted decoration was observed. Simple fingertip impressions occurred with some frequency on large vessels, either on the rim or on a raised band around the neck. Large jars also sometimes had on their necks raised zigzag lines. Incised lines of various kinds, as well as impressed dots, shallow grooves, and impressed points, were found on the smaller vessels. On a few sherds fine incised lines were filled with a white paste. A few bore stamped decoration. Graphite was applied to the surface of a number of sherds, sometimes in bands and sometimes covering the entire surface.

Little will be said here about the typological and chronological affiliations of the pottery; such analysis will be presented in another context. For present purposes suffice it to say that the pottery corresponds closely to that from other settlements in the vicinity that are dated to the phases Hallstatt A, B, and C in the relative chronological scheme for central Europe, particularly to Hallstatt B, dated 1000 to 700 B.C. (Gersbach 1951, 1961; Müller-Karpe 1959a). Numerous well-studied cemeteries, such as Kelheim (Müller-Karpe 1952a), Gernlinden, Grünwald, and Unterhaching (Müller-Karpe 1957), Straubing (Hundt 1964), Manching (Rochna 1962), Altessing (Rochna 1965), and Steinkirchen (Müller-Karpe 1975), and settlements, such as the Bogenberg (Hundt 1955), Künzing (Herrmann 1974–1975), and Hienheim (Kruyff and Modderman 1979) in southern Bavaria, provide abundant typological comparisons for the pottery from Hascherkeller. Since forms of ceramic vessels became very standardized over large areas during this period, the Hascherkeller material can be compared with assemblages from other parts of central Europe as well (see especially the syntheses in Kimmig 1940 for Baden, Müller-Karpe 1948 for Hanau, Herrmann 1966 for Hessen, Hennig 1970 for Oberfranken, Dehn 1972 for north Württemberg, Unz 1973 for southwest Germany and Switzerland, Eggert 1976 for Rheinhessen, Šaldová 1981 for Bohemia, and for the whole of central Europe in Müller-Karpe 1959a. Along with the general typological comparison with other dated contexts, the Hascherkeller material can be dated on the basis of a series of six radiocarbon dates, which provide good fixed points for the chronology that agree with the chronological assessment based upon the pottery forms (see chapter 4).

The principal concern here is in asking what information about the prehistoric community can be derived from the pottery. Since all of the pottery came from pits, ditches, and the humus layer, there is little direct evidence pertaining to the uses of the vessels except in the case of the supposed storage pits. And in most cases individual vessels are represented by only a number of sherds, sometimes by just a single sherd. Hence, means were required that could derive useful information from individual sherds, most of them in secondary contexts. The principal advantage of the pottery assemblage at Hascherkeller is the substantial quantity of sherds, making numerical patterns significant.

From his study of the temper of the Hascherkeller pottery, John Stubbs (chapter 8) is able to argue that virtually all of the pottery found on the settlement was made there from local materials, a pattern consistent with the results from the small number of other settlement assemblages that have been examined from this perspective.

Some information about general purposes for different ceramic vessels can be derived from the sherds. Although no complete vessels were recovered and very few vessels could be substantially reconstructed from the sherds available, many large rim sherds provide an indication of the general form of the vessels from which they came. Since only a small proportion of the walls of vessels was usually ascertainable from the sherds, only the most rudimentary morphological typology can be suggested. The principal vessel forms represented are the following, defined for purposes of discussion here:

Bowls — vessels with mouth diameter greater than height and mouth diameter nearly as large as the greatest diameter of the vessel (hence without a constricted neck).
Jars — broad-bodied vessels, often globular in form, with wide mouth diameter, and with greater height than mouth diameter.
Cups — small bowls with handles.
Beakers — vessels with greater heights than mouth diameters, and with mouth diameters at greatest only slightly less than maximum diameters.
Plates — round, nearly flat vessels.

The most abundantly represented of the vessel forms are bowls and jars, as is the case at other settlements of the period elsewhere in Europe (e.g., Bradley et al. 1980). The largest vessels are the big jars, the smallest the cups and beakers. A few other forms occur in small numbers, such as strainers (fig. 49d) and children's toys (fig. 56o).

Since little of the pottery was in its primary location when recovered, there is not much evidence concerning the functions of the different vessels in the archaeological context of the settlement, a situation similar to that at other sites. The best information from which function can be judged comes from the earliest realistic representations of people involved in everyday activities, the situla art of the East Alpine region dating principally from the sixth to fourth centuries B.C. (Kastelic 1965), and from later, medieval contexts where similar vessels were used in everyday food preparation and consumption. Analogous vessel forms persisted from the period of Hascherkeller to early modern times, and there is no reason to think that the functions of the various vessels changed substantially over this time. Cups, beakers, and small bowls were used principally for drinking liquids (Kossack 1964). The majority of bowls were probably used for cooking, serving, and eating foods. Plates were used for serving dry foods. Jars were used for serving liquids and for cooking dishes involving liquids, such as soups, stews, and porridges. Large jars were used principally as storage vessels to hold grain and beverages. (For information about the uses to which vessels are likely to have been put, see Solheim 1960, p. 327; Kossack 1964, 1970, pp. 132–138; Clarke 1976; Pauli 1978, pp. 71–73; Bradley et al. 1980, p. 250; Jaanusson 1981, pp. 66–93, 111–112; Šaldová 1981.)

Working with this rough, but probably generally correct, association between vessel form and principal function, it was necessary to devise a means of assessing the relative quantities of different categories of vessels represented in the sherd assemblages from the different pits on the settlement. A sample of about one-hundred sherds was studied with the aim of developing some metrical technique for assessing the quantities involved. A strong correlation was found between the thickness of sherds from vessel walls and forms and sizes of the vessels. The small vessels, including cups, beakers, and small bowls (all of which generally have much finer and more highly polished surfaces than other forms), have thin walls. Large vessels of coarse texture, with rough, unsmoothed surfaces, have thick walls. Most of the bowls and some of the jars have walls of intermediate thickness and have surface finishes intermediate between those of the thinnest and the thickest categories of vessels.

Further experimentation and sorting of sherds in the field laboratory in 1981 permitted the metrical definition of three main categories of pottery, based upon the thickess of sherds. Similar tripartite divisions of sherds of settlement pottery have been employed by archaeologists working on settlements of this period in southern Britain (Bradley et al. 1980, p. 232) and may be applicable to all prehistoric Euro-

pean contexts (Clarke 1976, pp. 462–464). These measurements were taken from portions of the vessel walls of sherds whenever possible; if the sherds represented only part of a rim or base, an estimation of the thickness of the vessel wall was made on the basis of comparison with other sherds for which both parts of the vessel were present. In borderline cases, several different measurements were taken from different parts of the sherds, and the results were averaged. (See discussion about measuring the thickness of sherds in Jaanusson 1981, pp. 63–65.) The thinnest category was defined as having a thickness of less than 4.5 mm, the intermediate category from 4.5 to 9.0 mm, and the thickest category greater than 9.0 mm. These measurements were chosen because they conformed to natural divisions in the pottery assemblage according to wall thickness. Few sherds were close to 4.5 mm or 9.0 mm thick; the great majority fell near the middle of the first two categories (0 to 4.5 mm and 4.5 to 9.0 mm thick) or were considerably thicker than 9.0 mm. The association between vessel form (and surface finish) and wall thickness was found to be very consistent.

During the 1981 field season all of the sherds recovered from each context during the four seasons of excavation by the Peabody Museum were sorted into these three categories with a fourth category of split sherds — sherds broken longitudinally and missing the interior or exterior surface and hence not assignable to one of the three categories. The sherds were measured with calipers. For every recorded find-unit (e.g., each 10-cm level of each half of each pit), all of the sherds in each of the three metrically defined categories and in the split category were counted and weighed. The statistics resulting from these countings and weighings are presented in table 1. This numerical picture of the pottery in each of the principal pits provides much information concerning the use to which the different pits were put. Reduced to simplest terms, the vessels of the thinnest category can be assumed to have been used principally for drinking beverages, those of the middle category for preparation and serving of food, and those of the thickest category for storing foods. In a small community such as that at Hascherkeller, it is very unlikely that social distinctions played any part in the usage of different kinds of pottery. Only very few vessels did not fall into the expected morphological category on the basis of wall thickness; hence, the function of vessels represented by individual sherds could be broadly ascertained by these measurements. (Other studies have similarly used counts and weights of sherds from settlements to derive economic information and should be consulted for comparison to the results presented here. See

Table 1.
Pottery in the principal pits: quantitative data.

	No. of sherds	Wt. of sherds (grams)	Avg. wt. per sherd (grams)	% sherds by N	% sherds by wt.	% splits by N	% splits by wt.
BV							
Fine	4	15	3.75	1.32	0.17		
Intermediate	163	3,285	20.15	53.62	36.60		
Thick	137	5,675	41.42	45.07	63.23		
Subtotal	304	8,975					
Split	19	35				5.88	0.39
Total	323	9,010					
C							
Fine	9	10	1.11	6.82	0.79		
Intermediate	101	670	6.63	76.52	52.76		
Thick	22	590	26.82	16.67	46.46		
Subtotal	132	1,270					
Split	18	35				12.00	2.68
Total	150	1,305					
DIII							
Fine	134	320	2.39	20.62	7.03		
Intermediate	472	3,620	7.67	72.62	79.47		
Thick	44	615	13.98	6.77	13.50		
Subtotal	650	4,555					
Split	78	145				10.71	3.09
Total	728	4,700					
L							
Fine	47	65	1.38	17.87	4.68		
Intermediate	208	1,170	5.63	79.09	84.17		
Thick	8	155	19.38	3.04	11.15		
Subtotal	263	1,390					
Split	55	110				17.30	7.33
Total	318	1,500					
N west extension							
Fine	39	190	4.87	9.42	1.72		
Intermediate	314	7,560	24.08	75.85	68.35		
Thick	61	3,310	54.26	14.73	29.93		
Subtotal	414	11,060					
Split	40	110				8.81	0.98
Total	454	11,170					
N north end							
Fine	24	125	5.21	6.84	3.07		
Intermediate	240	1,590	6.63	68.38	39.02		
Thick	87	2,360	27.13	24.79	57.91		
Subtotal	351	4,075					
Split	170	155				32.63	3.66
Total	521	4,230					

	No. of sherds	Wt. of sherds (grams)	Avg. wt. per sherd (grams)	% sherds by N	% sherds by wt.	% splits by N	% splits by wt.
S red pit							
Fine	23	95	4.13	12.50	4.03		
Intermediate	130	1,135	8.73	70.65	48.09		
Thick	31	1,130	36.45	16.85	47.88		
Subtotal	184	2,360					
Split	30	55				14.02	2.28
Total	214	2,415					
S north end							
Fine	34	40	1.18	18.78	4.94		
Intermediate	129	600	4.65	71.27	74.07		
Thick	18	170	9.44	9.94	20.99		
Subtotal	181	810					
Split	21	40				10.40	4.71
Total	202	850					
S south end							
Fine	45	100	2.22	21.43	6.39		
Intermediate	157	1,230	7.83	74.76	78.59		
Thick	8	235	29.38	3.81	15.02		
Subtotal	210	1,565					
Split	61	105				22.51	6.29
Total	271	1,670					
W							
Fine	955	2,480	2.60	17.76	3.82		
Intermediate	3,591	42,390	11.80	66.78	65.26		
Thick	831	20,085	24.17	15.45	30.92		
Subtotal	5,377	64,955					
Split	2,221	4,990				29.23	7.13
Total	7,598*	69,945*					
AAI							
Fine	19	20	1.05	8.37	0.37		
Intermediate	172	3,820	22.21	75.77	70.09		
Thick	36	1,610	44.72	15.86	29.54		
Subtotal	227	5,450					
Split	19	40				7.72	0.73
Total	246	5,490					

*Plus roughly 5,000 fragments weighing 3,290 g.

especially Solheim 1960; Lüning 1972; Evans 1973; Orton 1975; Hinton 1977; Bradley et al. 1980; Bradley and Fulford 1980; Jaanusson 1981, pp. 45–60; Vince 1977.)

A total of 14,853 sherds belonging to the main period of occupation, weighing a total of 146,220 g, were found in the course of the Peabody Museum excavations (table 1). Of these, 11,025 sherds, weighing 112,285 g, were found in the closed contexts of the 11 principal pits in levels below the top of the loess subsoil. The other 3,828 sherds of the main occupation were recovered in the tops of these pits, where the possibility of mixing by plow cannot be excluded, in the smaller features, in the ditches, in the humus, and on the surface of the rest of the areas excavated.

Of the 11,025 sherds in the 11 pits, 7,598 of them were recovered in the large pit containing kiln debris in Trench W. The other 10 pits contained between 150 and 728 sherds each. The variation in numbers of sherds in the other 10 pits is regular, showing a normal distribution (fig. 26). In terms of the weights of the sherds recovered, there is a greater range of variation, but the distribution of weights is also normal (fig. 27).

The comparisons that can be made between the assemblages of sherds in the different pits can only be relative, involving proportions of different

Table 2.
Average weights of pottery categories, main occupation phase.

	Avg. wt. per sherd (grams)	% each category (N = 11,734)[*]	% by wt.[*]
Fine	2.59	13.87	3.02
Intermediate	10.72	70.44	63.34
Thick	25.45	15.69	33.54
Split	2.10		

[*]Excluding splits.

Table 3.
Quantities of pottery recovered, main occupation phase and Bronze Age.

	No. of sherds	Wt. of sherds (grams)
Main occupation phase		
Fine	1,627	4,220
Intermediate	8,266	88,600
Thick	1,841	46,855
Subtotal	11,734	139,675
Split	3,119	6,545
Total	14,853[*]	146,220[*]
Bronze Age (Trench BV, pit in SE wall; Trench P, pit at S end; Trench V, pit in W wall)		
Fine	194	1,130
Intermediate	721	7,235
Thick	64	2,275
Subtotal	979	10,640
Split	168	300
Total	1,147	10,940

Note: Of all prehistoric pottery (main occupation and Bronze Age, but not Roman or medieval), 92.83 percent belongs to the main occupation by number of sherds and 93.18 percent by weight of sherds.
[*]Plus roughly 5,000 fragments in Trench W, weighing 3,290 g, making a grand total of 149,510 g.

categories of vessels. Absolute numbers of vessels have little meaning here because of the varying ways in which pottery entered the pits and because material from the tops of some pits but not others may have been removed by plows. Another difficulty in working with absolute numbers of pots is the problem of differential use-lives for different kinds of vessels. Foster (1960) and David (1972; with David-Hennig 1971a and 1971b) note that in ethnographic contexts vessels used for cooking and serving food generally last only a couple of years, whereas storage vessels often last tens of years. This same pattern is reflected in the sherds at Hascherkeller where 70 percent (by count) of all of the sherds are of the intermediate category, bowls and small jars probably used principally in food preparation and serving.

Besides the counting and weighing of all of the sherds in each of the three categories, an attempt was made on the basis of the rim sherds to estimate the minimum number of vessels represented in each pit. This attempt met with only limited success. It was rarely possible to reconstruct much of any indi-

vidual vessel because not enough sherds were present in most cases. In some instances where it was possible to reconstruct much of a vessel, it was clear that all parts of the rim were not homogeneous; two rim fragments of a single vessel would not easily have been identified as having come from the same vessel. Sherds from one vessel were often of very different surface colors because of local variations in firing conditions. Thus the pottery was not homogeneous enough to permit good assessments of what sherds belonged to what vessel.

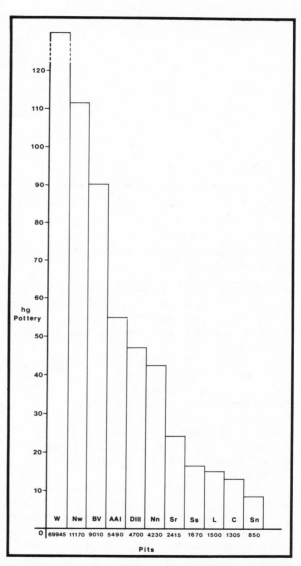

Figure 27. Histogram of weights of sherds in the 11 major pits.

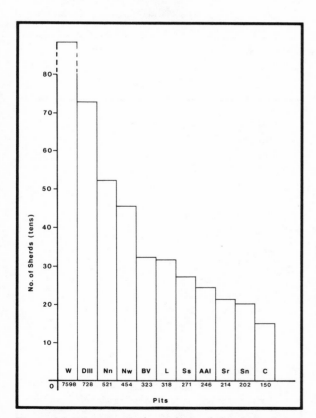

Figure 26. Histogram of numbers of sherds in the 11 major pits.

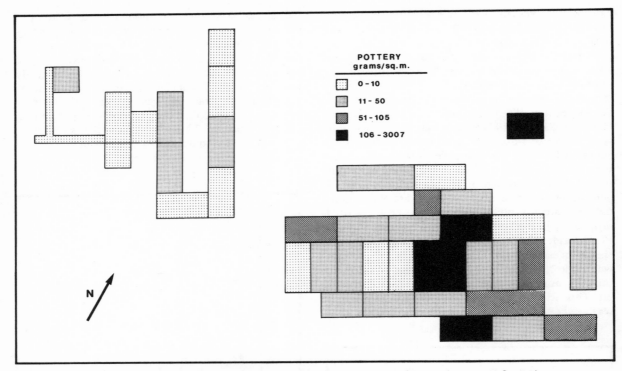

Figure 28. Plan showing the distribution of quantities of pottery over the site (compare fig. 10).

The following is a count of the definitely identifiable vessels:

N west extension — 20 vessels: 10 jars, 5 bowls or cups, 4 bowls, and 1 cup. Rim sherds of 3 or 4 additional vessels were also present.

N north end — 13 vessels: 7 bowls, 3 jars, 2 bowls or cups, and 1 cup.

DIII — 27 vessels: 17 bowls, 9 jars, and 1 cup.

L — 6 vessels: all bowls.

C — 6 vessels: 5 bowls and 1 jar.

BV — 17 vessels: 12 jars and 5 bowls.

S north end — 10 vessels: 7 bowls and 3 jars.

S red pit — 6 vessels: 3 bowls and 3 jars.

S south end — 12 vessels: 11 bowls and 1 jar.

W — 41 vessels: 25 jars and 16 bowls.

Daub from the Pits. Daub occurs all over the settlement as chunks of various sizes, the remains of the clay plaster forming the walls of the structures that stood on the site (see chapter 9). It is particularly well represented in some of the pits, and the different quantities preserved in different pits provide important evidence for the location and character of structures (fig. 29).

Daub is generally preserved archaeologically

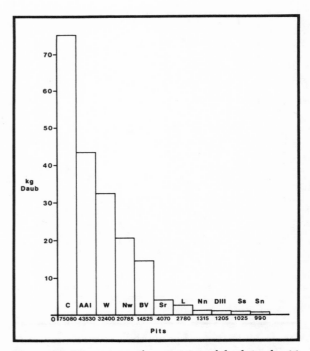

Figure 29. Histogram of quantities of daub in the 11 major pits.

Table 4.
Numbers of rim sherds from pits.

Pit	No. rim sherds	No. rim sherds from cutting above pit
BV	40	29
C	7	10
DIII	55	6
L	8	10
N	63	4
west extension	38	
north end	25	
S	48	65
red pit	11	
north end	10	
south end	27	
W	253	–
AAI	15	0

only if it has been fired. On prehistoric settlements daub was probably baked most often when it was situated close to a regular source of heat, near or in association with a fireplace, oven, or furnace. It could also have been fired when a building with wattle-and-daub walls burned. Experiments have demonstrated that when a structure burns, not all parts of the daub on walls and ceiling receive equal amounts of heat; certain parts are fired much more than others and hence are more likely to survive in the archaeological record (Schlichtherle 1977; Bankoff and Winter 1979; Reynolds 1980, p. 18).

The quantities of daub in the pits and the degree of fragmentation of the pieces relate directly to the proximity of buildings to the pits when they were open. The quantities of daub in the 11 principal pits, expressed in terms of weight, illustrate a significant pattern: Five pits contained large quantities of daub (over 14.5 kg), while the other six contained small quantities (under 5 kg). The large amounts of daub in the pits in Trenches C, AAI, and BV support the hypothesis, made on the basis of the form of the pits (see below), that they were cellars underneath houses. The quantities of daub here can be explained by the existence of structures standing over them and collapsing into them after abandonment or falling in upon burning. Some, but never very much, of the daub in the pits shows extensive signs of intensive burning, and no large deposits of charcoal are preserved in the pits. It is thus more likely that the surviving daub is from parts of structures exposed to the heat of fireplaces and ovens than that the buildings burned down in conflagrations.

The large amount of daub in Trench W proba-

bly derives from the structure of the kiln there. All of the upper parts of the kiln were destroyed, and the abundant daub is probably the fragmentary remains of the kiln. In the pit in the western extension of Trench N, the large quantity of daub also suggests a structure over the pit. The remains recovered in the pit of materials associated with crafts (bronze casting, weaving) suggest that this structure may have served at one time as a workshop. This pit also yielded fragments of daub with white and red paint on them, suggesting that the daub remains are not exclusively of ovens or furnaces but are at least in part of walls of buildings.

The very small quantities of daub in the other pits suggest that buildings with wattle-and-daub walls did not stand directly above them or even close by, since some daub would be expected to have found its way into the pits, unless, of course, they were buildings such as sheds whose walls were never exposed to the heat of a fire. On grounds of shape, the pits in DIII and S south end are likely to have been outdoor storage pits for grain, and the low amounts of daub in them would not contradict this idea. Interpretation of the pit in Trench L as a borrow pit for clay would also be consistent with the small amount of daub. The outstanding characteristic of the red pit in Trench S was its fill of very reddish, apparently intensely heated, pebbles. The purpose of this pit is unknown, but the staining of the pebbles and of the surrounding soil suggests that intense heat was generated here, an activity consistent with an open part of the settlement rather than one with a structure over it. Judging by the form, the pit at the north end of Trench S was probably a grain storage pit like those in DIII and S south end, and its proximity to the palisade separating the western and central enclosures would be in keeping with such a purpose rather than an association with a building. To judge by its shape, the pit at the north end of Trench N is likely to have served as a borrow pit.

The quantities of daub in the various pits is thus consistent with other evidence, especially the form of the pits and their contents, in suggesting which of them were closely associated with buildings incorporating wattle-and-daub walls and which were not.

Other Cultural Material. The other categories of cultural material recovered at Hascherkeller were also best represented in the fill of the pits (fig. 30). A total of 11 ceramic loom weights were recovered. Six were found in the pits (two in W, two in BV, one in N west extension, and one in L), four in the inner ditch, and one in the plowsoil.

Seven bronze objects were found in the large pit in Trench W, two in DIII, one in C, and one in N north end. Other bronze fragments were recovered in the plowsoil.

The small iron cylinder in figure 56f was found in the pit at the south end of Trench S, and two iron fragments came from the pit in Trench AAI. Other small fragments of iron found on different parts of the site in the plowsoil could be of prehistoric date; but since large quantities of recent iron debris were also recovered in the plowsoil, such as nails, chains, horseshoes, and plow parts, it is possible that they

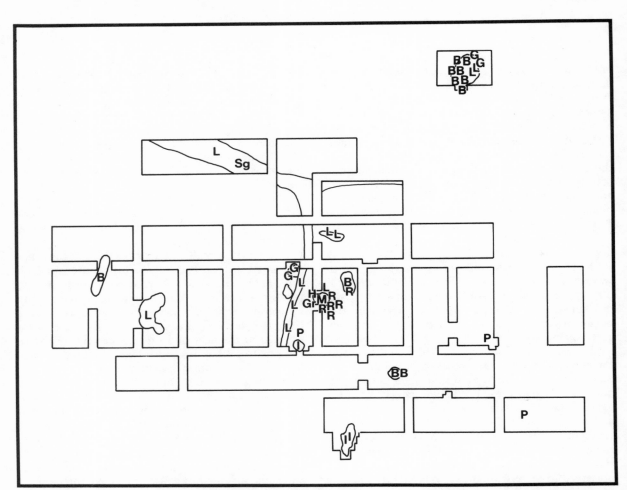

Figure 30. Plan showing the distribution of various categories of artifactual materials in the pits and ditches on the settlement. (Objects recovered in the plowsoil are not represented here.) L: loom weight. B: bronze object. I: iron object. R: ceramic ring (probably spindle whorl). G: glass bead. M: mold. H: hammerstone. Gr: grindstone. Sg: iron slag. P: cache of pebbles (perhaps slingstones).

are corroded fragments of modern materials. One lump of slag was found in the fill of the inner ditch in Trench EII, and four others were found in the plowsoil.

Clay rings were recovered in the two pits in Trench N, five in the pit in the west extension of N and one in the pit in the north end.

The most important tool made of stone, the sandstone mold for casting finger rings, was found in the pit in Trench N west extension. In this same pit were a fragment of a grindstone and a hammerstone made from a quartzite pebble. Two smooth, irregularly shaped stones were found in the pit in Trench AAI, perhaps used as polishing stones. None of the river pebbles interpreted as slingstones (see below) occurred in any of the major pits, though they were found in some of the small features and also just above the loess subsoil at the base of the modern plowsoil.

The Individual Pits: Character, Contents, and Interpretation

Pit in Trench W (figs. 36–39). The pit in Trench W was first identified as a potential feature of the prehistoric settlement on the basis of the magnetometer survey map, where it appeared as a major anomaly on the field (fig. 72). Removal of the modern humus revealed the top of the pit to be an irregular oval roughly 4 by 2.5 m (fig. 21). In Trench W the loess subsoil was reached at a depth of about 60 cm below the modern surface of the ground. The top 20 cm of plowsoil produced a very few sherds, but larger numbers appeared in the layer 20 to 40 cm below the modern surface, particularly over the center of the pit. Many also were recovered in the 40-to-60-cm layer, particularly over the center. At 60 cm down, the outlines of the pit were clear, and at this level the surface was scraped clean and the top of the pit was photographed and mapped.

The pit was bisected along a line running north-south on the grid system, and excavation began on the western half of the pit. The fill was removed in 10-cm levels and screened through the standard quarter-inch mesh hardware cloth. The north-south profile through the middle of the pit is shown in figures 25c and 31. The pit was about 1 m deep from the top of the loess subsoil and a little over 2.5 m wide at the bottom. Throughout the fill were large quantities of cultural materials, particularly pottery and daub, but also animal bone, seven bronze objects, two blue glass beads, and two loom weights. The cultural materials were particularly concentrated in two layers, both densely packed with pottery, charcoal, and daub, which were sepa-

Table 5.
Volume of the settlement pits.

Pit	Approximate volume (in cubic centimeters)
W	6,440,000
L	3,980,900
C	2,116,800
AAI	997,150
S south end	875,000
DIII	846,720
N north end	441,000
S north end	431,825
N west extension	346,500
S red pit	346,115
BV	103,950

Note: These are very rough approximations calculated as follows: maximum length of top surface × maximum width of top surface × depth of pit × 0.70. The volumes so calculated are not strictly comparable because of the different shapes of the pits. Since the tops of all pits were destroyed by subsequent agricultural activity, these figures do not represent the volumes of the original features.

Figure 31. North-south profile through the large pit in Trench W. The ranging rod is marked off in half-meter intervals. (Compare fig. 25c.)

rated by 10 to 15 cm of the brown pit fill. Study of the pottery indicates that the two layers are not distinct typologically or chronologically. The time difference between their depositions may have been a few minutes, if the separating layer was intentionally shoveled onto old debris to create a clean working surface, or a few years, if the pit remained open and humus washed and blew into it naturally. The time lapse between deposition of the two layers is unlikely to have been as long as a century since no typological differences could be recognized between the ceramics above and below the separating deposit.

The bottom of the pit was originally flat. Before much activity had taken place inside the pit, some of the loess that had been shoveled out fell back into the pit, forming the loess-humus mixture that now fills the bottom of the pit. No pottery, charcoal, or daub was recovered in this bottom zone, suggesting that the soil reentered the pit soon after it was dug and before it was put to its intended use.

The shape of the pit had originally been rectangular, as became apparent in the course of excavation (figs. 32, 33).

At a depth of about 60 cm below the top of the loess subsoil in the northern half of the pit, the remains of a roughly rectangular structure consisting of bright reddish-orange clay were encountered. At the top where it first appeared at a depth of 60 cm below the top of the loess, the structure was diffuse and the bright reddish-orange clay was largely mixed with humic soil, as if this portion of the original

structure had been severely damaged, either shortly after the end of its use or at a later stage in the history of the pit. Below this depth the structure became more coherent and distinct, and the edges more clearly defined. At about 70 cm below the top of the loess its form was clearest as an elongated rectangle about 55 cm across (measured from outer wall to outer wall) and some 70 cm long (fig. 34). At a depth of 80 cm below the top of the loess only the base of the structure remained.

Closely associated with this structure — within it, around it, and above it — were dense concentrations of broken pottery, much of it consisting of wasters (figs. 38m, 39h), charcoal, including the remains of whole carbonized logs, and fragments of daub. The association of numerous waster sherds and abundant charcoal with this structure suggests that it was the remains of a pottery kiln.

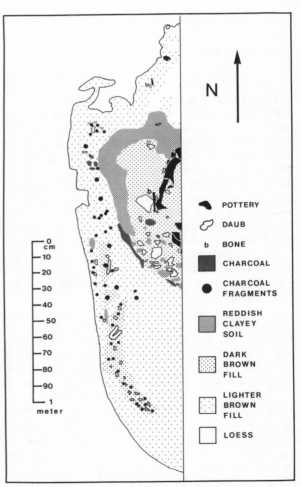

Figure 32. The western half of the large pit in Trench W, at 70 cm into the loess subsoil.

Figure 33. Plan of the western half of the large pit in Trench W, at 70 cm into the loess subsoil.

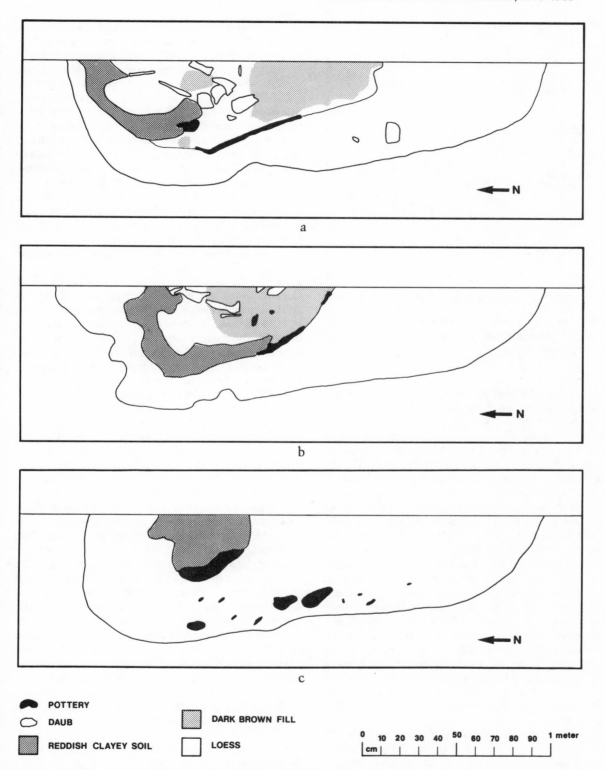

POTTERY

DAUB

REDDISH CLAYEY SOIL

DARK BROWN FILL

LOESS

Figure 34. The structure interpreted as the base of a kiln in the pit in Trench W. a. at 60 cm into loess subsoil. b. at 70 cm. c. at 80 cm.

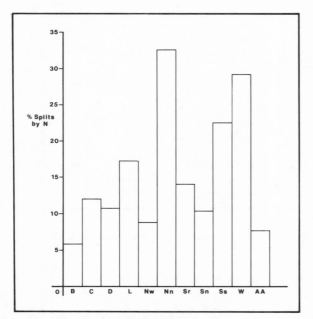

Figure 35. Histogram of the percentage of split sherds in the principal pits.

Other kilns that have been excavated from this period are round, such as those at Elchinger Kreuz (Pressmar 1979) and Sévrier (Bocquet and Couren 1974), but in the reports about these other sites little is said about the structures of the fireboxes beneath the domed firing chambers. At Hascherkeller the firing chamber was not preserved; the covering dome and the perforated surface on which the pottery stood were both missing, represented only by the large quantity of daub fragments in the pit. What survived in the bottom of the pit appears to have been the lower structure of the firebox, which was situated beneath the kiln and in which charcoal and wood were burned to provide the heat for the firing. This fragmentary structure is very similar in form and size to a feature at Elchinger Kreuz interpreted there as a baking oven (Pressmar 1979, pp. 21–23, pl. 26), a structure with the purpose of generating heat by fire. Kilns with domed firing chambers often had rectangular firing boxes beneath them (e.g., Hodges 1982, p. 119, fig. 29). Thus the missing upper portions of the kiln at Hascherkeller may well have been round like the other contemporaneous ones that have been excavated.

The quantities of the different categories of pottery in this pit (table 1; figs. 26, 27) support the interpretation of the structure as the remains of a kiln. The vast majority of the pottery from the 11 principal pits at Hascherkeller came from this one pit: 69 percent of all sherds by count, 65 percent by weight. This pit also had an exceptionally high proportion of split sherds (fig. 35) and of very small sherds, consistent with the presence of a sherd dump next to a kiln. Every firing of pottery produces some unusable vessels. Leach, a British potter, notes that in a firing of 284 pots done by him about 30 percent were useless and had to be discarded (cited in Pressmar 1979, p. 34). Even if we assume a failure rate of 20 percent or even 10 percent, a lot of pottery had to be discarded over a period of years. A pottery dump is more likely to contain large proportions of split and highly fragmented sherds than other contexts because many sherds are thrown together and thereby broken; a dump in the vicinity of a kiln would probably be trampled on frequently as well.

Many of the sherds from this pit were wasters that cracked in the firing process and were therefore discarded. Such wasters do not occur elsewhere on the site. In other numerical comparisons of the pits on the basis of the pottery in them, the pit in Trench W falls remarkably close to the center of the distributions. The pottery forms in Trench W are also very similar to those in all of the pits on the site. The two loom weights recovered in the pit, both fragmentary, may also represent misfirings.

The location of this pit outside of the enclosures and removed from the main settlement area is consistent with its interpretation as a kiln site. Pottery firing and metalworking were frequently done outside settlements, both because of the fire hazard involved and because of the unpleasant smoke and gases produced (see chapter 12). With the kiln situated north of the settlement, gases produced by firings would have been carried by the prevailing winds eastward past the settled area.

As the section drawing of the pit (fig. 25c) indicates, the bottom structure of the kiln was situated at the very bottom of the pit, suggesting (1) the pit was originally dug to accommodate the kiln and (2) the material situated stratigraphically above the remains of the kiln was deposited in the pit after the kiln had ceased to function and is not necessarily related to the kiln. Any depression on a settlement surface collects debris. A pit once used for a specific purpose, as in this case for firing pottery, after abandonment would have tended to fill with debris from the community living near it. Unless a pit interfered with the daily life of the community members, it is unlikely that anyone would have taken the trouble to fill it in.

The lower of the two layers of pottery and other cultural material was probably deposited during the use-life of the kiln or immediately after it. Wasters and other kiln debris were probably tossed aside by

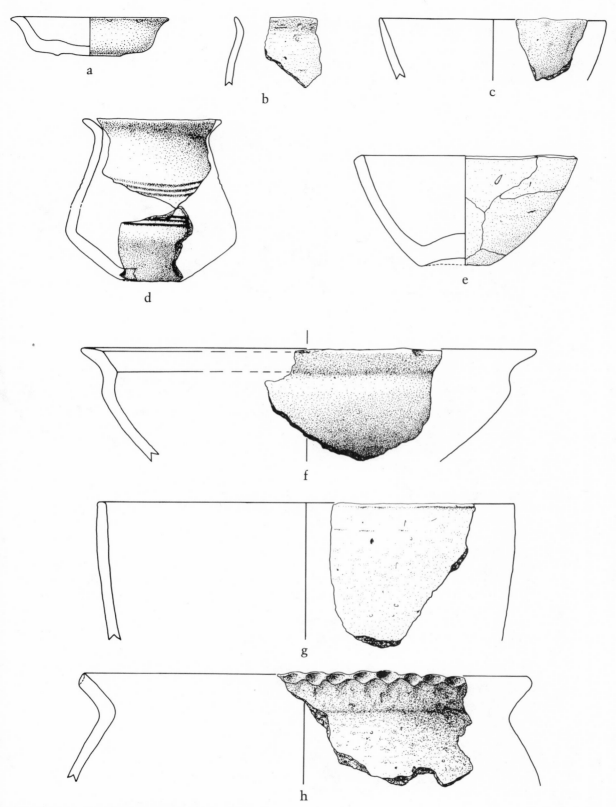

Figure 36. Pottery from the pit in Trench W.

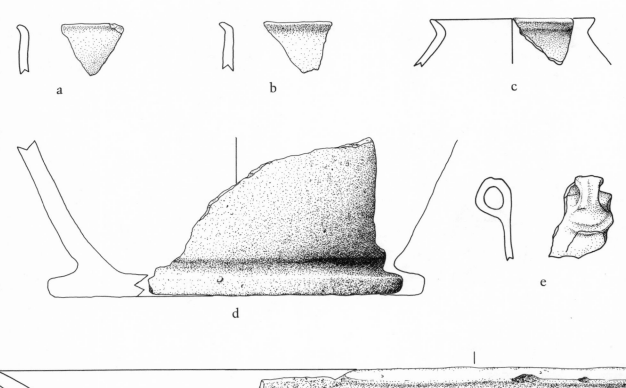

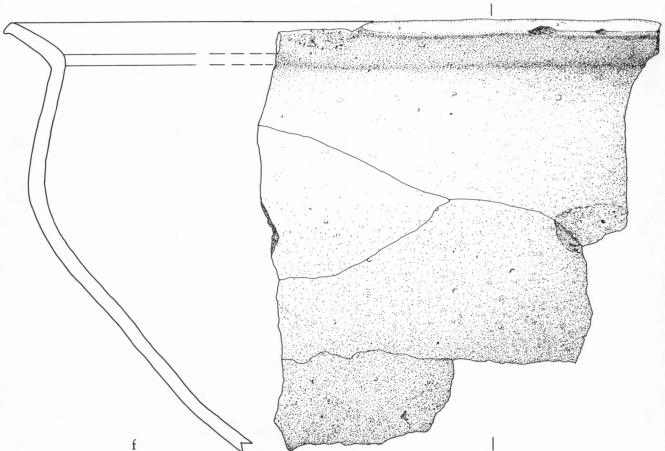

Figure 37. Pottery from the pit in Trench W.

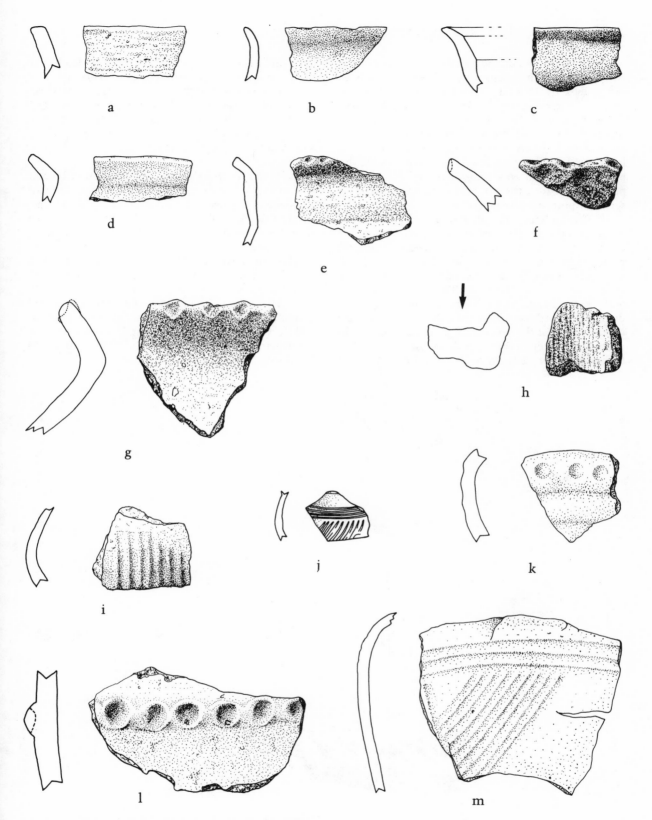

Figure 38. Pottery from the pit in Trench W. h. daub.

potters or piled up close by the kiln. The upper of the two layers, which is separated from the remains of the firebox by 10 to 15 cm of fill containing few cultural materials, was deposited after the kiln had ceased to be used. Since the material in this layer is typologically indistinguishable from that in the lower layer, it is likely that the pottery in this upper layer was tossed onto a discard pile just outside the pit when the kiln was being used and shoveled or pushed back into the pit when the kiln ceased to serve for pottery manufacture.

The daub from the pit was probably part of the dome over the firing chamber. No large fragments of daub survived in this pit, and no useful structural pieces indicated the form of the walls of the kiln.

The seven bronze objects recovered probably entered the pit accidentally. The bronze pin with lentil-shaped head and the small bronze ring with diamond-shaped section are the only complete bronze objects found at the settlement, and they were probably lost by their wearers, perhaps the potters. The five fragmentary bronze pins are unlikely to have been discarded on purpose and probably also found their way into this pit through some oversight.

Two beads of dark blue glass were found close to the top of the pit, and they need not have had anything to do with the operation of the kiln. They can only be regarded as objects lost by the wearer of a necklace or bracelet of beads.

Pit in Trench BV (fig. 41). The rich pit in Trench B, Cutting V became apparent in the top layer of plowsoil as a dense concentration of sherds appearing at a depth of about 15 cm. The soil around the sherds was left standing while the rest of the cutting was taken down to the top of the loess subsoil. The shallow pit was excavated with trowels and brushes so that the pottery and other cultural materials could be left in place for photography and drawing (fig. 40).

The pit was 2.65 m long and 0.80 m wide and extended only a few centimeters into the loess subsoil. It contained a dense deposit of broken pottery, along with daub fragments, animal bone, and two loom weights.

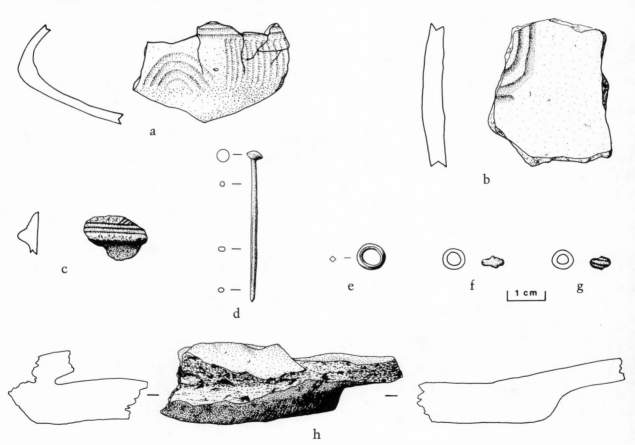

Figure 39. Trench W. a, b, c, h. pottery. d, e. bronze. f, g. greenish-blue glass.

Figure 40. Part of the fill of the long, narrow pit in Trench BV in the course of excavation, view looking north. Note particularly the numerous large sherds of pottery that are visible.

The pottery in this pit (fig. 41) consisted principally of large, thick-walled vessels. The situation of the pottery suggested that a row of such vessels, so close together as to be almost touching one another, had been crushed in place. The shape of the pit, the presence of large vessels apparently crushed in place, and the high concentration of daub (fig. 29) suggest that this feature was a cellar pit beneath a house, like that beneath the Early Iron Age house at the Lochenstein in Württemberg published by Bersu and Goessler (1924, pl. 24).

This interpretation is supported by the character of the pottery assemblage. As suggested above, the percentage of split sherds in pits may be an indication of the degree to which the sherds in the pit were knocked together. In the pit in Trench BV the proportion of split sherds is the lowest of any of the pits (fig. 35), suggesting that the pottery in this pit was knocked about much less than average at the site. The interpretation of the pit as a cellar containing large storage vessels is consistent with these data. The vessels were probably broken by the collapse of the structure above and by the subsequent pressure of the soil on them, but the sherds were not as greatly fragmented as they would have been had they been tossed into a rubbish area. A similar configuration is apparent in the pottery from the pit in Trench AAI (see below).

Another indicator in support of this interpretation is the very low proportion of fine pottery in Trench BV, the lowest of any pit on the site both in number of sherds and in total weight of sherds. Here again the numerical evidence supports the suggestion of a specific use for this pit that did not involve fine pottery.

Interpretation as a storage cellar to hold large ceramic vessels containing foodstuffs is further supported by the exceptionally high percentage of sherds of thick pottery (45.07 percent by count and 63.23 percent by weight), both substantially higher than for any other pit. Here again, the figures support the hypothesis that (1) this pit was a special-purpose structure rather than a catchall trash receptacle and (2) this function was one of food storage, involving predominantly pottery of the thick category.

Pit in Trench C (fig. 42). Materials from the pit in Trench C appeared in the overlying plowsoil and on the surface; chunks of daub and sherds of pottery were recovered in an area directly above this feature. At 0 to 20 cm below the ground surface, the northern end of the pit, situated in Trench BII, became apparent as a dark, humus-filled feature. Much daub from the pit was scattered throughout the plowsoil in the 0-to-20-cm level below the surface in the eastern half of Trench BII. Similarly, in the early stages of humus removal from Trench C abundant chunks of daub were found in the northwest corner in and above the pit.

Once the humus topsoil was removed, the pit

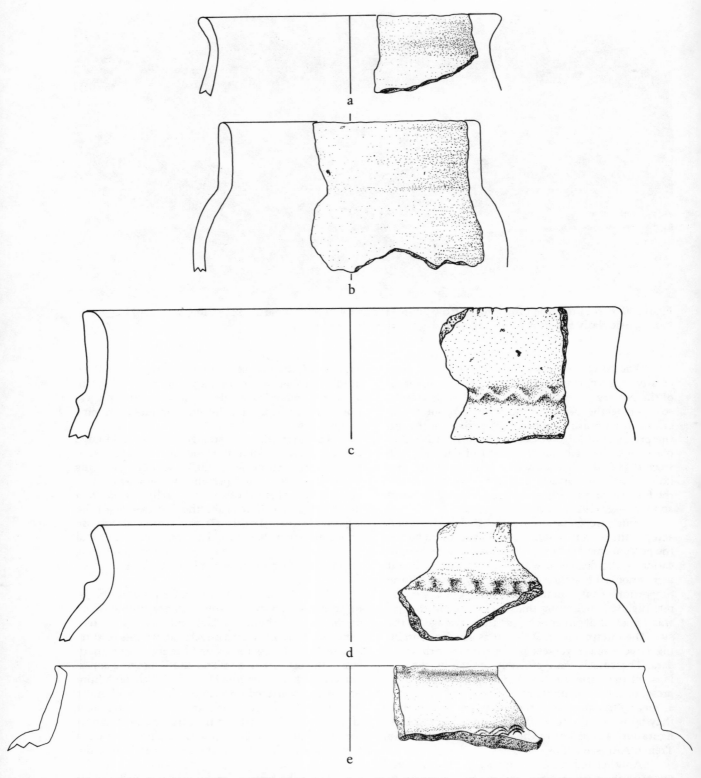

Figure 41. a, b, c. pottery from the long, narrow pit in Trench BV. d, e. sherds from the plowsoil near the pit.

became clear as a long, narrow, and symmetrical feature filled with dark brown humus intruding into the loess subsoil. It was 4.9 m long and about 1 m wide, and it extended 0.90 m from the top of the loess down. In section it was cup-shaped and symmetrical.

The most striking of the pit's contents was the daub, of which 75,080 g were recovered, nearly twice as much as in the pit with the next most daub (fig. 29). This aspect alone strongly suggests that a building had stood above the pit. The form of this pit also points to a function similar to that in Trench BV, a cellar hole beneath a building. Like the one in BV, this pit contained very little fine pottery (fig. 42).

This pit yielded a small fragment of bronze recovered during screening.

Pit in Trench DIII (figs. 43–45). The settlement pit in Trench D, Cutting III was presaged by pottery and daub in the plowsoil layers above the subsoil. Just above the level at which the pit became visible in the subsoil, especially large quantities of daub and sherds were recovered in the humus. When the surface of the loess was cleaned off with hoes and trowels, the pit appeared as an almost round feature 1.3 m in diameter. In section, the pit was found to have

a remarkably straight wall on one side and an overhanging one (perhaps because of a wall collapse) on the other. The bottom of this pit was flat. Such a flat bottom could not have been produced unintentionally but must have been purposely dug in that fashion. The shape of this pit, compared with those on other settlements, suggests that it was dug for storage of grain. Whether it was lined or not is unknown; no lining residue survived, nor were any other indications of lining observed.

The very small quantity of daub recovered in this pit is consistent with the hypothesis that it was a grain storage pit at some remove from any building. The 728 sherds of pottery (figs. 43–45), the most numerous assemblage on the site after that from Trench W, are best interpreted as being a result of secondary deposition, as the numerical patterns in the three categories of sherds suggest. The intermediate category of pottery, the one best represented on the site both in numbers and weight, is better represented than the average in this pit, as is the fine pottery. The amount of thick pottery is well below the average for the site. If it is correct that the intermediate category of pottery principally comprised everyday eating utensils, then this kind of pottery would have been most frequently broken (Foster

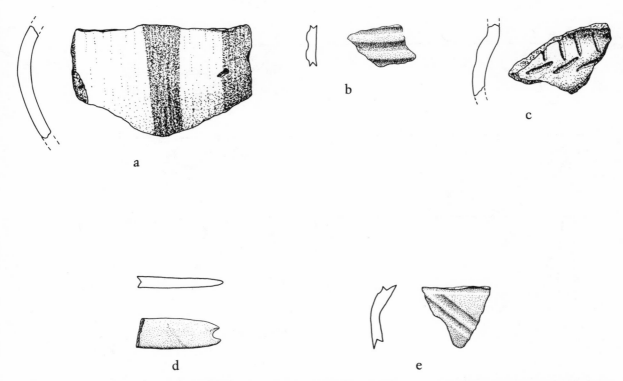

Figure 42. a, b, c. pottery from the pit in Trench C. Sherd a has a decoration of graphite bands; b has graphite coating on the exterior. d, e. bone object and sherd from the plowsoil above the pit.

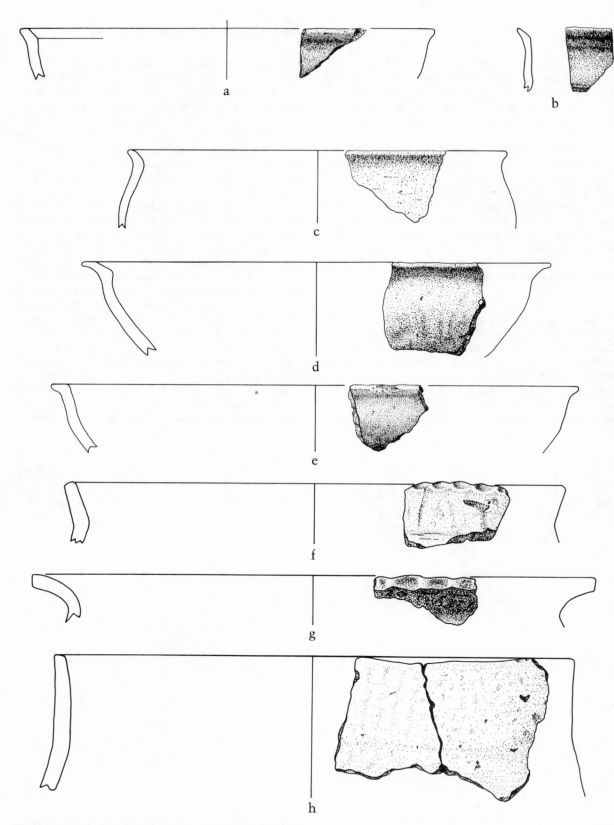

Figure 43. Pottery from the pit in Trench DIII.

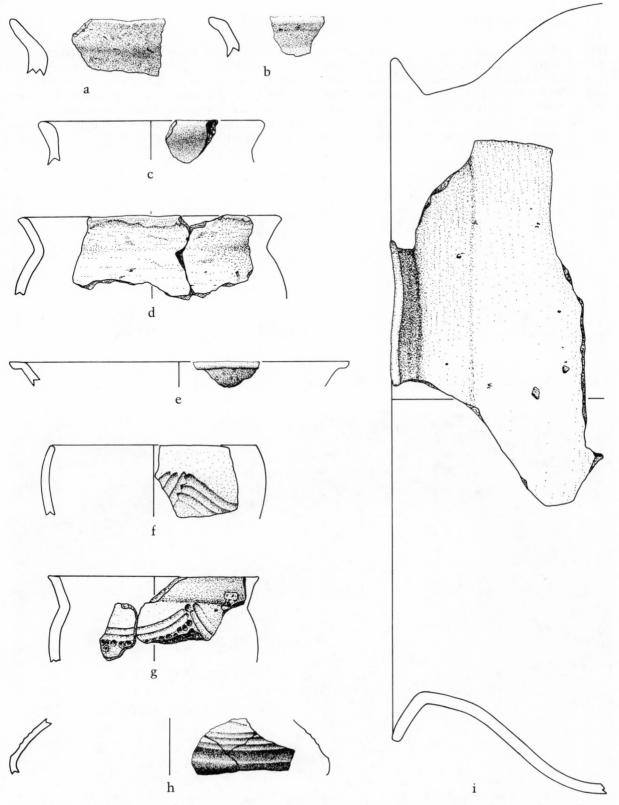

Figure 44. Pottery from the pit in Trench DIII. Sherds g and h have graphite coating on the exterior surfaces.

1960; David 1972) and hence best represented in trash contexts. If the thick ware served principally for storage of food, these vessels would rarely have been moved or lifted. Thus, the thick pottery would not be expected to occur frequently in secondary trash deposits. Since it was kept in underground cellars, it would have broken principally when a destroyed or abandoned house collapsed on top of it.

Most likely, the occupants of Hascherkeller simply tossed broken sherds into any convenient hollow in the ground, such as this disused storage pit, or they may have thrown them aside to the ground surface. Those sherds which found their way into hollows survived intact until recovery; those

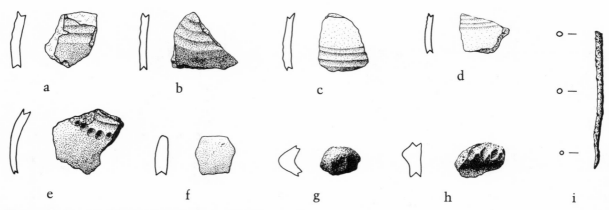

Figure 45. Material from Trench DIII. a–h. pottery. i. bronze.

Figure 46. The large pit in Trench L.

which did not were crushed underfoot or pulverized by plows over the millennia.

Besides the pottery, daub, and animal bones, two bronze objects were recovered in this pit: a long fragment of a pin and a small piece of sheet bronze.

Pit in Trench L (fig. 48). Cultural material from the pit in Trench L became evident in the humus layers, and at a depth of about 60 cm the top of the loess subsoil around the pit was reached. Surface cleaning yielded a large, irregularly shaped pit consisting of dark brown fill (fig. 46) with numerous fragments of cultural materials, particularly pottery, daub, and charcoal, apparent on the top surface (fig. 47). The feature measured 4.4 m long by 2.8 m wide, and it extended down about 45 cm from the top of the loess subsoil. Four different sections were cut through this large feature in order to obtain a variety of different profile views and to examine variations in structure and fill. The feature contained little daub relative to other pits on the settlement, and the pottery, with 318 sherds, was the median quantity of the 11 pits (fig. 26). The pit was a shallow hollow with sloping sides and was probably a borrow pit, dug for the procurement of clay for the manufacture of pottery, loom weights, and daub.

The small amount of daub in the pit (fig. 29) suggests that a building was probably not immediately associated with it. The pottery (fig. 48) shows a high proportion of split sherds by weight (as high as for Trench W), suggesting that the ceramic material in the pit was subjected to a considerable amount of battering (fig. 35). Like the pit in Trench DIII, that in Trench L is characterized by a very high proportion of sherds of intermediate thickness (the highest on the site) and a very low proportion of those of the thick category (the lowest on the site). The arguments put forward in connection with Trench DIII hold for this pit as well. The secondary function of this pit accounts for the character of its contents. Having been dug as a borrow pit and then left, this hollow in Trench L was a catchall for settlement rubbish, including animal bones, broken pottery, and other material. The fact that rubbish was tossed in or unintentionally kicked or washed in is suggested by the high proportion of split sherds (fig. 35).

This pit also yielded a ceramic loom weight in fragmentary condition.

Pit in Trench N North End (fig. 49). Pottery associated with this pit began to appear in the humus layer. Close to the top of the pit was found a perfect bone button (fig. 49j) at a depth of about 35 cm below the modern ground surface. At this level, it cannot be said with certainty that the button belonged to

the prehistoric pit; it could have entered the deposit at any later time up to the present and been moved down to this depth by plows. A similar bone button has been found at the Heuneburg, also in a stratigraphically uncertain context, as Dr. S. Sievers informs me.

The top of the loess subsoil was reached in Trench N at a depth of between 35 and 40 cm below the modern surface. At this depth the pit was clearly apparent as a roughly rectangular intrusion measuring 2.2 m long by 1.1 m wide and filled with dark brown humus (fig. 17). Sectioning showed it to be a very shallow pit, at the deepest 25 cm and with a flat bottom. The pit yielded very little daub, suggesting that no building of wattle-and-daub construction was associated. It produced a considerable quantity of sherds (fig. 49), the third most of all the pits. The large quantity of split sherds is striking (fig. 35).

The most likely explanation for this pit is that it was dug as a borrow pit. Its shallowness argues against any function such as grain storage, while the shape (wide and shallow instead of narrow and deep) argues against a cellar hole as does the small quantity of daub. The high proportion of split sherds is consistent with a secondary use of this hollow as a trash receptacle.

Also found in this pit were a fragmentary bronze tool (fig. 49k) and a ceramic ring.

Pit in Trench N West Extension (figs. 52–55). Material associated with the pit in the west extension of Trench N appeared in the upper humus layer. This pit was rich in several different kinds of

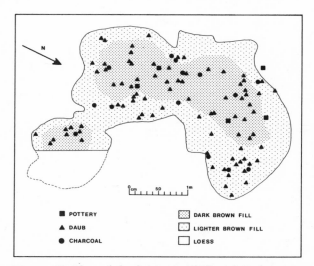

Figure 47. Plan of the large pit in Trench L showing the distribution of cultural debris on the surface (at the level of the top of the loess).

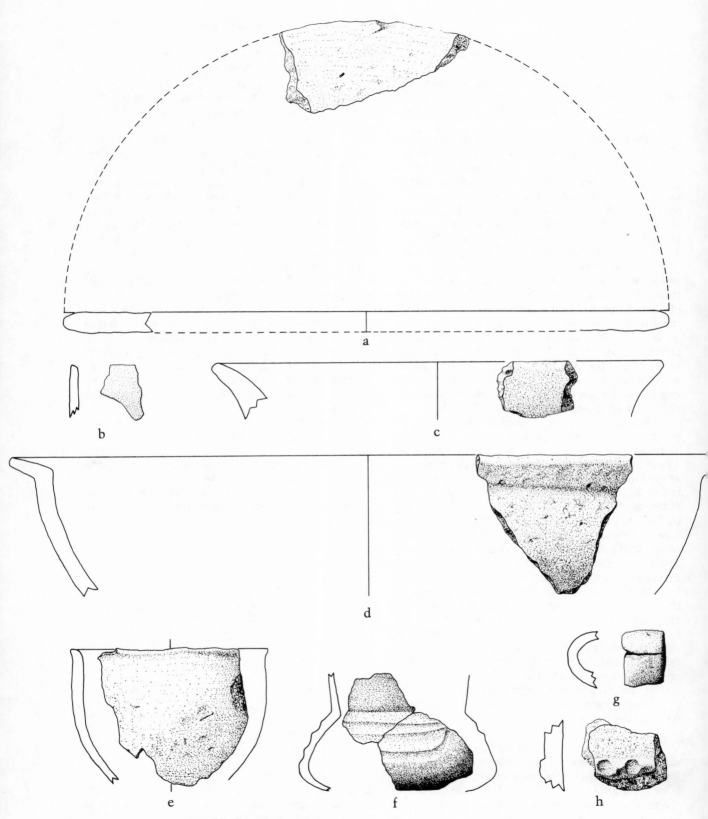

Figure 48. Pottery from the pit in Trench L.

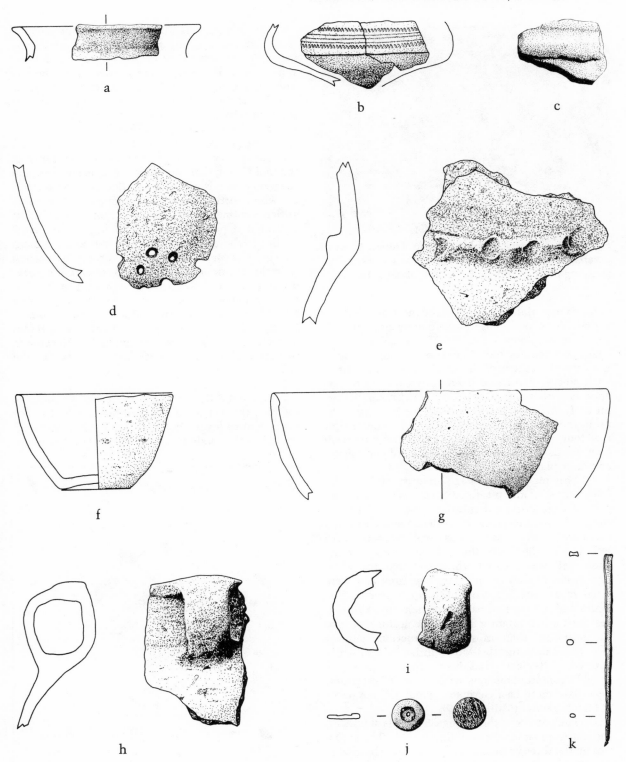

Figure 49. Cultural material from Trench N north end. a–i. pottery. j. bone. k. bronze.

Figure 50. The surface of the pit in Trench N west extension, at the level of the top of the loess subsoil, showing pottery and daub. View looking south.

cultural material. The form of the pit at the level of the top of the loess subsoil was roughly circular with a diameter of about 1.1 m (figs. 50, 51). The pit was shallow, extending only 20 cm down from the top of the subsoil. Because of the special nature of the fill, with pieces of cultural debris often on top of one another with little soil between them (much like the pit in Trench BV), it was decided not to section the pit in the usual fashion but instead to divide the pit into four quadrants, remove the material from each by hand, using trowels and brushes, and photograph and draw plans at frequent intervals.

This pit yielded a large quantity of daub, the fourth most of any pit (fig. 29), suggesting the presence of a structure either directly above or close to the pit. Numerous pieces of daub had white paint on them, frequently in as many as three layers separated by layers of plain daub (fig. 52), indicating that the daub wall was painted white and that the walls underwent repairs in the course of time and were often repainted. Some of the daub fragments had white and red painted bands on them (fig. 53), suggesting a much brighter and more colorful aspect to the buildings than most reconstructions suggest (e.g., those in Reinerth 1936). Similar red and white painted wall plaster has been reported from the roughly contemporaneous settlement of Rottelsdorf near Eisleben in East Germany, about 350 km north of Hascherkeller (Müller 1959).

The pottery in the pit (figs. 54, 55) is abundant, the fourth most on the site (figs. 26, 27). The statistics on the three categories of pottery are remarkably close to the average for the whole site. The proportion of split sherds is low, suggesting that the pit did not serve as a trash receptacle.

Particularly significant from this pit are the traces of manufacturing activity. The sandstone mold (fig. 66) was found in this pit, as were a loom weight, five of the six ceramic rings from the site (the other, from the pit at the north end of this same trench, may have entered that borrow pit from the same activity area as these), a fragment of a grindstone, and a quartzite pebble hammer.

The proliferation of daub suggests that a structure stood over or close to the pit. The presence of the mold, complete and undamaged, is puzzling and suggests that this part of the settlement, and perhaps the whole settlement, was abandoned suddenly. It is difficult to imagine that a perfect mold would be left behind if departure was not in haste. The same applies to the complete ceramic rings and the loom weight. The pit must have been directly associated with these craft activities, perhaps as part of a weaving area and/or of a bronze casting area. The fact that these two different crafts are represented in this one pit suggests that different crafts were carried out in a single location, perhaps by a jack-of-all-trades craftsperson or by different individuals who came to the same place in the settlement to work in the different media.

Trench S Red Pit (fig. 56b–e). Unlike many of the pits, this feature did not become evident in the upper humus levels, but first at a depth of about 35 cm below the modern surface. It first became appar-

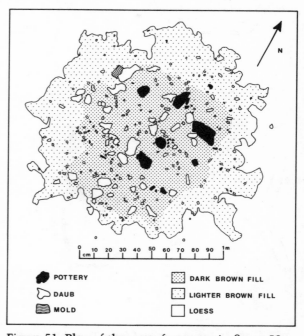

Figure 51. Plan of the same feature as in figure 50.

0   1

cm

Figure 52. Fragment of daub showing three layers of whitewash.

ent as a concentration of red soil, red pebbles, pottery, and daub. The most striking aspect of this pit, distinguishing it from all other features on the site, was the abundance of pebbles stained red, some up to 10 cm in length but most less than 2 cm long. Much of the humic fill of this pit was also this peculiar red color, particularly in the top 20 cm of the pit; below that depth the fill was brown humus similar to that in the other pits.

The form of the pit at the level of the subsoil was irregularly oval, with maximum dimensions of 1.45 m long and 1.1 m wide. The pit had relatively steep sides and a flat bottom, attaining a depth of 32 cm below the top of the loess subsoil. It contained a small amount of both daub and pottery (fig. 56–e). The proportions of the three categories of pottery are close to the average for the whole site, suggesting that the pottery in this pit probably does not indicate anything about the specific functions of this pit but rather represents trash that accumulated in it after it had served its primary purpose.

The purpose of the pit must relate to the presence of the strongly burned soil and the burned pebbles. The shape also suggests that it was dug to serve a particular purpose, not just to obtain clay. Since the red staining of the pebbles and soil suggests intense heat, it is odd that little charcoal was found in the pit. If a fire had burned just above the present top of the pit, all traces of the fire may have been obliterated by the plow. The red material in this pit may have migrated down from above.

Pit in Trench S South End (fig. 56f–n). All of Trench S contained an abundance of cultural material in the humus layers, and in the southern part of

the trench much of this material derived from the pit in the southern wall and some from the ditch running just west of it. Since the humus covering the site became deeper toward the edge of the terrace, it was not until excavation had reached a depth of 55 cm below the modern ground surface that the outline of this pit became clear in the loess subsoil. At this depth, the top of the pit was oval, 1.25 m by 1.0 m across. The pit extended 80 cm down into the loess subsoil (135 cm below the modern surface). In its upper portions the pit was shaped like a shallow basin, then at a depth of 20 cm below the top of the subsoil it became narrow and steep-sided. It contained pottery and daub all the way to the bottom. Numerous fragments of charcoal were found throughout the fill, including some close to the bottom. These charcoal fragments were used to obtain a radiocarbon determination.

The total quantity of daub in this pit was small because the fragments were all very small pieces. The 271 sherds of pottery are just below the median for the 11 pits. The proportion of intermediate pottery is above the average for the site, that for the other two categories below the average. As in the case of Trench DIII, the form of this pit suggests that it was dug to serve a particular purpose, while the archaeological material in it suggests that there was no building above or next to it and that the purpose of the pit does not relate to the proportions of pottery in it. In this pit and in that in Trench DIII, the pottery reflects secondary use as trash receptacles. The form of each would be consistent with an original function as a grain storage pit.

This pit also yielded a small cylindrical object of iron (fig. 56f), recovered in the process of screening the pit fill from a depth of 40 to 60 cm below the top of the loess subsoil (95 to 115 cm below the modern surface).

Pit in Trench S North End (fig. 56a). The top of this pit became evident in the level of the plowsoil

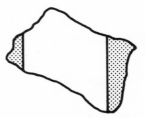

Figure 53. Fragment of daub showing bands of white and red paint. The drawing is based on a sketch from the excavation record book. Shown at actual size.

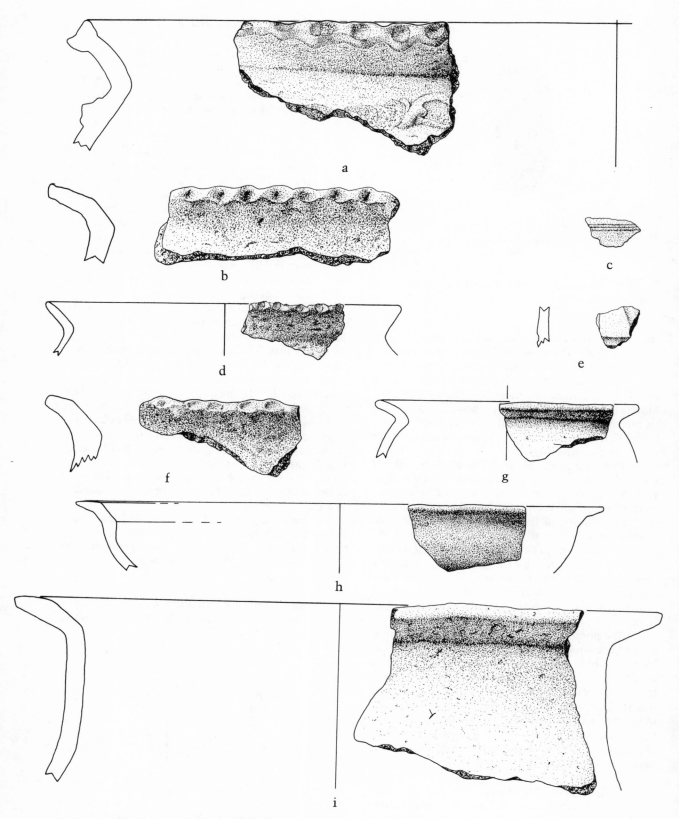

Figure 54. Pottery from Trench N west extension.

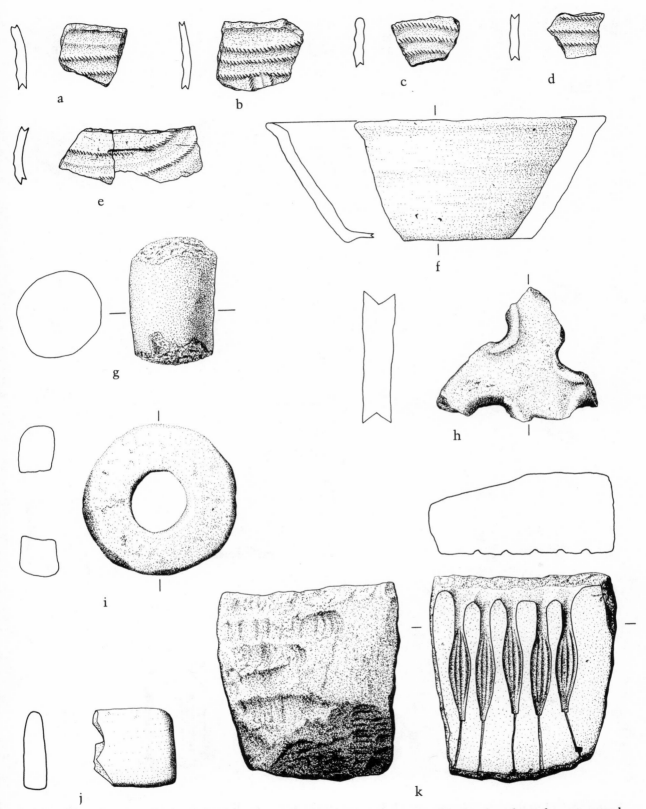

Figure 55. Cultural material from Trench N west extension. a–f, h, i. pottery. Sherds a through e are coated with graphite. g, j, k. stone.

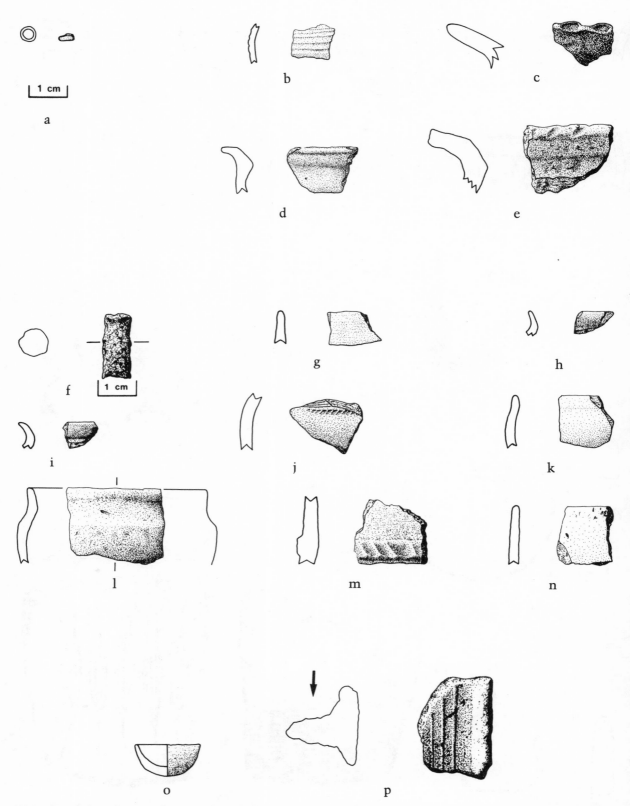

Figure 56. Cultural materials from Trench S. a. from pit at north end. b–e. from red pit. f–n. from pit at south end. o, p. from ditch fill. a. greenish-blue glass. f. iron. p. daub. The rest is pottery.

20 to 40 cm below the surface. Since the pit had been cut into by the ditch next to it, it was difficult to distinguish ditch fill from pit fill at the upper levels. Both were identical in color and consistency, and no boundary between the two was visible. At 60 cm below the modern surface the outlines of the ditch and pit could be discerned, but the nature of the intersection was still impossible to determine. At a depth of 70 cm below the modern surface, the boundary between the two features became distinct. It was apparent that the ditch was dug subsequent to the pit and had cut through its eastern edge. From this depth on it was possible to separate the cultural material coming out of the two features with confidence.

The width of the pit at the level of the loess was 0.95 m; its original length was probably around 1.4 m before it was cut by the ditch. Its shape was oval. The pit contained the smallest amount of daub of any of the pits, and the quantity of pottery was also very small. In part these low quantities stem from the fact that material at the top of the pit could not be assigned with assurance to either the pit or the ditch and was therefore left out of these computations. Yet in the course of removing and screening the fill from this pit, it was observed that the sherds were generally much smaller than those from other pits, and this observation during excavation is confirmed by the average weights of the sherds from this pit (table 1). The average weight of thick sherds

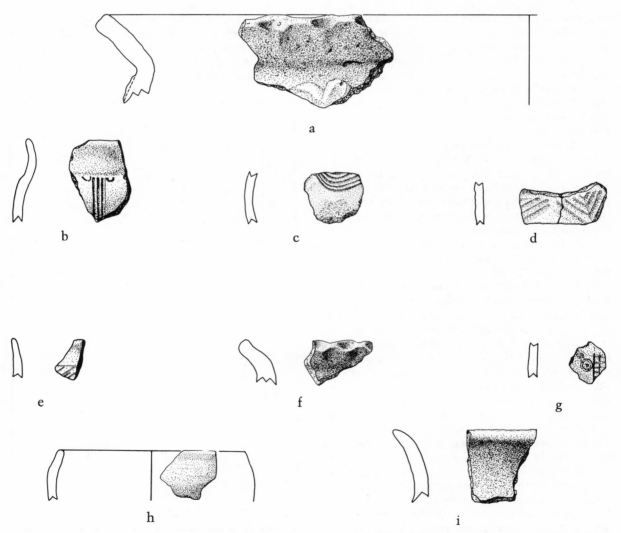

Figure 57. Pottery from the plowsoil in Trench S. Sherds b, e, and g contain traces of white paste in the grooves.

here is less than half that of the thick sherds from any other pit, and the average weight of intermediate sherds is less than for any other pit (fig. 58). Thus the debris in this pit appears to have been exceptionally fragmented.

The pit had a flat bottom and nearly vertical sides. Its depth was 55 cm below the top of the loess subsoil.

Like the pits in Trenches DIII and S south end, and for the same reasons, this pit is likely to have been a grain storage facility containing a secondary fill of general trash from the settlement surface.

Two small glass beads of greenish-blue color were found in the fill of this pit, one complete and one fragmentary.

Pit in Trench AAI. Material from this pit began to appear in some quantity in the level 20 to 40 cm below the surface. In the 40-to-60-cm level below the surface large quantities of daub, which were associated with a number of sherds, appeared at the top of the pit. The dimensions of this pit were roughly 3 m long by 1 m wide. In section, it was cup-shaped, like the pits in Trenches BV and C, with steep, curving sides, and it reached a depth of 35 cm below the surface of the loess subsoil.

The pit contained large quantities of daub, including some very large fragments (fig. 59). The total weight of daub here was 43.53 kg, the second most of any pit after the pit in Trench C (fig. 29). The pit contained in its upper parts some large sherds of thick-walled pottery reminiscent of the pit in Trench BV in both the character of the pottery and the apparent crushing-in-place of large vessels. Some of the sherds were very similar to sherds from that other pit. Here again the impression created was that large vessels had been crushed in place, then covered by daub from a collapsed building. On the basis of strong similarities to the pit in Trench BV, this pit is also likely to have been a cellar beneath a building.

The statistics of the pottery support this hypothesis. Like the Trench BV pit, this pit has a very low proportion of split sherds, suggesting that little bashing and splintering occurred. They are both high in average sherd weights of the intermediate and thick categories, also indicating little breakage of pottery in the pit. Additionally, they are both low in the proportion of fine pottery, but the Trench AAI pit is slightly higher than average in thick pottery and in intermediate pottery. It might be suggested, to account for the lower proportion of thick pottery and higher of intermediate than in the pit in Trench BV, that in the collapse of the building over the Trench AAI pit more of the general household pottery entered into the pit than was the case in the Trench BV pit.

This pit also yielded two small fragmentary objects of iron, which were too corroded to identify.

Summary of Pits

On the basis of the shapes and sizes of the pits, quantities of daub in them, proportions of different categories of pottery, and finds of other cultural materials, several different purposes can be suggested for the 11 principal pits on the settlement.

Grain Storage. The pits in Trenches DIII, S north end, and S south end are likely to have served as storage pits for grain. The characteristics of such pits have been discussed at length by Bouzek and Koutecký (1964), Reynolds (1974, 1979a), and Coles (1979).

At Hascherkeller, the special aspects of these pits are steep sides, flat bottoms, small quantities of daub (perhaps reflecting no direct associations with buildings), and cultural debris of secondary (highly fragmented) character.

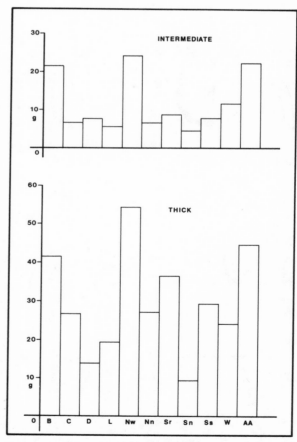

Figure 58. Average weights of intermediate and thick sherds (see table 1).

Cellar Storage. The pits in Trenches BV, C, and AAI were probably storage cellars beneath buildings. The form of each compares with that of a cellar pit beneath a house at the Lochenstein (Bersu and Goessler 1924, pl. 3). The features of these pits at Hascherkeller are a long, thin, symmetrical shape with a cup-shaped vertical section. Large quantities of daub in them suggest that structures stood above them. On settlements of this period in central Europe where postholes survive, houses are usually shown to have been aligned north-south (Herrmann 1974–1975, p. 70). The pits in Trenches C and AAI are both very close to north-south, and that in Trench BV is very close to east-west. The orientation of these three pits thus supports the hypothesis that they were cellars beneath buildings. The high proportion of thick pottery indicates the presence of storage vessels. Few split sherds occur, reflecting relatively little fragmentation. Fine pottery is poorly represented. Pottery proportions as a whole are not close to average for the site but are concentrated toward the thick end of the spectrum.

Borrow Pits. The pits in Trenches N north end and L were probably borrow pits. These pits were dug for the procurement of clay and thus had no characteristics indicative of specific functions. They were shallow and had gently sloping walls. They were long (and in the case of the Trench L pit also wide) in proportion to their depth. Pottery, daub, and bone were all highly fragmented, suggesting secondary (trash) deposition. Daub is not abundant, and proportions of the three categories of pottery are close to the averages for the site as a whole.

The digging of the other pits intended for special uses also produced clay, which could have been used for pottery and daub, and in this sense all pits on the site may have served as borrow pits.

Kiln. Trench W contained the remains of a pottery kiln, including structural remains of the kiln, wasters, much charcoal, and a moderate quantity of daub.

Workshop. Trench N west extension contained numerous objects indicative of crafts activity, particularly bronze casting and weaving. Large amounts of daub, including painted fragments, indicate the presence of a structure above the pit.

Uncertain. The purpose of the Trench S red pit is unclear. The intense burning indicated by the red staining of the soil and pebbles suggests that a hot fire burned nearby, perhaps in connection with melting bronze, but the lack of other evidence makes interpretation problematical.

Figure 59. Section cut through the pit in Trench AAI showing the large chunks of daub throughout the central part of the pit.

CULTURAL MATERIALS RECOVERED

Ceramics

Pottery. The principal characteristics of the pottery from the settlement have been discussed above. The pottery is all of plain character, with minimal ornamentation. Comparison with pictorial representations of vessels in Early Iron Age contexts and with similar vessels used in later times suggests that the various vessels were used principally for cooking, serving, eating, drinking, and storing food and beverages. The basic forms, with the exception of the large storage vessels, are very similar to the forms of pottery in household use in central Europe throughout medieval and into early modern times. The substantial quantity of large vessels of coarse fabric, most likely storage vessels, is of special interest. Wyss (1971a, p. 138) has interpreted the frequency of such large storage vessels on Bronze Age settlements as indicating an increase in agricultural production. The use of large storage containers can be understood in conjunction with the evidence for longer-term occupation of settlements during this period than previously (Bouzek et al. 1966) to indicate a more systematic and controlled approach to the storage of foodstuffs and maintenance of field fertility, all pointing to an increased degree of control over the environment and the food supply.

Loom Weights. Eleven baked ceramic loom weights were recovered at Hascherkeller, all in fragmentary condition though some were still intact enough to have been used (fig. 62). Two were recovered in the pit in Trench W, one in Trench L, two in the long pit in Trench BV, one in Trench N west extension, three in the inner boundary ditch in

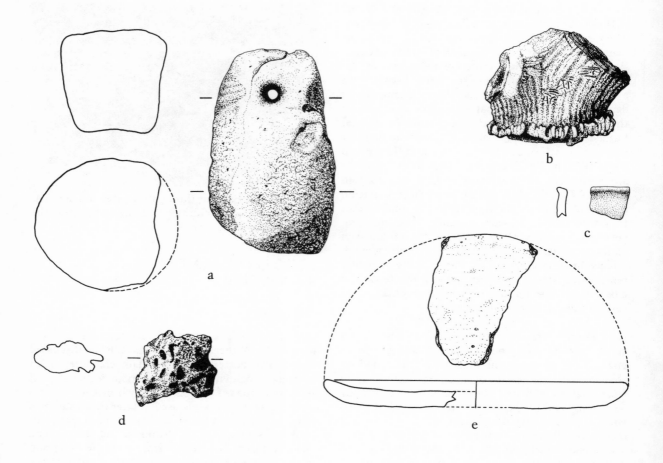

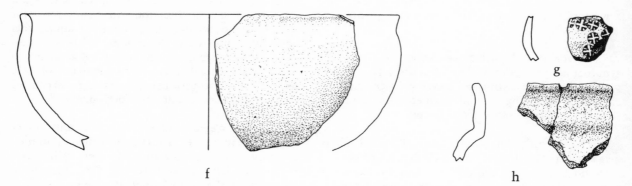

Figure 60. Cultural materials from the fill of the inner ditch of the western enclosure. a–e. from Trench EII. f–h. from Trench FI. a, c, e–h. pottery. b. antler *(Cervus elaphus)*. d. iron slag. g. pottery coated with graphite.

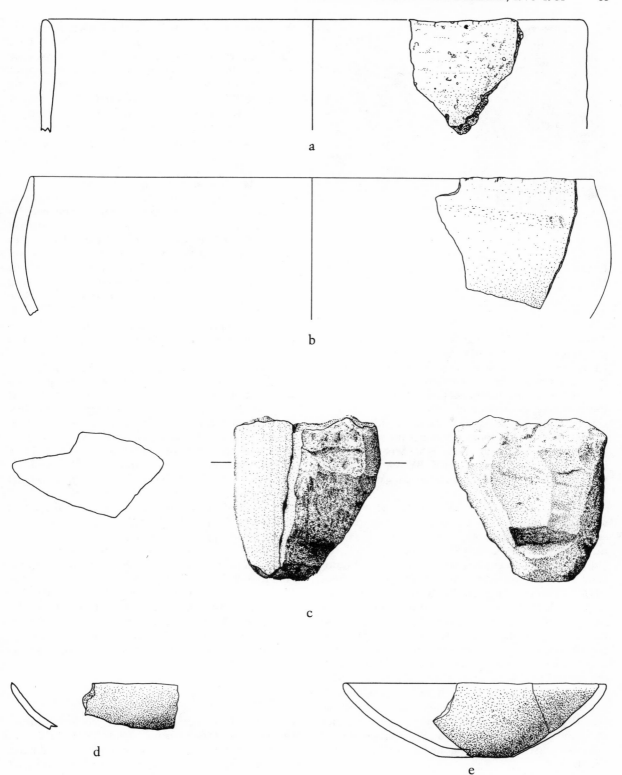

Figure 61. Cultural material from the plowsoil. a, b. from Trench D, balk between Cuttings I and II. c. from Trench EII. d, e. from Trench T. c. stone. The rest is pottery.

a   b

0   5

cm

Figure 62. Two fragmentary loom weights of baked clay.

Trench S, one in the ditch in Trench EII, and one in the plowsoil of Trench BIV. All have the same rounded pyramidal shape with a flat bottom and a large hole near the top, and all are light tan in color.

The distribution of these 11 loom weights on the settlement is relatively dispersed rather than concentrated; hence, there is no clear indication of the location of the loom or looms on which they were used. Seven of the 11 weights were recovered in the contiguous cuttings BIV, BV, N, and S, and weaving may have been done on this part of the settlement.

Loom weights of this form or of roughly similar shape are common at Late Bronze and Early Iron Age settlement sites (e.g., those from the Schlossberg near Kallmünz in Bavaria [Müller-Karpe 1959b, pl. 19], from the Cronenbourg in Alsace [Hatt and Zumstein 1960] and from Stillfried in Austria [A. Eibner 1974]). Pictorial evidence shows how such weights were employed to hold the warp threads taut on vertical looms. The most informative scenes are those on a ceramic vessel from Sopron-Ödenburg in western Hungary (Frey 1976, p. 581, fig. 2) and on the sheet bronze tintinnabulum from the Tomba degli ori at the Arsenale Militare in Bologna (ibid., p. 583, fig. 4). Similar vertical looms have been studied ethnographically in the Faroe Islands (Hald 1950, p. 206, fig. 207). In some unusual instances a whole series of loom weights have been found together as they fell from a disused and abandoned loom (ibid., p. 204, fig. 206a).

The loom weights are important evidence that textile weaving was done at Hascherkeller and that the inhabitants thus filled their own needs for clothes and did not rely on imports. No textile remains survive at the site, as is generally the case in central Europe. Contemporaneous textiles from the bogs of Denmark (Hald 1950) and from the salt mines at Hallstatt in Austria (Hundt 1970; Mefford 1981) show that weaving skills were highly developed by this time. Both wool and linen were being woven in different patterns and dyed in different colors.

Clay Rings. Six rings of baked clay were recovered, five in Trench N west extension and one in Trench N north pit (fig. 63). All are between 7.5 and 8.5 cm in diameter. The principal variation among them is in the size of the central hole. No two are exactly alike, and it would seem that the six specimens represent six different versions of an object that did not require a specific form. Or, the variations in the size of the interior hole may denote different uses.

Such clay rings are common at Late Bronze Age settlements in central Europe (e.g., Herrmann 1966), and in the southeast Alpine region they frequently occur in graves (e.g., Pahič 1972, pl. 2,4; Staré 1975, pl. 11,9; 17,11). Most investigators describe them simply as clay rings and do not suggest what purpose they served, but others propose that they were associated with weaving. Wyss (1971a, p. 134) considers them to have been loom weights. Two objects of stone that are very similar in form and size to the Hascherkeller rings are thought by Kostelníková (1980, p. 79, fig. 1,1) to have been spindle whorls. An object of sandstone of Late Iron Age date from Karlstein bei Bad Reichenhall very similar in shape and size to some of the Hascherkeller rings is considered by Menke to have been a spindle whorl (1977, pp. 230, fig. 5,1, 277). In this connection it is significant that none of the baked clay objects usually considered to have been spindle whorls have been found at Hascherkeller. For the rings with small central holes, at least, an interpretation as spindle whorls is the most likely. In the scene on the tintinnabulum from Bologna (Frey 1976, p. 582, fig. 3), the spindle has a weight on it that resembles the rings from Hascherkeller.

Bronze Objects

A total of 18 bronze objects were recovered during the four field seasons from 1978 to 1981 (fig. 64). In three instances (fig. 64c, g, k), fragments found close together probably belonged to the same original objects; hence, the number of complete objects represented by the finds is probably 14. One fragmentary piece (fig. 64l) is of rhomboid shape and has grooves and ridges around three edges. This object was found on the modern surface of the ground just east of Trench FI; it cannot be dated and thus is left out of discussion here. The tetrahedral lump (fig. 64j) and another, smaller piece were found in the plowsoil of Trench M and similarly cannot be confidently ascribed to the principal occupation.

The remaining 11 bronze objects were recovered in pits belonging to the principal occupation of the settlement. Six are pins, one complete and five fragmented. One (fig. 49k) is probably a fragmentary tool; it could possibly be a pin, but its rectangular section at the larger end suggests a tool. One object is a complete small ring with a diamond-shaped section (fig. 64i). One is a small fragment of sheet bronze (fig. 64f). Two small bronze fragments are unclear as to the form of the original objects (fig. 64b, c).

The distribution of the bronze objects in the pits is as follows:

Pit in Trench W: complete pin, complete ring, fragments of four other pins, two similar fragments of bronze probably not from pins.

Pit in Trench DIII: large fragment of pin, small fragment of thin sheet bronze.

Pit in Trench C: small triangular fragment of flat bronze.

Pit in Trench N north end: fragmentary tool.

The bronze objects found at Hascherkeller are similar to those from other contemporaneous settlements in central Europe. Pins are the best-represented metal objects on Late Bronze Age settlements (Dehn 1972, p. 37, fig. 8a; Primas 1977a, p. 48). The fragment of thin sheet bronze is of special interest because sheet bronze objects are not often found on settlements. This fragment was probably part of a piece of jewelry or a vessel. The complete pin, 8.2 cm long with a lentil-shaped head, from the pit in Trench W is of a form common in graves of the period. Two similar specimens were found in Grave 42 at Unterhaching (Müller-Karpe 1957, pl. 20, A,9.10) and two in Grave 41 at Grünwald (ibid., pl. 11, D,1.2). Both sites are south of Munich. Similar pins have been recovered from graves all over central Europe dating from the earlier part of the Urnfield Period to the Early Iron Age (e.g., Herrmann 1966, p. 31, pl. 99, C22; Kossack 1970, pl. 4, B10; Wells 1981, p. 133, fig. 2e). In Urnfield graves these pins most often occur singly and less often in pairs. Since the burial practice involved cremation and subsequent placement of goods in the urn or next to it, there is little information available about where these pins were worn on the body. Similar pins occur in both

a

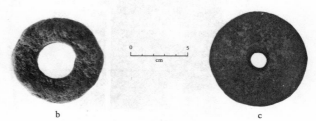

b   c

Figure 63. Three baked clay rings.

men's and women's graves, so the specimen from Hascherkeller may have been worn by a member of either sex.

The bronze ring, which has an external diameter of 1.3 cm, is also of a form common in graves of the period. An example from nearby came from a grave at Steinkirchen on the Danube (Müller-Karpe 1975, p. 173, fig. 2, B3). Such rings are common in graves and also occur on settlements, as at Buchau (Kimmig 1979, p. 54, fig. 19b) and Auvernier (Rychner 1979, vol. II, pl. 95,51–86) and in hoards, such as that from Winklsass (Müller-Karpe 1959a, pl. 148,45). They frequently occur singly in the graves, sometimes in pairs, and occasionally in larger numbers. Very similar rings were found in the rich Early Iron Age Grave 1 at Grosseibstadt in northern Bavaria, dated at around 675 B.C. (Kossack 1970, pl. 39,78–81).

The bronze rod in figure 49k, found in the pit at the north end of Trench N, appears to be fragmentary at the larger end. In its present condition it is 10.35 cm long. The larger end has a rectangular section measuring 0.4 by 0.2 cm. About 1.5 cm from this end, the section changes from rectangular to round, and here the round section is 0.35 cm in diameter. The rod tapers the rest of its length, round in section all the way. The larger end looks as if it may once have been shaped as a chisel. The form of the object resembles that of a bronze piece with a

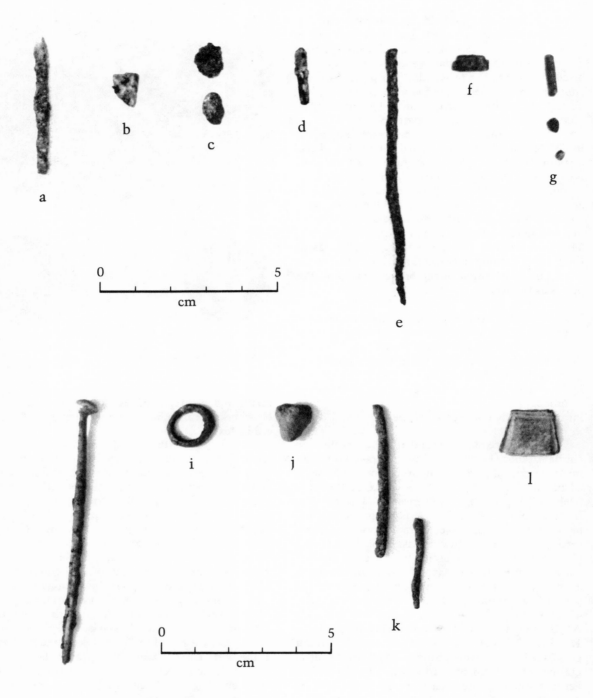

Figure 64. Bronze objects. a, c, d, g, h, i, k. from Trench W. b. from Trench C. e, f. from Trench DIII. j. from Trench M plowsoil. l. stray find from the surface, east of Trench FI.

chisel end from the Roseninsel in the Chiemsee (Müller-Karpe 1959a, pl. 193,36.37) and of two specimens from Auvernier (Rychner 1979, vol. II, pl. 126,13.17). The rectangular section of the larger end suggests that the object was not a decorative pin because such pins have round sections along the entire shaft. The object from Hascherkeller was probably a chisel or similar tool.

Iron Objects

Four iron objects were found in settlement features belonging to the principal period of occupation. These are the lump of iron slag in figure 60d from the top 20 cm of the ditch fill in Trench EII, the small cylindrical object from the pit at the south end of Trench S (figs. 56f, 65a), and two heavily corroded fragments from the pit in Trench AAI (fig. 65b, c). Two other small, badly corroded fragments of iron were found at a depth of 40 to 60 cm below the modern surface in Trench AAII; these may date from the principal occupation, but they were not associated with any identified feature. Lumps of iron slag were also found in the plowsoil of Trenches BIV, BII, and C and in the top of the rich pit in N west extension (20 to 40 cm below the modern surface, hence possibly a later intrusion introduced by the plow). Although these four pieces of iron slag are likely to date from the principal occupation, since they were recovered above rich pits and above the inner ditch of the settlement, their position within 40 cm of the modern ground surface makes the attribution uncertain. Much modern iron was found in the plowsoil all over the site, particularly nails and fragments of horseshoes, chains, and various tools.

The small cylindrical object from the pit at the south end of Trench S was found at a depth of 95 to 115 cm below the modern ground surface in association with pottery belonging to the principal occupation, along with daub, charcoal, and animal bone. A radiocarbon determination was obtained from charcoal in this pit (chapter 4). The cylinder is 1.8 cm long and has a diameter of 0.7 to 0.8 cm. The original form of the object is difficult to determine because of the corrosion. This piece is the only iron fragment found that clearly has a form indicating a finished object and the only iron piece from a pit that yielded a sample for radiocarbon analysis.

The presence of iron objects at Hascherkeller is of special interest in light of the relatively early radiocarbon dates for the site. The number of iron objects from central European contexts dating before 1000 B.C. is growing at a steady pace (Rieth 1942, p. 7; Butler 1976; Pleiner 1980, pp. 376–378), and for the latter half of the Urnfield Period, roughly 1000

Figure 65. Iron objects. a. from Trench S south end. b, c. from Trench AAI.

to 700 B.C., iron objects are fairly numerous (Kimmig 1964, pp. 274–281; recent distribution map in Pleiner 1981, p. 124, fig. 11). The objects being made of iron at this time were principally inlay for bronze and blades in composite tools with bronze handles. Iron inlay occurs in bronze swords, rings, and pins; and iron blades were often set into bronze handles to make swords and knives. Such implements have been recovered at some of the Swiss lakeshore settlements of the late Urnfield Period (Rieth 1942, pp. 10–12; Vogt 1949–1950). Cemeteries of this period often contain small iron objects such as rings and knives (Wells 1981, pp. 102, 104, table 7).

The evidence suggests that iron was being worked at many different locations in central Europe several centuries before the beginning of what is traditionally designated the Iron Age. At this stage, iron was being employed exclusively for the manufacture of prestige goods such as weaponry, jewelry, and occasional special tools such as knives (R. Pleiner, pers. comm.), as well as small tools for working bronze (Bouzek 1978). Tools involved in food production and crafts, such as sickles and hammers, were still being made of bronze. It was not until the fifth and fourth centuries B.C. that iron began to replace bronze as the principal material for tools.

The occurrence of iron objects at Hascherkeller, which clearly dates before 800 B.C. if the radiocarbon dates are accepted, indicates that the inhabitants were able to obtain, probably through their own production efforts, luxury items of this new metal. The fragments recovered do not suggest large objects such as swords, but rather some kinds of ornaments. The lump of slag from the ditch in Trench EII suggests that ironworking took place on the site.

Glass Beads

Four glass beads were recovered at Hascherkeller, all of approximately the same greenish-blue color (three complete ones in figs. 39f, g, 56a). Two were found in the pit at the north end of Trench S and two in the pit in Trench W. All were recovered in the process of screening soil, two in dry-screening on the site and two during wet-sieving for recovery of plant remains at the field laboratory. Such beads are probably often overlooked in the excavation of settlement sites of the period because they are so small, yet many settlements and graves have yielded such beads, sometimes in considerable quantities (Haevernick 1978, p. 147). Similar beads were also in common use during the Early Iron Age (Haevernick 1974).

The three complete beads measure 0.4, 0.5, and 0.6 cm in external diameter; the fourth, fragmentary bead was within this size range. All three complete beads have two small pointed protrusions marking the place where the two ends of the glass rod from which they were made were joined (Haevernick 1978, pp. 146, 147). On the basis of spectrographic analysis of such beads from other sites, Neuninger and Pittioni suggest (1959, 1961) that they were manufactured in the north Tirol in crafts industries associated with the smelting of copper ores.

The beads recovered at Hascherkeller were probably lost from bracelets or necklaces. Perhaps a whole string of such beads broke, the beads fell to the ground, and the owner collected all he/she could find, but some of the tiny objects were missed.

Stone Objects

The Mold (fig. 66). The mold was found in the pit in the western extension of Trench N lying face-down near the western edge of the pit in close association with large quantities of daub, including some pieces with white paint on them, pottery, and bone fragments (fig. 51). The object is made of gray, fine-grained homogeneous sandstone. Since the sides are uneven, a single precise measurement of the piece cannot be given. It is 10.5 to 11.0 cm long, its maximum width is 9.8 cm, and its maximum thickness is 4.5 cm. The front, or working face, measures about 10 by 9 cm. This surface is very smooth and has fine casting indentations cut into it. Along the top of this face the stone is cut away obliquely, providing a trough into which molten metal could be poured when the mold was placed vertically against a flat matching piece. From this trough extend five smooth funnel-shaped channels about 0.4 cm wide. There is no sharp boundary between the channels and the spaces in which the objects were cast, and it is apparent that the solidified bronze objects had to be further worked once removed from the mold. The ends

of the objects toward the channels had to be filed or cut away.

The five casting spaces are about 4.5 cm long and 0.9 cm wide at the middle. Each casting space has three longitudinal ridges, a straight one in the center and one on either side of it, these two curving outwards in the middle. The objects cast would have thus had three grooves in them. The five casting spaces are very similar, but not identical. It is clear that the craftsperson who made the mold was attempting to produce five identical casting spaces. Since the final products were probably finished with chisel and file, differences in the form of the rings made by bending the castings into circles probably resulted more from final touch-ups than from the minor differences in the casting spaces in the mold. The bottom ends of all five casting spaces are squared off and measure 0.2 cm across. A very shallow and narrow groove runs from the end of each to the bottom of the mold. These grooves were apparently intended to allow air to escape as the metal entered, thus preventing the formation of air bubbles in the castings.

The front of the mold is grayish-tan in color. At the top of the mold, on the edges of the sides next to this face, and on the bottom next to this face, the stone is colored a darker gray, perhaps as a result of the heat to which the rock was exposed. The back of the mold is dark gray in color, and the surface is uneven. On the left side of the back (as viewed in fig. 66) are marks of working the stone, broad shallow grooves about 1.3 cm wide, which are apparently the result of chiseling to remove unwanted parts.

The top of the mold is relatively flat, but very uneven and rough. The angle of slope from the top surface to casting face of the mold is about 45 degrees. The bottom of the mold is rough and uneven, and it shows the same kind of grooves as the back of the object, probably also caused by chiseling.

Although the left side of the mold has a shape that suggests that it might have been broken and hence made useless, such is not the case. The trough running along the front edge of the top of the mold, from which the five funnel-shaped channels lead down into the casting spaces, ends on both the left and right sides in a clear boundary. If the left side had been broken off, the boundary would not be preserved.

The mold must have had a completely flat, smooth matching piece, against which it was pressed vertically and held firmly in place for the casting, perhaps by being bound to the other slab with leather thongs.

Molds for casting bronze objects are relatively

Figure 66. The mold from Trench N west extension, showing front, back, and oblique views. The front view is shown actual size.

0   3

cm

Figure 67. Hammerstone of quartzite from Trench N west extension.

common from settlements of this period, though they are rarely found in well-delineated contexts. Like this one, most are made of sandstone, though some other kinds of stone were used; and complex objects such as socketed axes were sometimes cast in clay or metal molds (Wyss 1967a and b; Goldmann 1981). A mold that bears some resemblance to this one from Hascherkeller was recovered at the Early Iron Age settlement at the Heuneburg (Bittel and Rieth 1951, pl. 11,5). The Heuneburg mold is also of sandstone and is of roughly the same shape as the Hascherkeller specimen, though it is slightly smaller. The Heuneburg mold is thought to have been used for casting earrings. Like the Hascherkeller

mold, in the Heuneburg mold five rings were cast at one time.

The objects cast in the Hascherkeller mold were probably finger rings, or possibly earrings, of a form well represented in burials. The cemeteries south of Munich at Gernlinden and Grünwald have yielded several such rings (Müller-Karpe 1957, pl. 7,25; pl. 37,11), and rings of similar form have been found in graves in neighboring regions of central Europe (e.g., Kimmig 1940; Herrmann 1966; Dehn 1972; Eggert 1976) and at a few settlements such as Buchau (Kimmig 1979, p. 52, fig. 17q, r) and Auvernier (Rychner 1979, vol. II, pl. 96,14–18).

The Hammerstone (fig. 67). The stone in figure 67 was recovered in the pit in the western extension of Trench N. It consists of white quartzite and is cylindrical in shape, measuring 7.0 cm in length and 4.5 cm in diameter. The body of the stone is smooth, having the characteristic form and outer surface of a waterworn pebble. Each end is heavily battered, indicating that each was used for extensive pounding or grinding. No stone occurs naturally in the loess on which the settlement is situated, and this pebble was probably collected from a stream bed, most likely from the Isar.

Similar hammerstones made from river pebbles have been found at other contemporaneous settlements, for example, at St. Veit near Schwarzach (Salzburg) in Austria (Hell 1971, p. 43, fig. 5,10) and from the Hohlandsberg in Alsace (Jehl and Bonnet 1968, p. 12, fig. 6, bottom left).

The Slingstones. Caches of egg-size river pebbles were found in three locations on the settlement surface: at the southern end of Trench S, in the southeast corner of Trench V, and in the western half of Trench AAIII. About 50 were found in Trench S, 31 in Trench V, and 111 in Trench AAIII. Some of the pebbles from the southeast corner of Trench V are shown in figure 68, and their lengths and weights are represented in figure 69.

These pebbles, like all stones recovered on the site, were brought there intentionally; no stones occur naturally in the loess soil. Not one of the caches of pebbles was situated in one of the principal pits, though that at the south end of Trench S was very close to the the pit there, and some of the pebbles were located in the bottom of the plowsoil just above the pit. These pebbles may have been associated with that pit before the plow disturbed the top of it.

No evidence was observed at the settlement or on the pebbles themselves to suggest what they were used for. They may have been slingstones. The majority correspond closely in weight (fig. 69) to the tens of thousands of slingstones from caches at Maiden Castle (Wheeler 1943, p. 49), which were also for the most part natural pebbles. Roman slingstones made of baked clay are also of similar weight (Maier 1979, p. 166). River pebbles believed to have been used as slingstones are reported in the hundreds from the Early Iron Age fortified hilltop settlement at Mont Lassois on the upper Seine in France (Haffner 1973, p. 171; Joffroy 1976, p. 801) and from Early Iron Age graves in the Middle Rhineland, which contained other weapons as well (Haffner 1971, 1973). A pit at the Urnfield settlement of Efringen-Kirchen (Lörrach) in southwest Germany contained a large number of such pebbles (Dehn 1967, p. 47), and they are reported from many other late prehistoric settlements (Joachim 1980, p. 369, n. 37).

Very little is known about the use of the sling in this period. The stones at Hascherkeller may have been used in warfare, for hunting, or for both purposes.

Flint Flakes. Occasional flakes of flint were recovered on the settlement, both in the plowsoil and in the ditch and pit fill. Since the terrace was occupied throughout prehistoric times, it is not possible to assign these to the principal period of occupation of the settlement. Flint flakes have been recovered from many settlements of the Late Bronze Age (e.g., Herrmann 1966, pp. 11–12; von Brunn 1968, p. 258); hence, some or all may belong to that period.

Antler and Bone

Two large fragments of antler were recovered — the base of a red deer *(Cervus elaphus)* antler with the two tines cut off, from the ditch fill in Trench EII (fig. 70c), and a large fragmentary antler with two tines, from the southwestern edge of the large pit in Trench W (fig. 70a). Two objects cut from antler or bone were recovered, neither in a securely closed context. The button in figure 49j was found at a depth of 35 cm at the very top of the pit in the north end of Trench N. It probably belonged to the fill of that pit, but because of its shallow depth it may have entered the deposit subsequently through plow

0   5

cm

Figure 68. Pebbles, perhaps slingstones, from the small pit in the southeast corner of Trench V.

activity. A similar button was found at the Early Iron Age settlement at the Heuneburg, there too in a stratigraphically uncertain context (S. Sievers, pers. comm.). The fragmentary polished bone object in figures 42d and 70b, the purpose of which is unclear but which may have been part of a small shuttle used in weaving (see La Baume 1955; Wells 1980a, p. 326, n. 34), was found in Trench BII at a depth of 13 cm below the modern surface in the plowsoil near the large pit in Trenches C and BII. The location of this object close to the rich pit in Trench C and the fact that much daub and pottery from that pit was found above it in the plowsoil and on the surface suggest that this object probably belonged with that pit.

Figure 70. Antler and bone objects. a. from Trench W, small pit at the southwestern edge of the main pit. b. from the plowsoil above the pit in Trenches BII and C. c. from Trench EII ditch fill. Objects b and c are at the same scale.

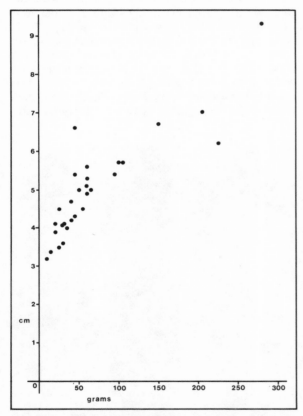

Figure 69. Scatter diagram showing the lengths and weights of pebbles interpreted as slingstones.

4

The Radiocarbon Dates

Charcoal was collected for purposes of radiocarbon dating whenever large enough fragments could be recovered in the settlement pits. Substantial quantities of charcoal were found only in the large pit in Trench W. The pit in Trench BV also contained some large chunks of charcoal (larger than a cubic centimeter), and the pit at the south end of Trench S contained many small fragments (smaller than one cubic centimeter) scattered throughout the fill. In the other pits only very small fragments of charcoal were preserved, for the most part too small to be used for standard radiocarbon determinations. Since the original surface of the prehistoric settlement no longer survives, none of the charcoal from cooking fires was preserved in situ. The only charcoal recovered in situ was that which had entered open pits, for example, the charcoal produced in the process of firing pottery in the kiln in Trench W.

Charcoal samples were collected with a clean steel trowel and transferred directly from the soil to packages made of clean aluminum foil. In the field laboratory the charcoal samples were separated from adhering soil and roots with a clean steel knife blade, then repacked in new aluminum foil for submission to the radiocarbon dating laboratory or for storage.

Six samples were submitted for radiocarbon dating analysis, all to Beta Analytic Laboratories of Coral Gables, Florida. The samples submitted were selected on the basis of their adequate size for analysis and their association with cultural materials, particularly pottery, in the principal pits. One sample came from the pit in Trench BV, one from the pit at the south end of Trench S, and four from the pit in Trench W.

Beta-1262: 2830 ± 120 B.P. (= 880 bc). The pit at the south end of Trench S contained fragments of charcoal throughout its fill, none of them alone large enough to provide a reasonable determination. This sample therefore consisted of many small charcoal fragments collected in the fill of the pit between 1.15 and 1.35 m below the modern ground surface. Pottery of the principal occupation together with daub

and animal bone occurred throughout the pit down to its bottom, 1.35 m below the surface.

Beta-1263: 2760 ± 80 B.P. (= 810 bc). Among the sherds, daub, and other materials in the pit in Trench BV were many chunks of charcoal up to and over a cubic centimeter in size. A package of these fragments constituted the second sample for analysis.

Beta-1722: 3040 ± 65 B.P. (= 1090 bc).
Beta-1846: 3050 ± 90 B.P. (= 1100 bc).
Beta-1847: 2705 ± 100 B.P. (= 755 bc).
Beta-2406: 2690 ± 100 B.P. (= 740 bc).

These four samples all came from the large pit in Trench W containing the remains of a kiln. All came from the lower of the two levels which contained dense deposits of pottery, daub, and charcoal (figs. 25c, 31).

However the dates are interpreted, they provide at least a good general impression of the absolute chronology of the settlement, and they support the dating of the principal occupation on the basis of the pottery to the period Hallstatt B, roughly 1000 to 700 B.C. (Müller-Karpe 1959a, fig. 64). Four of the dates are close together: 740, 755, 810, and 880 bc. The other two, 1090 and 1100 bc, are very close to each other but not to the other four. The dates in each of the two groups are statistically indistinguishable from one another, and there is even some question whether the difference between the two groups is statistically significant (M. Tamers, pers. comm.).

The issue of calibration is still problematical. It is evident that the dates obtained from the laboratory must be calibrated to bring them into line with calendar years, but there still exists considerable disagreement among physicists and archaeologists about the best formula for calibration (see Ralph et al. 1973; Clark 1975; Suess 1979). Further confusion is added by the fact that in a number of specific cases in European prehistory the uncalibrated dates seem to correspond better to the accepted chronol-

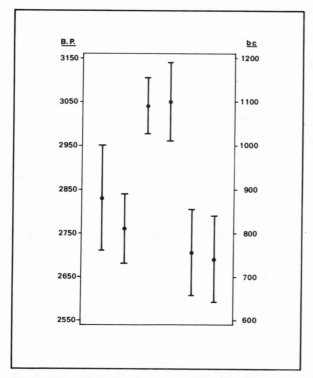

Figure 71. Diagram showing the six radiocarbon determinations from Hascherkeller.

ogies than any of the suggested calibrations of the dates (Snodgrass 1975; Schwabedissen 1978; Coles and Harding 1979, pp. 379, 380; Harding 1980). It may be that the accepted chronologies are often incorrect and radiocarbon determinations can be used to correct them (Beer et al. 1979); if so, much of the current understanding of European prehistory would have to be revised (C. Renfrew 1973).

According to the recent calibration tables published by Suess (1979), the four most recent dates from Hascherkeller can be ascribed to the period 1000 to 800 B.C. and the two older ones to the period 1400 to 1200 B.C. On the basis of the dates obtained through radiocarbon analysis, then, the principal occupation of the site dates within the period 1000 to 800 B.C. Four of the six dates indicate this period. The two earlier dates both come from the pit in Trench W that also yielded two of the more recent dates.

The existence of the two earlier dates along with the two more recent ones from Trench W, which agree closely with those from the two other dated pits, requires some discussion. It is possible that the difference between the dates is a statistical

one and that no actual difference is signified. Yet because the two later determinations from Trench W are very close to each other, with just 15 years difference, and the two earlier ones are only 10 years apart, it would seem that the differences between the earlier and later dates reflect a real chronological variation. All four samples were taken from the same level of the pit, the lower of the two zones of dense cultural debris. Most likely, the different dates are to be explained by the presence of old and new wood in the pit when it was filled in.

At the time that Hascherkeller was occupied, trees were growing in central Europe that attained ages of 400 years (B. Becker, pers. comm.). If the people living at Hascherkeller had felled and cut up trees of such age, it is possible that wood from the inner layers of the tree and from the outer parts could have ended up as charcoal in the same layer of the pit. The different dates would then reflect the ages of different parts of a large and old tree.

It is also possible, and perhaps more likely, that the old wood in the pit came from old implements, which had been in use by the occupants of the settlement and finally found their way into a fire. From sites such as Hascherkeller in the environment of central Europe, virtually no wood survives that has not been carbonized; but from other contexts such as the lakeshore settlements of southwest Germany and Switzerland, numerous wooden implements are well preserved and attest to the importance of wood in the material culture of the period (e.g., Speck 1955; Wyss 1971a; Primas and Ruoff 1981). To judge by medieval and early modern farming communities in Europe (e.g., Fél and Hofer 1972; Hartley 1979), most implements in use at Hascherkeller and at other settlements were made of wood. Many items such as chairs, tables, boxes, chests, bowls, ladles, and handles for shovels and axes probably remained in use for several centuries, passing down from one generation to the next. In the course of time, some would have been broken beyond repair and used for firewood. A radiocarbon determination from the charcoal of such an object would reflect the year that the tree from which the object was made was felled and hence would be much earlier than the time at which the object burned. It may be this kind of situation that is reflected in the two earlier radiocarbon dates from Hascherkeller.

It is the four later determinations, 880 bc, 810 bc, 755 bc, and 740 bc, however, that provide the basis for the dating of the principal occupation. Radiocarbon dating has still not been extensively used in later European prehistory, though much valuable information has emerged from the determinations that have been made, especially in ascertaining chronological relationships between archaeological sites in different parts of Europe where the typological patterns may be different. A few published radiocarbon determinations from sites approximately contemporaneous with Hascherkeller will be noted here.

Central Europe

Zug-Sumpf settlement (Switzerland), earlier phase (Hallstatt A2 and B1 in the relative sequence):

K-997: 880 ± 100 bc
K-998: 930 ± 100 bc
K-1121: 990 ± 100 bc

Zug-Sumpf settlement, later phase (Hallstatt B2 and B3):

K-996: 740 ± 100 bc
K-1112: 710 ± 100 bc

(See Lanting 1976 for discussion of all of the above dates; see Speck 1955 about the settlement).

Dornholzhausen settlement (Hessen, West Germany) (Lanting 1976, p. 60; about the settlement see Janke 1971):

GrN-7238: 930 ± 45 bc

Hallstatt (Upper Austria), from the galleries of the salt mines (Barth et al. 1975):

VRI-267: 970 ± 100 bc
VRI-258: 860 ± 90 bc
VRI-345: 860 ± 90 bc

Northern Continental Europe

Elp settlement (Netherlands) (Waterbolk 1964; Lanting 1976):

GrN-2881: 805 ± 65 bc

Angelsloo settlement (Netherlands):

GrN-4173: 910 ± 60 bc

Scandinavia

Hallunda settlement (central Sweden), Site 13:

Thirteen dates, ranging from 845 to 485 bc

Hallunda settlement, Site 69:

Six dates, ranging from 975 to 715 bc

(See Jaanusson 1981, p. 26 for the above dates.)

Britain

Aldermaston Wharf (Berkshire, England) (Bradley et al. 1980, pp. 224, 248):

BM-1591: 835 ± 35 bc

Runnymede Bridge (Surrey, England) (Needham and Longley 1980, p. 401):

HAR-1834: 800 ± 70 bc
HAR-3112: 750 ± 70 bc
HAR-3113: 720 ± 70 bc

Mucking (Essex, England) (Jones and Bond 1980, p. 475):

HAR-1630: 840 ± 90 bc
HAR-1634: 820 ± 110 bc
HAR-1708: 860 ± 70 bc
HAR-2911: 750 ± 80 bc

5

The Magnetometer Survey

by Helmut Becker

Until recently archaeological prospection with magnetometer in Germany was limited to the Rhineland, where in combination with aerial photography it was used in the mapping of hundreds of previously unknown sites (Scollar 1975). Development of these modern survey techniques in the Rhineland was stimulated by the threatened destruction of many archaeological sites by rapid expansion of modern settlements and industrial sites. With traditional excavation methods effective protection of the archaeological sites would have been impossible; many were not even known, and limitations of time and money presented serious constraints. Similar situations exist in modern industrial regions everywhere.

Since 1977 the Institut für Allgemeine und Angewandte Geophysik of the University of Munich, with financial assistance from the Volkswagen Foundation, has been developing a Laboratory for Archaeological Prospection and Archaeomagnetism. The emphasis of this work is on exploring the potential of archaeomagnetism as a chronological tool. An instrument for the magnetic prospection of large surfaces was already tested in 1977. Since spring of 1982 this magnetic prospection system has been employed routinely in archaeological survey work in Bavaria. The use of the magnetometer at Hascherkeller is exemplary for the combination of aerial photography and magnetism. In this instance the advantages of the application of magnetometer survey work are clear: Archaeological structures are recognizable by the magnetometer even when they are not identifiable in aerial photographs because of the humus cover.

Viewed physically, an archaeological site presents a complex heterogeneity of magnetic properties of the upper soil layers. A disturbance, or anomaly, has been caused in the magnetic field of the earth, and it can be measured. Measurement can pinpoint traces of various human activities even after millennia.

The success of magnetometry in archaeological prospection depends upon the utilization of a variety of physical effects, the causes of which lie in the magnetization of the soil. One of the most important is the Le Borgne Effect. A characteristic division of magnetic susceptibility develops in soil disturbed by man, with the highest values in the upper layers. Susceptibility, a physical property that depends upon the composition of soils and upon the proportion of magnetic minerals, signifies the magnetizability. The magnetic field of the earth, with intensity F, induces magnetization in a material with susceptibility X (X times F) in the direction of the field. A part of the induced magnetization forms not spontaneously, but after prolonged exposure to the magnetic field. This part is designated *viscous magnetization*.

The development of the highest level of susceptibility in the upper layers of the soil is explained by the transformation of the weakly magnetic minerals of the soil (iron oxides) into strongly magnetic phases such as magnetite and maghemite, especially through the repeated use of fire. A disturbance of this uppermost, strongly magnetized layer — for example, by the digging of a ditch — results in a measurable negative geomagnetic anomaly. If such a ditch is left to the natural processes of sedimentation, the strongly magnetized surface soils wash in, forming a concentration of material with high magnetization. A positive geomagnetic anomaly forms, such as was measured over the ditches on the settlement of Hascherkeller. As the excavations have demonstrated, the strong magnetization of the ditch fill can also be understood in terms of the high proportion of burned clay materials contained in it, such as daub and pottery. Positive anomalies are also observed in the pits. Especially in the cases of storage and trash pits, the strongly magnetic maghemite formed by the decay processes seems to play a role. This formation of maghemite can also account for the positive anomalies shown by postholes (Aitken 1974).

Iron causes strong geomagnetic disturbances.

On archaeological sites such disturbances are most often caused by recent metal. Iron is readily recognizable because of the strength and form of the anomaly; hence, modern iron rubbish can be quickly identified and avoided. Burned clay in large quantities is also easily identified because fired clays exhibit a strong thermoremnant magnetization (Becker 1978). The majority of the archaeologically interesting anomalies are, however, so weak that they are only measurable with very sensitive instruments such as the proton magnetometer and cesium magnetometer (for information about the measuring techniques, see Stuart 1972). A further difficulty lies in the superposition over these anomalies of much stronger and chronologically variable disturbances, both natural and artificial. Part of the variation, especially the natural variation, comes from above the ground. Much of it depends upon the time of day and upon magnetic disturbances. Aside from the strong disturbances caused by magnetic storms, they can be eliminated without difficulty. More serious are the artificial disturbances caused mainly by electrical currents and transient magnetic variations. In the vicinity of high tension lines, industrial plants, and cities, magnetometer prospection is problematical.

These geomagnetic variations can be eliminated by means of a differential measurement using two probes. One probe is used as a stationary basis and the other as the actual measuring instrument on the surface of the site. Since the external disturbances work identically on both probes, they can be eliminated from the values being measured. The survey is carried out as a measurement of the ground surface, with intervals of 0.5 or 1.0 m between measuring points. An assistant moves the probe along marked measuring lines. The proton magnetometer requires three seconds to measure one point. If measurements are taken at intervals of 1.0 m, a hectare of land can be surveyed in about three days. At Hascherkeller, one-half hectare was surveyed using intervals of 0.5 m between points and 1.0 m between measuring lines; readings were taken at 10,000 points. The survey took about ten hours. It had to be carried out over three days because at certain times the strong disturbances caused by the city of Landshut made work with the proton magnetometer impossible.

The measured data were read directly into a digital cassette. Besides saving time in the field, this procedure makes possible automatic evaluation and graphic representation of the results by computer. A magnetometer survey produces an enormous quantity of data, which must be transformed into a graphic representation in order to make visible the geomagnetic anomalies. Contour maps and shadings are well suited for this purpose and can be drawn automatically by computers. Although contour maps provide a quantitatively good picture of the morphology of the anomalies and thus are essential for a precise calculation of disturbances, the representation of the anomalies in a point-density distribution drawing permits the recognition of extended archaeological structures, even when all other disturbances are much stronger. Here the remarkable capability of the human eye is utilized to recognize order in an otherwise incomprehensible profusion of points. The point-density distribution map, which is generated by covering each measured value with a specific number of dots, when much reduced gives the impression of a photographic illustration of the soil beneath the surface. A stronger anomaly shows up as a greater darkening of the points in the picture. The point-density distribution map of the results of the magnetometer survey at Hascherkeller shown here (fig. 72) was drawn by hand. Even this somewhat incomplete representation of the raw data permits a preliminary archaeological interpretation. Its accuracy is demonstrated by its agreement with the archaeological results.

The course of the series of double ditches is clearly visible. Noteworthy is a slight shift toward the south of the maximum of the anomalies, caused by the inclination of the earth's magnetic field. The ditches thus run just north of the anomaly, 0.5 to 1.0 m from it. The anomalies in the western part of the surveyed area are weaker than those in the eastern part. This difference may be explained by more intensive erosion in the western area, which would also suggest a deeper destruction of the archaeological remains. Since the anomaly of the inner ditch of the eastern enclosure is considerably stronger than that of the outer, it can be concluded that the inner is wider and deeper. This observation agrees with the results of excavation, which showed the inner ditch to have been renewed. Both magnetometer and excavation showed that the ditches became narrower toward the south. The same pattern probably holds for the inner ditch of the middle enclosure with its stronger anomaly. For the western enclosure, this pattern is not apparent in the magnetometer data.

Besides the double ditches, a small disturbance caused by a single ditch cutting across the outer ditch of the middle enclosure deserves mention. The anomalies along the path north of the settlement are typical for modern underground pipes; here these are water pipes. The actual structure of the settlement cannot be revealed in any detail with this relatively

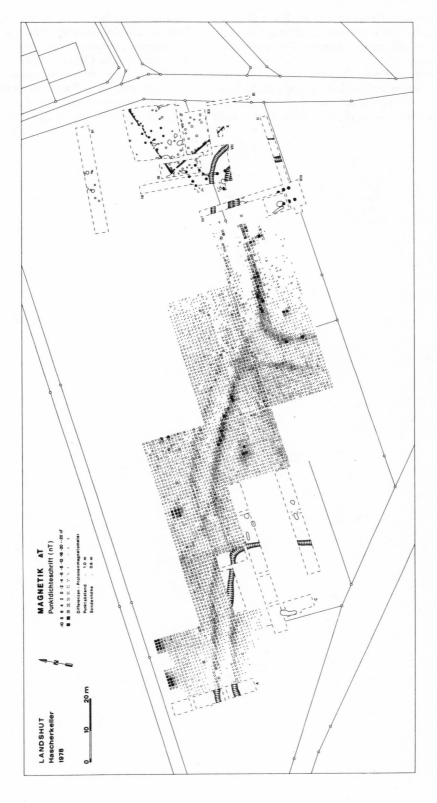

Figure 72. Plan of the results of the magnetometer survey showing the outlines of the three enclosures bounded by the double ditches. At the left are the trenches opened by the Peabody Museum in 1978; at the right are those excavated by the Bayerisches Landesamt für Denkmalpflege in that year (see Christlein 1979). Plan courtesy of Helmut Becker and Rainer Christlein.

coarse measuring interval of 1.0 m. For a detailed settlement plan comparable to that obtained through excavation, a much greater density of points would have to be measured.

The limits of the capabilities of magnetometer survey as a means of archaeological mapping lie principally in the precision of measurement of the magnetometer used and in the density of points at which readings are taken. The proton magnetometer used here is actually too imprecise and too slow. Hence, the magnetometer survey program has converted to a cesium magnetometer, with substantially better results in terms of the precision and speed of taking readings. With this device the optimal conditions for a magnetometer survey of detailed archaeological structures can be achieved, even for routine surveys.

6

The Plant Remains

by C. Caroline Quillian

Sixty palaeoethnobotanical samples were collected at Hascherkeller during the first three excavation seasons. Twenty-one were collected in 1978, varying in amount from one to two liters each. The samples taken during the 1979 and 1980 field seasons were all ten liters. All flotation of samples presented in this report was carried out during the 1979 and 1980 field seasons.

COLLECTION

The palaeoethnobotanical samples were collected from the features on the site. Of the 60 samples taken, 7 were from ditches and 52 were from pits. One sample was taken from the interior of a complete vessel of Early or Middle Bronze Age date from the pit in the west wall of Trench V. The humus close to the surface of the site had been disturbed regularly by plowing and therefore was not suitable for sampling. The exact sampling area within each feature was determined by the location of the sections through the ditches and of the bisections of the pits. At least one sample was collected from each suitable pit, and more were taken if the amount of visible charcoal was greater than usual.

The method of collecting palaeoethnobotanical samples during the 1979 and 1980 seasons was the following. A 30-by-30-cm square was marked in the soil with a trowel, and the exact location of the square within the cutting was recorded on a standardized form. Clumps of soil were removed from this square with a trowel and transferred to a clean 10-liter plastic bucket. Breakage of carbonized material was minimized by removing the soil in large clumps. Ten liters of soil were collected in most cases. Depending upon the density of the soil, the 30-by-30-cm block ranged from 7 to 8 cm in depth.

After the sample was taken, the bucket was covered with a clean plastic sheet to prevent contamination. At the field laboratory detergent (general cleaner) and water were added to the sample, which was then allowed to soak for several hours. The

Figure 73. Wet-sieving in the field laboratory in 1979, with four sieves stacked on top of one another.

detergent helped to break up the clumps of soil, making it easier to separate the dirt during the wet-screening process. Breakage of the carbonized material was minimized because clumps did not have to be broken by hand. Soil consisting of a loess-humus mixture tended to be very loose and did not need much detergent, while the pure humus in some pits remained in clumps and sometimes needed about one-half cup of detergent.

The wet-sieving and flotation apparatus consisted of four circular, size-differentiated sieves that fit tightly on top of one another. The mesh sizes were 10 mm, 2 mm, 1 mm, and 0.6 mm. Each sample was slowly poured into the top of the set of sieves. The dirt was then forced through each layer by means of a hose adjusted to medium power (fig. 73). Although no carbonized material was usually found in the 10-mm sieve, faunal and ceramic remains were recovered there and placed into labeled containers. With a mod-

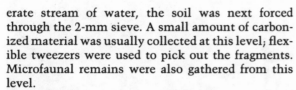

Figure 74. Charcoal floating to the surface in a pan and being poured into a small sieve.

Figure 75. Cleaning carbonized plant materials in a sieve.

erate stream of water, the soil was next forced through the 2-mm sieve. A small amount of carbonized material was usually collected at this level; flexible tweezers were used to pick out the fragments. Microfaunal remains were also gathered from this level.

The procedure was slightly different for the 1-mm and 0.6-mm sieves. After the dirt clumps in each sieve were broken up, the remaining sediment was gathered in one area of the sieve. It was then transferred to a rectangular pan with the use of a low-powered hose on the opposite side of the sieve. The sediment, together with a small amount of water, was swirled in a circular motion several times around the rectangular pan, allowing the carbonized material to float out into a smaller handheld sieve (fig. 74). At this stage the material in the handheld sieve consisted of carbonized plant remains, small modern snail shells, bones, and roots. Using a shallow bucket of clean water and swirling hand movements, the roots and heavier sediments were separated from the carbonized materials in the handheld sieve (fig. 75). It is important that the roots be removed at this stage because they tend to attach to the carbonized material during drying, and specimens may be damaged if the roots are removed later. Lighter colored particles that were the same weight as the carbonized materials were not removed. Such fragments could be calcified plant parts. They were saved along with the carbonized plant remains.

The samples were next placed in clean, dry cloths in labeled containers. Sections of diapers were used because of their close, even weave. The samples were allowed to dry slowly and were not exposed to direct sunlight at any time. They needed to be completely dry before being packed away in order to prevent formation of mildew.

ANALYSIS

The first stage in the analysis of the samples consisted of the separation of plant remains from charcoal. This separation was done under a binocular microscope with the aid of a fine paintbrush and flexible tweezers. The plant remains were stored in small plastic boxes, and the identified seeds were placed in clear gelatin capsules or plastic containers of similar size.

The following discussion of plant remains at Hascherkeller deals only with the materials from the principal period of occupation. The results of the analysis of remains from the Bronze Age pits are listed in the two charts. These results will not be discussed in detail here, as they do not differ greatly from the floral remains from the principal occupation. To judge by the limited sample available, the plants in use during the Early Iron Age and the Bronze Age were very similar.

Domesticated Plants

The three major food crops represented in the samples from Hascherkeller are millet *(Panicum miliaceum)*, wheat *(Triticum* sp.), and barley *(Hordeum* sp.). Twenty-five specimens of millet were identified, as were five grains of wheat and two of barley. Although only a small number of wheat and barley grains could be definitely identified, many other fragments in the samples could be identified as either wheat or barley. The abundance of millet agrees with the conclusions of Knörzer (1971) in his comparison of plant material from eight Early Iron Age sites in the Rhineland. Millet was probably one of the major food plants during the Early Iron Age in central Europe. Unfortunately, the relative importance of millet, wheat, and barley cannot be ascertained at Hascherkeller because of the small numbers of specimens in the samples.

Measurements listed below for the individual species were taken according to the guidelines set by Helbaek (1970, p. 191):

L = Length: in cereal grains from the embryo point (radicle) to the apex; in round seeds the greatest dimension parallel to the cotyledons.

B = Breadth: in cereal grains the maximum dimension between the flanks; in discoid seeds (such as lentil) the greatest diameter.

T = Thickness: in cereal grains the maximum dimension from the dorsal to the ventral sides, the latter being the surface bisected by the ventral furrow; in leguminous seeds (lentil) the maximum dimension at right angles to the cotyledon plane.

Measurements are listed in the text as follows: average length (range of lengths) × average breadth (range of breadths) × average thickness (range of thicknesses).

Panicum miliaceum: Broomcorn millet 1.71 (1.25–2.10) × 1.46 (1.00–1.60) × 1.35 (1.10–1.60) mm.

Twenty-five seeds from nine samples are probably *Panicum miliaceum.* They were identified on the basis of their spherical shape, the absence of a ventral furrow, and the grooves along the palea left by the margins of the lemma (fig. 76). The grooves can be seen on both the dorsal and ventral sides. The measurements compare well with those from Knörzer's study of Early Iron Age sites in the Rhineland (1971, p. 48). The Hascherkeller millets are much smaller than most of the prehistoric *Panicum* measurements taken from impressions and listed by J. Renfrew (1973, p. 100). The size difference probably results from the fact that her measurements were taken from impressions and not from carbonized seeds.

Panicum miliaceum grows well in most soils and has a lower water requirement than most of the large-grained cereals (J. Renfrew 1973, p. 100). Ethnographically known uses of millet include porridge, leaven, and fermented beverages (J. Renfrew 1973, p. 101).

Triticum sp.: Wheat 4.54 (3.05–5.80) × 2.69 (1.65–3.40) × 2.25 (1.25–2.75) mm.

Hordeum sp.: Barley 4.85 × 2.32 × 1.75 mm.

Five grains of wheat and two of barley were identified from the samples. Seventy-two fragments of cereal grains are either wheat or barley but cannot

be identified definitely as one or the other. Of these, sixteen are more likely barley. (Cereal grains generally undergo some distortion during carbonization, making accurate species identification difficult; see Hopf 1955.) Twenty-two rachis fragments were also found. Most appear to be *Triticum dicoccum* (emmer wheat), but their small size suggests that they might be *Triticum monococcum* (einkorn). One glume base may be from *Triticum spelta* (spelt).

Lens esculenta: Lentil.

Eight lenticular fragments were found in four samples at Hascherkeller. These are most likely from lentils or wild legumes, to judge by their general characteristics, though no part of the testa is preserved with the hilum. Lentils have been found in central Europe since the early Neolithic and were widely cultivated during the Iron Age (J. Renfrew 1973, p. 113).

Oil-bearing Plants: Perhaps Domesticated

Camelina sativa Crantz: Gold of pleasure.

One carbonized seed of *Camelina sativa* was

0   .2

cm

Figure 76. Seeds of *Panicum miliaceum* (millet).

found in the Hascherkeller samples. The seeds of this plant were used in prehistoric times because of their high oil content (Knörzer 1971, pp. 55, 56). They were often associated with fields of flax and may have been cultivated. The earliest finds of *Camelina sativa* come from Neolithic contexts in southeast Europe (Knörzer 1978). These seeds are commonly found at sites in northern Europe, particularly from the Bronze and Iron Ages. They were found in the stomachs of the Tollund and Grauballe men from the Danish bogs (J. Renfrew 1973, p. 169). According to Schlichtherle (pers. comm.), the seeds of *Camelina sativa* have rarely been found in central Europe, in part because sieves with small enough mesh have not been used. An important Early Iron Age find of this plant (14 seeds) was made at the site of Nettesheim in the Rhineland (Knörzer 1971, p. 43).

Papaver somniferum: Opium poppy.

The one example of *Papaver* from Hascherkeller is calcified, not carbonized. This type of preservation cannot be definitely dated to the principal period of occupation of the settlement, but it is likely that this calcified seed is the same age as the carbonized material from the site.

Wild Plants

Wild plants were also important in the diet at Hascherkeller. Hazelnuts *(Corylus avellana)* were found in abundance. One stone of a wild plum or blackthorn *(Prunus* sp.) was found. Other wild species recovered, all of which are considered weeds today, include cleavers *(Galium* sp.), sorrel *(Rumex* sp.), and fat hen or goose foot *(Chenopodium* sp.). It is unclear whether these wild plants represent only the refuse from the harvesting of major cereals, or whether they actually played a role in the diet.

Corylus avellana: Hazelnut.

Twenty-one fragments of hazelnut shells were identified on the basis of the tubular parallel form of the nerves, the characteristic ovoid shape, and the thickness of the woody pericarp. Most of the samples that contained fragments of hazelnut shells also contained thin carbonized barklike pieces, which may have come from the inside of the shells. This suggestion is based on comparison of the cell structures of these barklike pieces with modern carbonized samples.

Hazelnuts are one of the most common fruits represented on archaeological sites in Europe. Whole fruits are rarely found. Identifications are usually based on fragments of the shells, which were prob-

ably broken when the nuts were eaten. It is unlikely that the shells were broken after charring, because charring causes the pericarp to become extremely hard (Dimbleby 1978, p. 34). The hazel tree only flowers freely when it receives full light, although it is a component of the deciduous forest. Dimbleby (1978, p. 128) suggests that prehistoric man probably took steps to grow hazel trees in open clearings, where they would flower and produce fruit in abundance. The many hazelnut fragments found at Hascherkeller suggest that this practice may have been followed there.

The recovery of hazelnuts in most of the graves of the great Hohmichele tumulus at the Heuneburg, dating to the sixth century B.C., suggests that hazelnuts may have had some kind of ritual significance beyond their use as food (Riek 1962).

Galium sp.: Cleavers 2.63 × 2.20 × 2.35 mm.

Fifteen fruits of *Galium* were identified in the samples from Hascherkeller. Although most had a reticular pattern on the epidermis, some had smooth surfaces. The distinctive large aperture of *Galium* was present in all the fruits. Cleavers are annual plants that characteristically grow among shrubs, on open slopes, or in fields, and they are especially common in fields of flax (Helbaek 1955, p. 689). Although we do not know if the fruits of *Galium* were of any importance in prehistoric times, suggestions have been made for uses of other plant parts. The roots of *Galium boreale*, bedstraw, can be used to make a red dye (Dimbleby 1978, p. 52). *Galium palustre*, goose grass, could have been used in the curdling of milk (Milisauskas 1978, p. 81).

Rumex sp.: Sorrel, dock.

Five carbonized specimens of *Rumex* were identified from three samples at Hascherkeller. As modern specimens of *Rumex* were also common in the Hascherkeller samples, it was necessary to puncture each seed with a sharply pointed instrument to determine whether it was carbonized. These modern seeds were probably brought into the samples by rodents or were blown in during the taking of samples in the field or during the wet-sieving and flotation processes.

Sorrel usually grows in meadows or damp areas (J. Renfrew 1973, p. 184). Seeds of *Rumex* have been found in large quantities at early Neolithic sites in Bulgaria. Because of the purity of the Bulgarian samples, Dennell concludes that *Rumex* was used there as a food resource (1976, p. 238). A good source of carbohydrates, *Rumex* seeds may have been ground into flour. The leaves could have been used as a spinach (Dennell 1976, p. 238; J. Renfrew 1973, p. 184). The roots of *Rumex* can be made into a red dye (Dimbleby 1978, p. 31).

Chenopodium cf. *album*: Fat hen, white goose foot.

Three carbonized seeds of *Chenopodium* were identified from three Hascherkeller samples; one calcified seed was also recovered. Modern seeds of *Chenopodium album* were found in almost every sample. These modern fruits can be easily distinguished from the carbonized seeds because they do not have a carbonized interior.

Although *Chenopodium album* is thought of today as a weed, it may have been cultivated separately or collected in prehistoric times to supple-

ment the diet. It has been found on archaeological sites in central Europe dating from the Neolithic on (Willerding 1966, p. 53). The seeds of *Chenopodium album* were identified in the stomachs of the Tollund and Grauballe men in Denmark (J. Renfrew 1973, p. 170). Because of their large embryo, the seeds have a high protein and fat content (J. Renfrew 1973, p. 170). The leaves can be boiled and used as greens (Dimbleby 1978, p. 31; J. Renfrew 1973, p. 170), and in historic times the seeds were ground and mixed with wheat in bread meal (Dimbleby 1978, p. 31).

Prunus sp.: Wild plum, blackthorn 6.15 × 5.45 × 4.20 mm.

One specimen of *Prunus* sp. was found at Hascherkeller. It is probably either *Prunus spinosa*

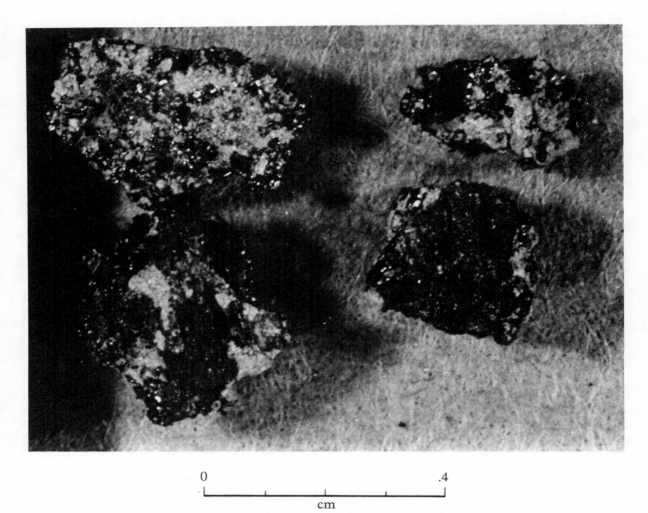

0   .4
|_____|_____|_____|
              cm

Figure 77. Plant material fused with charcoal, probably remnants of a porridge.

(blackthorn) or *Prunus institia* (wild plum). The stones of *Prunus spinosa* have been found in central Europe dating from the Neolithic Period on. Today the fruits are used to make sloe wine or sloe gin (J. Renfrew 1973, p. 144). The stones of the wild plum are generally slightly larger than the specimen from Hascherkeller. However, stones from the Neolithic site of Ravensburg near Lake Constance have measurements very similar to the stone from Hascherkeller (J. Renfrew 1973, p. 144). *Prunus institia* is a deciduous tree whose stones have been found on sites dating from the Neolithic Period on in Europe.

Three other samples, all from the pit in Trench C, contained what appear to be plant remains fused with charcoal. Each piece consisted of a bubbled portion, with no visible cell structure, attached to a piece of charcoal with obvious wood cells (fig. 77). The absence of cell structures and clear shapes of plant materials suggests that these fused fragments may represent the remains of porridge made from ground grains. Porridge may have been spilled into a fire, heated, and then fused with the surrounding charcoal.

CONCLUSION

The results of this study combined with those of similar investigations such as Knörzer's in the Rhineland provide information for a general reconstruction of subsistence economy at Hascherkeller. The settlement was ideally situated on fertile loess soil. Several species of millet, wheat, and barley, the principal crops, were probably grown in fields near the settlement, as were lentils. Domesticated plants found at contemporaneous settlements include oats, beans, and peas; these may also have been grown at Hascherkeller. The occupants of the settlement may have cultivated or collected gold of pleasure and opium poppy for their oil. Flax may also have been grown.

The crops were most likely threshed by crushing or grinding, and parching may have been used to free some of the grains from their spikelets. The seeds of the wild plants, which may have grown on the stalks of the harvested cereals, may have been removed by sorting or sieving. Some of the wild plants that occurred in the Hascherkeller samples, now considered to be weeds, may have been deliberately cultivated then. Uses for cleavers, sorrel, and white goose foot are recorded ethnographically. Hazelnuts and wild plums were consumed at Hascherkeller, and other fruits such as apples, pears, and cherries, all represented at sites of the same period in central Europe (see Wyss 1971a), may have been gathered from the lands around the settlement.

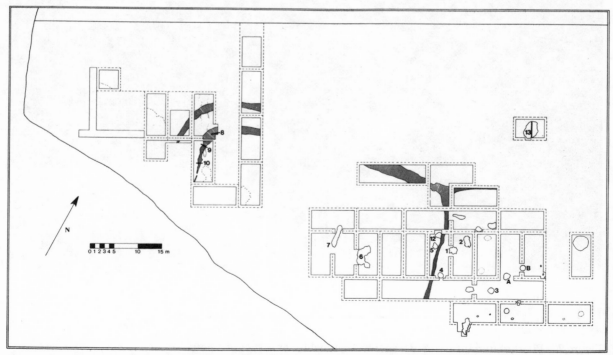

Figure 78. Plan showing the locations of samples taken for wet-sieving and flotation. The arabic numerals and letters A and B correspond to the sample numbers (table 7).

Table 6.
Plant species represented at Hascherkeller.

Sample area	No. of liters	*Panicum miliaceum* (millet)	*Triticum* (wheat)	*Hordeum* (barley)	*Lens esculenta* (lentil)	*Camelina sativa* (gold of pleasure)	*Papaver* (poppy)	*Corylus avellana* (hazelnut)	*Galium* (cleavers)	*Rumex* (sorrel)	*Chenopodium album* (fat hen)	*Prunus* (wild plum)
Main occupation phase												
1	40	11 (3)	– –	– –	5 –	– –	– –	9 –	5 –	4 –	– –	1 –
2	20	– –	– –	– (3)	– –	– –	– –	– (2)	1 –	1 –	1 –	– –
3	6	1 –	1 –	– (1)	– –	– –	1 –	2 –	2 –	– –	– –	– –
4	30	– –	– (3)	– (6)	– –	– –	– –	1 –	– –	– –	– –	– –
5	10	2 –	– –	– (1)	– –	– –	– –	– –	– –	– –	– –	– –
6	30	1 –	– –	– –	– –	– –	– –	– –	1 –	– –	– –	– –
7	11	– –	1 –	– (3)	– –	1 –	– –	– (2)	– –	– –	– –	– –
8	30	– –	– (1)	– (1)	– (3)	– –	– –	7 (3)	1 –	– –	– –	– –
9	4	– –	– –	1 –	– –	– –	– –	– –	1 –	– –	1 –	– –
10	4	– –	– –	– (1)	– –	– –	– –	– –	– –	– –	– –	– –
11	10	– –	– (2)*	– –	– –	– –	– –	– –	– –	– –	– –	– –
12	40	– –	– (3)*	– –	– –	– –	– –	– –	2 –	– –	1 –	– –
13	77	10 –	3 (47)*	1 –	– –	– –	– –	2 –	2 –	– –	1 –	– –
Bronze Age												
A	20	– –	5 –	1 –	1 –	– –	– –	– –	6 –	– –	1 –	– –
B	11	– –	1 (1)*	– –	– –	– –	– –	– –	– –	– –	– –	– –

Note: Under each plant name, the left column records definitely identified specimens, the right column records probably identified ones.

*Identified as either *Hordeum* or *Triticum*.

Table 7.
Contents of palaeoethnobotanical samples.

Location*	Depth (cm below surface)	Identified	Possibly identified
Main occupation phase			
1. Trench N, pit in west extension			
Sample 30	20-40	3 *Galium* sp. 7 *Corylus avellana* 3 *Panicum* sp.	Barklike pieces from *Corylus avellana* 1 rachis fragment
Sample 35	38-48	2 *Lens esculenta* 1 *Galium* 2 *Rumex*	Burned mollusk 1 rachis fragment
Sample 36	45-50	6 *Panicum miliaceum* 1 *Lens esculenta* 2 wild legumes 2 *Corylus avellana* 1 *Prunus* sp. 2 *Rumex* sp. 1 *Galium* sp.	3 *Panicum miliaceum* 3 rachis fragments
Sample 37	Approx. 50	2 *Panicum miliaceum* 1 wild grass 1 rachis fragment	
2. Trench N, pit in north end			
Sample 31	47-54	1 *Galium* sp. 1 *Chenopodium* (calcified)	1 *Hordeum*
Sample 32	50	1 *Rumex* 1 glume base	2 *Hordeum* sp. 2 *Corylus avellana* 1 rachis fragment
3. Trench D, Cutting III, pit			
Sample 24	70	1 *Panicum miliaceum* 1 *Corylus avellana* 1 *Galium*	1 *Hordeum* 1 twig fragment
Sample 14	80	--	--
Sample 16	90	--	2 rachis fragments
Sample 15	100-110	1 *Corylus avellana* 1 *Galium* sp. 1 *Triticum* sp.	1 *Polygonum persicaria*
Sample 20	110-120	1 *Papaver* (calcified) 1 glume base	1 *Solanaceae*
Sample 18	120-130	--	--

*For locations of samples, refer to figure 78.

Location	Depth (cm below surface)	Identified	Possibly identified
4. Trench S, pit in south end			
Sample 43	75-83	1 *Corylus avellana*	6 *Hordeum* 3 *Triticum*
Samples 41, 42	95-123	1 glume base 2 wild grass	--
5. Trench S, red pit			
Sample 39	45-50	2 *Panicum miliaceum*	1 *Hordeum* 1 *Solanaceae*
6. Trench L, pit			
Sample 27	56-64	1 *Panicum* sp. 1 wild grass	1 rachis fragment
Sample 28	62-70	--	--
Sample 29	63-71	1 *Galium*	--
7. Trench C, pit			
Sample 3	0-10	--	--
Sample 9	40	1 *Triticum* sp.	--
Sample 6	42-52	1 *Camelina sativa*	3 rachis fragments 1 *Polygonum* sp.
Sample 26	44-54	Fused charcoal/ plant material	2 *Corylus avellana* 1 rachis fragment 1 *Hordeum* or *Triticum*
Sample 12	46	Fused charcoal/ plant material	--
Sample 7	52-62	Fused charcoal/ plant material	2 *Hordeum* or *Triticum*
Sample 25	54-64	--	2 rachis fragments
Sample 17	56	--	--
Sample 8	62-72	--	1 rachis fragment
Sample 19	66	Fused charcoal/ plant material	--
Sample 13	82	--	--

Table 7 (continued).

Location	Depth (cm below surface)	Identified	Possibly identified
8. Trench F, Cutting I, ditch fill			
Sample 1	Approx. 40	--	2 *Corylus avellana*
Sample 4 (rounded ditch)	50-58	6 *Corylus avellana*	1 *Triticum* 1 *Hordeum* 3 *Lens esculenta* 1 *Corylus avellana*
Sample 5 (pointed ditch)	50-58	1 *Corylus avellana* 1 *Galium* sp.	--
9. Trench F, Cutting II, ditch fill			
Sample 2	Approx. 60	1 *Hordeum* sp. 1 *Galium* sp. 1 *Chenopodium album*	--
10. Trench F, Cutting II, ditch fill			
Sample 11	10-20 below trench surface	--	1 *Hordeum*
11. Trench S, ditch fill			
Sample 45	55-61	--	2 *Hordeum* or *Triticum*
12. Trench S, pit in north end			
Sample 47	50-57	1 *Galium* sp.	--
Sample 48	65-71	--	1 *Hordeum* or *Triticum*
Sample 54	70-77	--	--
Sample 60	80-85	1 *Galium* sp. 1 *Chenopodium album* 1 rachis fragment	2 *Hordeum* or *Triticum*
13. Trench W, pit			
Sample 46	60-70	1 *Triticum* sp. 2 *Galium* sp.	6 *Hordeum* or *Triticum*
Sample 49	70-77	1 *Triticum* sp. 2 *Panicum* sp. 3 rachis fragments	13 *Hordeum* or *Triticum*
Sample 50	80-90	1 *Triticum* sp. 1 spikelet fragment 6 *Panicum* sp. 1 *Chenopodium album*	22 *Hordeum* or *Triticum*
Sample 52	120-130	2 *Panicum* sp.	4 *Hordeum* or *Triticum*

Location	Depth (cm below surface)	Identified	Possibly identified
13. Trench W, pit (continued)			
Sample 51	120-130	2 *Corylus avellana*	--
Sample 57	130-133 (from intense concentration of red claylike soil)	--	1 *Hordeum* or *Triticum*
Sample 59	130-140	--	--
Sample 56	130-140 (from intense charcoal concentration)	--	(several burned bone fragments)
Sample 55	140-144	1 *Hordeum* sp.	1 *Hordeum* or *Triticum*
Bronze Age			
A. Trench P, pit in south end			
Sample 34	47-54	1 *Hordeum* sp. 4 *Triticum* sp. 2 *Galium* sp. 1 rachis fragment	2 rachis fragments Cereal fragments
Sample 40	55-62	1 *Triticum* sp. 4 *Galium* sp. 1 *Lens esculenta*	2 rachis fragments 5 cereal fragments
B. Trench V, pit in west wall			
Sample 58	--	*	*
Sample 53	48-58	1 *Triticum* sp.	1 *Hordeum* or *Triticum*

*This sample consisted of half of the contents of a complete ceramic vessel and contained only charcoal fragments.

7

The Faunal Remains

by Brenda R. Benefit

Over 1,435 bone fragments were collected and analyzed from features of the principal occupation at Hascherkeller and from the earlier Bronze Age pits. Preservation of all bone was poor. Only 253 bones from the principal occupation and 29 from the pits of Early and Middle Bronze Age date were fully identifiable by body part and species, representing 20 percent of the total assemblage, a percentage typical for central European open settlement sites (P. Bogucki, pers. comm.). This relatively small percentage can be ascribed to the great extent of bone fragmentation during the occupation of the settlement and to excavation procedures that resulted in the recovery of even minute pieces of bone. The majority of the identifiable bones were fragmentary, and only a small proportion were measurable (table 15). Of the unidentifiable fragments, 46 percent were classified as small (less than 1 g), 15 percent as medium (1 to 2 g), and 39 percent as small burnt pieces (less than 0.5 g).

SPECIES PRESENT

The sample of identified bones from the principal occupation consists of 87 percent domestic and 13 percent wild animals. Of the domestic fauna, 37 percent has been attributed to pig *(Sus scrofa)*, 33 percent to sheep/goat *(Ovis aries/Capra hircus)*, 24 percent to cattle *(Bos taurus)*, 5 percent to dog *(Canis familiaris)*, and 1 percent to horse *(Equus caballus)* (see table 8). Among the sheep and goat remains, Prof. Joachim Boessneck identified 13 specimens as coming from sheep and 9 from goat. Besides the domestic animals, the inhabitants of the settlement exploited red deer *(Cervus elaphus* — 5 percent of the total animal bones), fish (species unidentified — 3 percent), and quail *(Coturnix coturnix)*. Hare *(Lepus europaeus)* and hedgehog *(Erinaceus europaeus)*, representing respectively 9 percent and 6 percent of the wild animal bones, may have been exploited as well, although there is no direct evidence in the form of cut, chewed, or burnt bone.

Microfaunal remains were collected using wet-sieving and flotation. Species identified were *Talpa europaea* (mole), *Arvicola terrestris* (water vole), *Apodemus sylvaticus* (wood mouse), and *Apodemus flavicollis* (yellow-necked mouse). The mole and water vole are burrowing animals and may have entered the features at any time after deposition. The mice were probably deposited during the time of human occupation of the settlement. Both the wood mouse and the yellow-necked mouse raid crops today, and they probably did during the Bronze and Iron Ages as well.

Of the 29 identifiable bones from Early and Middle Bronze Age pits, 21 are from mammals and 8 are from toads *(Bufo viridis)*. Of the 21 mammal bones, 17 are from domestic species and 4 are from wild. Among the Bronze Age mammals, 6 pigs are represented, as are 4 sheep/goats, 3 goats, 1 sheep, 1 cattle, and 2 dogs. One deer is present. Microfaunal remains of mouse, mole, and toad were recovered through wet-sieving and flotation.

AGE AT DEATH

Ages at death of the domestic animals from the principal occupation were estimated by identifying tooth wear stages defined by Grant (1975) and Payne (1973). All pig teeth with distinguishable wear were aged, including 6 mandibles, 2 partial maxilla, and 15 loose teeth, these representing 5 to 20 individuals (probably closer to 20). Of these, 3 mandibles and 7 loose teeth came from animals under 6 months of age; 2 mandibles and 4 loose teeth came from animals between 16 and 23 months old; 1 mandible, 2 maxillary fragments, and 2 loose teeth came from pigs about 24 months old; and 1 loose tooth came from an animal older than 24 months. Only 2 of the 34 postcranial remains had unfused epiphyses. The low number of juvenile postcrania is likely to be the result of differential preservation. As mentioned in a previous report (Wells et al. 1981), it has long been common practice in Europe to allow pigs to forage for themselves during the spring, summer, and fall, but to supplement their diet with stored grain during the winter. Pigs are usually slaughtered before they reach 24 months of age because pigs beyond that age yield less meat relative to the amount of grain needed to maintain them. A few females may be kept beyond this age for breeding purposes, but in general pigs are fast-breeding animals with an early onset of reproductive maturity, making even this measure unnecessary. The kill-off pattern at Hascherkeller with a high infant death rate probably caused by slaughter and seasonal (winter) slaughter of animals around two years old, is similar to that observed at other archaeological sites in Europe and elsewhere (Fél and Hofer 1972, p. 134).

The sheep/goat remains from the principal occupation were aged in a similar fashion, using all loose teeth and partial jaws with distinguishable wear. Of this sample, 4 loose teeth were from very young animals; 2 were from animals between 1 and 2 years old; 2 were from animals between 2 and 3 years old; 1 mandible, 1 maxillary fragment, and 1

loose tooth were from 3-to-4-year-old animals; 3 mandibles, 1 maxillary fragment, and 1 loose tooth were from 4-to-6-year-old animals; and 1 loose tooth was from a 6-to-8-year-old animal. Of the 17 postcranial elements, 3 have unfused articular ends, the small number again possibly due to reduced chances of unfused bone being preserved. The sheep-goat age curve at Hascherkeller is unlike that for meat production, in which the fewest individuals between 4 and 6 years old are present in the assemblage, but closely resembles that for wool production (Payne 1973). Numerous artifacts that may have been used in the production of wool textiles have been recovered from the settlement. Goats and sheep may also have been kept for dairy products.

Among the small assemblage of cattle bones, there are 3 loose teeth from juveniles, 2 loose teeth from middle-aged adults, and 1 partial jaw and 2 loose teeth from old adults. No postcranial elements have unfused articular ends. The cattle at Hascherkeller may have been used for traction and milk during life and for leather and meat after death.

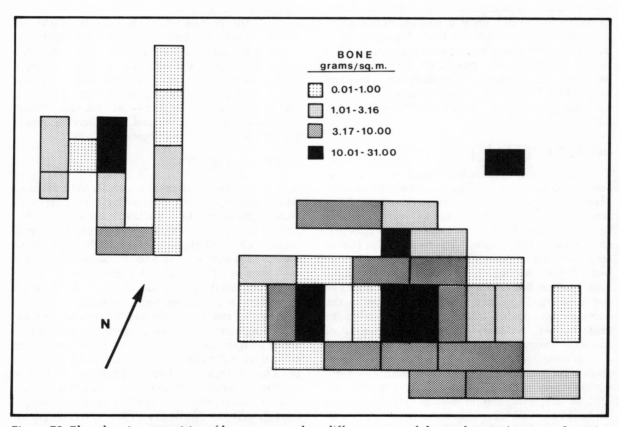

Figure 79. Plan showing quantities of bone recovered on different parts of the settlement (compare fig. 10).

DISTRIBUTION OF BONE

The distribution of species, skeletal elements, burnt bone, bones with cut marks, and fragmentary bone was studied to aid in identifying activity areas on the site. The distribution of all bone is given in table 11. Most of the identifiable fragments came from the pits in Trenches S (21 percent), N (16 percent), W (16 percent), and DIII (16 percent). Small unidentified fragments (less than 1 g) comprised 72 percent of all bone recovered from ditches and 70 percent of bone recovered from pits. Medium-sized unidentified fragments (1 to 2 g) comprised only 5 percent of all bone obtained from ditches and 14 percent of bone from pits. The higher percentage of small bone fragments in pits than in ditches suggests that bone in pits was subjected to more trampling and other breakage during or after deposition. The one pit that shows an exceptionally high degree of fragmentation is that in Trench L, which contained 75 percent small, 9 percent medium, and 2 percent small burnt bone fragments. The high percentage of small fragments in the pit in Trench L supports the hypothesis that much of its contents represent trash unintentionally deposited in the open hollow.

Burnt bone came predominantly from the pits in Trenches W (38 percent), N (26 percent), and DIII (4 percent). All of the ditch segments together contributed only 3 percent of the burnt bone. Whether the burnt bone is the result of cooking or burning after discard is not known. It is probable that the bone in at least one pit, that in the western extension of Trench N, was burnt after deposition. Few of the bones show signs of butchering or cooking. Those that do have cut marks are sliced deeply and regularly in a way that indicates that the cuts were made with a metal knife rather than with a stone implement. The pit in Trench W contained three identifiable burnt bones — the proximal metacarpal and proximal radius of deer and the radius of a cow — as well as one sliced lumbar vertebra of pig and a pig astragalus that had been chewed. The pits in Trench S contained two burnt bones — the distal radius of a cow and the distal metacarpal of a pig — and the chewed radius of a pig. The ditch segment in Trench EII contained the distal metacarpal of a deer that showed obvious cut marks and the distal femur of a cow that was burnt. The pit in Trench N contained a burnt cow astragalus and a burnt molar germ from a pig. The pit in Trench BV contained a distal cow phalanx that had been chewed. The pit in Trench L contained a chewed distal phalanx from a sheep. Dogs and pigs were probably responsible for the chew marks on the bone.

The number of skeletal elements preserved for each species is given in table 12. Since sheep and goat are distinguishable mainly on the basis of postcranial elements, it is necessary to consider the combined samples of the two taxa, of which 36 percent are cranial elements and 64 percent are postcranial. Loose teeth are the most common of the sheep/goat cranial elements, constituting 63 percent of that sample. The pig sample is composed of 60 percent cranial elements and 40 percent postcranial. Loose teeth comprise 69 percent of the cranial elements. Pig teeth and skull fragments survive well at most archaeological sites because they are especially sturdy (Halstead et al. 1978). Samples of both cattle and deer are represented by at least 73 percent postcranial elements. Unlike the other species, the cranial sample of cattle is composed of 50 percent loose teeth and 50 percent skull fragments. The only cranial elements of deer that are preserved are antler, which may have been collected after they had been shed. Foot bones make up a majority, 67 percent, of the deer bones. Boessneck has noted that few teeth and cranial elements of deer are ever found on Iron Age sites (pers. comm.).

The distribution of species and skeletal elements is shown in tables 13 and 14. Halstead, Hodder, and Jones (1978) propose that the distribution of species and skeletal elements in pits and ditches could help to identify activity areas within a site. They suggest that ditches and pits containing such elements as skull and foot bones (referred to as butchering waste) are indicative of butchery and cooking areas. Pits associated with eating or table areas would be characterized by the presence of the following elements considered under the rubric of meat-bearing bones: whole skeletons of juvenile animals, ribs, vertebrae, limbs, pelves, scapulae, and meat-bearing joints. This distinction is better applied to cattle, sheep, and goats than to pigs, the heads and feet of which are often eaten. An attempt was made to see if the pits and ditches at Hascherkeller held more butchering waste or meat-bearing bones.

Each domestic species was found to have a distinctive pattern of distribution. Most of the meat-bearing cattle remains came from pits rather than ditches. The pits in Trench L and in the western extension of Trench N — and to a lesser extent the pit in the south end of Trench S, that in Trench W, and the ditch segment of Trench EII — stand out as containing most of the meat-bearing cattle bones with one or no cranial elements. The only pits containing no cattle bones were the red pit in Trench S and that in the north end of Trench S. Pits containing a large number of pig meat-bearing bones were those in the north end of Trench N and in the south end of Trench S. The ditch segment in Trench EII contained two pig meat-bearing bones and no cranial elements, whereas all other ditch segments contained only cranial remains. The pits in Trenches DIII, L, and W contained more cranial than postcranial remains of pig. In total, 55 percent of the pig remains from pits and 85 percent from ditches were cranial. The largest number of sheep/goat postcranial bones came from the pit in Trench DIII, the pit in Trench C, and to a lesser extent from the pit at the south end of Trench S. Only 26 percent of the sheep/goat remains in pits were cranial, while 57 percent of the bones of these species in ditches were teeth and skull fragments.

Although the pattern of bone distribution does seem to suggest that more waste products were deposited in ditches, it is difficult to conclude what the functional areas of the site may have been. In terms of the total number of bones, the pit in Trench BV and the red pit in Trench S have so few bones that they probably had little to do with cooking and butchering activities. Pits containing equal numbers of cranial and postcranial remains, those from Trenches DIII and W, are both located away from the center of the settlement. They may have functioned more as general waste areas than as centers of cooking or butchering activities. The ditch segments in Trenches A, BIV, and DII also contained relatively equal numbers of postcranial and cranial fragments and similarly may not have been involved with specific animal processing activities. The long pit in Trench C and the pit in the western extension of Trench N each have more meat-bearing than non-meat-bearing bones and therefore may have been associated with eating areas according to the model proposed by Halstead, Hodder, and Jones. Ditch segments from Trenches EII and E-B contain high numbers of meat-bearing bones. Since the ditch segment in Trench EII is also the only ditch segment to contain bone with cut marks and burnt bone, it may have been associated with areas of food preparation. The remaining pits are more difficult to interpret.

The large pit in Trench L, that in the north end of Trench N, and that in the south end of Trench S all have more postcranial than cranial bones, suggesting proximity to areas where food was prepared. Because the size of the bone assemblage is small, it is difficult to substantiate the interpretations offered here. In combination with the analysis of artifact distribution, results from the above analysis of bone may contribute to more meaningful interpretations about the function of each pit.

SUMMARY

On the basis of the frequency of identified specimens, pig, sheep, goat, and cattle seem to have been the most important domestic species exploited, in that order. On the basis of information from this and other sites of the period (see chapter 13), pig would have been the principal meat animal, sheep would have been raised primarily for wool, goats for dairy products, and cattle for pulling plows and for dairy and leather products. The within-site distribution of species, skeletal elements, burnt bone, bone with cut marks, and fragmentary bone does not lead to any concrete conclusions about functional areas in the settlement. In general, bone in ditch segments was more fragmentary, unburnt, and composed of more non-meat-bearing skeletal elements than bone in pits. The one ditch segment that did not follow the pattern was that in Trench EII, which may have been associated with an area of food preparation. Among the pits, that in Trench L is unusual in containing a high percentage of fragmentary bone, which is consistent with the hypothesis that it had been a borrow pit and had filled gradually with sediment and loose rubbish from the settlement surface. This pit is also unusual in containing the largest number of meat-bearing cattle bones, which may have been table scraps. Pits in the central area of the site contained a higher ratio of meat-bearing to non-meat-bearing elements than did those in peripheral areas. The pits in Trenches DIII, N, S, and W contained the largest number of identifiable bones as well as burnt bones.

Table 8.
Domestic animals represented, main occupation phase.

	Cattle A*	Cattle J*	Pig A	Pig J	Sheep/goat A	Sheep/goat J	Sheep A	Sheep J	Goat A	Goat J	Dog A	Dog J	Horse A	Horse J
Cranial														
Horn-core	-	-	-	-	-	-	-	-	2	-	-	-	-	-
Skull fragments	3	-	5	3	-	-	2	-	-	-	5	-	-	-
Mandible														
With teeth	1	-	3	3	4	-	-	-	-	-	2	-	-	-
Without teeth	2	-	2	-	-	-	-	-	-	-	-	-	-	-
Maxilla														
With teeth	-	-	2	-	2	-	-	-	-	-	1	-	-	-
Without teeth	1	-	-	-	1	-	-	-	-	-	-	-	-	-
Loose teeth	4	3	21	8	11	4	1	-	-	-	1	-	-	-
Postcranial														
Vertebra	5	-	2	-	4	-	-	-	-	-	1	-	-	-
Rib	6	-	5	1	9	-	2	-	-	-	-	-	-	-
Scapula	4	-	-	-	1	-	2	-	-	-	-	-	-	-
Humerus	1	-	2	-	3	-	-	-	-	-	-	-	-	-
Radius	4	-	1	-	2	-	1	-	-	-	-	-	-	-
Ulna	2	-	1	-	-	-	-	-	-	-	-	-	-	-
Radiocarpal	-	-	-	-	-	-	-	-	1	-	-	-	-	-
Os carpalis	-	-	-	-	1	-	-	-	-	-	-	-	-	-
Metacarpal	1	-	1	-	-	-	-	2	-	-	1	-	-	-
Pelvis	1	-	2	1	1	-	-	-	-	-	-	-	-	-
Femur	5	-	-	-	-	-	-	-	-	-	-	-	-	-
Tibia	-	-	-	-	2	-	-	-	-	-	-	-	1	-
Fibula	-	-	-	-	-	-	-	-	-	-	1	-	-	-
Patella	-	-	-	-	-	-	-	-	-	-	-	-	-	-
Magnum	1	-	-	-	-	-	-	-	-	-	-	-	-	-
Astragalus	2	-	4	-	1	-	-	-	-	-	-	-	-	-
Calcaneum	-	-	1	-	-	-	1	-	-	-	-	-	-	-
Metatarsal	3	-	1	-	-	-	-	-	1	1	-	-	-	-
Metapodial	1	-	3	-	1	-	1	-	2	-	-	-	-	-
1st phalanx	-	-	6	-	1	-	-	-	-	-	-	-	1	-
2nd phalanx	-	-	1	-	1	-	-	-	-	-	-	-	-	-
3rd phalanx	2	-	2	-	1	-	1	-	2	-	-	-	-	-
Sesamoid	1	-	-	-	-	-	-	-	-	-	-	-	-	-
Total of each species	53		81		50		13		9		12		2	
Percentage of Total**	24		37		23		6		4		5		1	

*A indicates permanent dentition or fused epiphyses; J indicates deciduous dentition or unfused epiphyses.
**Percentage based on a total of 220 bones.

Table 9.
Wild animals represented, main occupation phase.

	Hare A*	Hare J*	Deer A	Deer J	Hedgehog A	Hedgehog J	Vole A	Vole J	Mole A	Mole J	Mouse A	Mouse J	Quail A	Quail J	Fish
Cranial															
Antler	–	–	3	–	–	–	–	–	–	–	–	–	–	–	–
Skull fragments	–	–	–	–	1	–	–	–	–	–	–	–	–	–	1
Mandible															
With teeth	–	–	–	–	1	–	–	–	–	–	–	–	–	–	–
Without teeth	–	–	–	–	–	–	–	–	–	–	1	–	–	–	–
Maxilla															
With teeth	–	–	–	–	–	–	–	–	1	–	–	–	–	–	–
Without teeth	–	–	–	–	–	–	1	–	–	–	–	–	–	–	–
Loose teeth	–	–	–	–	–	–	–	–	–	–	1	–	–	–	–
Postcranial															
Vertebra	–	–	–	–	–	–	–	–	–	–	1	–	–	–	6
Rib	1	–	–	–	–	–	–	–	–	–	–	–	–	–	–
Radius	1	–	1	–	–	–	–	–	–	–	–	–	–	–	–
Metacarpal	–	–	2	–	–	–	–	–	–	–	–	–	–	–	–
Pelvis	–	–	1	–	–	–	–	–	–	–	–	–	–	–	–
Femur	–	–	–	–	–	–	1	–	–	–	1	–	1	–	–
Tibia	–	–	–	–	–	–	1	–	–	–	–	–	–	–	–
Calcaneum	1	–	–	–	–	–	–	–	–	–	–	–	–	–	–
Metapodial	–	–	4	–	–	–	–	–	–	–	–	–	–	–	–
Metatarsal	–	–	1	–	–	–	–	–	–	–	–	–	–	–	–
Total of each species**	3		12		2		3		1		4		1		7

*A indicates permanent dentition or fused epiphyses; J indicates deciduous dentition or unfused epiphyses.

**Total for all species listed is 33 bones.

Table 10.
Domestic and wild animals represented, Bronze Age.

	Cattle	Pig	Sheep/Goat	Sheep	Goat	Dog	Deer	Mouse	Mole	Toad
Cranial										
Antler	-	-	-	-	-	-	1	-	-	-
Skull fragments	1	-	-	1	-	2	-	-	-	-
Mandible										
With teeth	-	-	-	-	-	-	-	-	-	-
Without teeth	-	1	-	-	-	-	-	-	-	-
Maxilla										
With teeth	-	1	-	-	-	-	-	-	-	-
Without teeth	-	-	-	-	-	-	-	-	-	-
Loose teeth	-	2	3	-	-	-	-	-	-	-
Postcranial										
Vertebra	-	-	1	-	-	-	-	-	-	-
Rib	-	1	-	-	-	-	-	-	-	-
Scapula	-	-	-	-	-	-	-	-	1	-
Pelvis	-	-	-	-	-	1	-	-	-	8
Femur	-	1*	-	-	-	1	-	-	-	-
Tibia	-	-	-	-	-	-	-	2	-	-
Radiocarpal	-	-	-	-	1	-	-	-	-	-
Carpal indet.	-	-	-	-	2	-	-	-	-	-
Total of each species**	1	6	4	1	3	2	1	2	1	8

*Juvenile.

**Total for all species listed is 29 bones.

Table 11.
Distribution of bones, main occupation phase.

	No. of bones in pit	% of total bones	No. identified	% identified	No. unidentified <1 g	1-2 g	burnt	% unidentified <1 g	1-2 g	burnt
Pit										
C	41	3	11	27	11	12	7	27	29	17
DIII	173	12	37	21	69	50	17	40	29	10
L	130	9	18	14	97	12	3	75	9	2
N	280	20	39	14	85	38	118	29	13	41
W	246	18	39	16	26	9	172	11	0.4	70
Ditch segment										
A	44	3	9	2	31	4	0	71	9	0
F	62	4	9	15	42	2	9	68	3	15
E	57	4	19	33	30	3	5	53	5	9
Pits and ditch segments combined										
B	44	3	6	14	5	20	13	11	45	30
S	312	22	50	16	135	23	104	43	7	33
Totals	1,389*		237*	17	531	173	448	38	12	32

* Sums are smaller than the total numbers of bones and identifiable bones (253) because some bone fragments could not be confidently attributed to a specific pit or ditch segment.

Table 12.
Distribution of skeletal elements in pits and ditches, main occupation phase.

	Cattle		Pig		Sheep/goat		Sheep		Goat		Dog		Deer		Hare		Horse		Total	
	P*	D*	P	D	P	D	P	D	P	D	P	D	P	D	P	D	P	D	P	D
Cranial	8	6	38	11	10	9	2	1	0	2	9	0	1	0	0	0	0	0	68	29
Percentage**	24	33	55	84	26	57					75		16						40	52
Postcranial	26	12	31	2	20	6	9	1	5	2	3	0	5	3	3	0	1	1	103	27
Percentage	76	67	45	16	74	43					25		84	100	100		100	100	60	48
Total number of bones***	34	18	69	13	30	15	11	2	5	4	12	0	6	3	3	0	1	1	171	56
Loose teeth	5	2	24	10	9	5	1	0	0	0	1	0	0	0	0	0	0	0	40	17
Vertebra	5	0	2	0	4	0	0	0	0	0	1	0	0	0	0	0	0	0	12	0
Rib	5	1	6	0	8	0	2	0	0	0	0	0	0	0	0	0	0	0	21	1
Scapula	1	1	0	0	1	0	0	1	0	0	0	0	0	0	0	0	0	0	2	2
Pelvis	0	1	3	0	1	0	0	0	0	0	0	0	1	0	0	0	0	0	5	1
Limb	5	6	4	0	3	1	0	1	0	0	1	0	1	0	1	0	1	0	16	8
Carpal and tarsal	2	1	5	1	1	1	2	0	1	0	0	0	0	0	1	0	0	0	12	3
Metapodial	4	1	6	0	0	1	2	0	2	2	1	0	3	3	0	0	0	0	18	7
Phalanx	2	0	6	1	1	2	1	0	2	0	0	0	0	0	0	0	0	1	12	4

*P indicates pits; D indicates ditches.

**Percentage of the bones of the species in the pits/ditches that are of the stated skeletal elements.

***These totals do not include several little-represented wild animals (see table 9).

Table 13.
Distribution of skeletal elements in pits, main occupation phase.

	BV			C			DIII			L			N west extension			N north end			S red			S north end			S south end			W		
	C*	P*	%**	C	P	%	C	P	%	C	P	%	C	P	%	C	P	%	C	P	%	C	P	%	C	P	%	C	P	%
Cattle	0	2	100	2	1	27	1	1	5	0	7	39	1	6	54	2	2	15	0	0	0	0	0	0	1	4	16	1	3	10
Pig	0	0	0	0	1	9	12	4	43	3	2	28	1	1	15	6	10	62	0	0	0	1	1	29	8	8	50	7	4	28
Sheep/goat	0	0	0	1	4	45	1	7	22	2	1	17	0	1	8	0	1	4	0	1	100	2	1	43	1	3	13	3	1	10
Sheep	0	0	0	0	1	9	1	0	3	0	2	11	0	0	0	0	5	19	0	0	0	0	0	0	1	0	3	0	1	3
Goat	0	0	0	0	0	0	0	3	8	0	0	0	0	0	0	0	0	0	0	0	0	0	0	0	0	1	3	0	1	3
Dog	0	0	0	0	1	9	0	1	3	0	0	0	0	0	0	0	0	0	0	0	0	0	0	0	1	0	3	8	1	23
Deer	0	0	0	0	0	0	0	2	5	0	0	0	0	0	0	0	0	0	0	0	0	0	0	0	0	0	0	1	3	10
Horse	0	0	0	0	0	0	0	0	0	0	0	0	0	0	0	0	0	0	0	0	0	0	0	0	0	0	0	0	1	3
Hare	0	0	0	0	0	0	0	1	3	0	0	0	0	0	0	0	0	0	0	0	0	0	0	0	0	1	3	0	1	3
Fish	0	0	0	0	0	0	0	3	8	0	0	0	0	0	0	0	0	0	0	0	0	0	1	14	0	3	9	0	0	0
Quail	0	0	0	0	0	0	0	0	0	0	0	0	0	1	8	0	0	0	0	0	0	0	0	0	0	0	0	0	0	0
Vole	0	0	0	0	0	0	0	0	0	1	0	6	0	2	15	0	0	0	0	0	0	0	0	0	0	0	0	0	0	0
Mole	0	0	0	0	0	0	0	0	0	0	0	0	0	0	0	0	0	0	0	0	0	1	0	14	0	0	0	0	0	0
Mouse	0	0	0	0	0	0	0	0	0	0	0	0	0	0	0	0	0	0	0	0	0	0	0	0	0	0	0	1	2	8
Total C & P**	2			11			37			18			13			26			1			7			32			39		
% of total faunal remains	0	100		27	73		40	60		33	67		15	85		31	69		0	100		57	43		37	63		54	46	

*C = cranial elements; P = postcranial elements; % = the percentage of the faunal remains within each pit.

**The total number of bones recorded in tables 13 and 14 is less than the total number of identified bones (253) because some fragments could not be confidently attributed to a specific pit or ditch.

Table 14.
Distribution of skeletal elements in ditches, main occupation phase.

	A			F			EII			E-B			BIV			S			DII		
	C*	P*	%*	C	P	%	C	P	%	C	P	%	C	P	%	C	P	%	C	P	%
Cattle	0	2	22	2	1	33	0	3	27	1	2	38	1	1	50	1	1	20	1	2	43
Pig	1	0	11	3	0	33	0	2	18	1	0	13	1	0	25	3	0	30	2	0	29
Sheep/goat	3	2	56	2	0	22	3	0	27	0	2	25	0	1	25	1	1	20	0	0	0
Sheep	0	0	0	0	0	0	1	0	9	0	1	13	0	0	0	0	0	0	0	0	0
Goat	0	0	0	0	1	11	1	0	9	1	0	13	0	0	0	0	1	10	0	0	0
Dog	0	0	0	0	0	0	0	0	0	0	0	0	0	0	0	0	0	0	0	0	0
Deer	0	0	0	0	0	0	0	1	9	0	0	0	0	0	0	0	0	0	0	2	29
Horse	0	1	11	0	0	0	0	0	0	0	0	0	0	0	0	0	0	0	0	0	0
Hare	0	0	0	0	0	0	0	0	0	0	0	0	0	0	0	0	0	0	0	0	0
Hedgehog	0	0	0	0	0	0	0	0	0	0	0	0	0	0	0	2	0	20	0	0	0
Vole	0	0	0	0	0	0	0	0	0	0	0	0	0	0	0	0	0	0	0	0	0
Mole	0	0	0	0	0	0	0	0	0	0	0	0	0	0	0	0	0	0	0	0	0
Mouse	0	0	0	0	0	0	0	0	0	0	0	0	0	0	0	0	0	0	0	0	0
Total	9			9			11			8			4			10			7		
% of total faunal remains	44	56		78	22		45	55		38	62		50	50		70	30		43	57	

*C = cranial elements; P = postcranial elements; % = the percentage of the faunal remains within each ditch.

Table 15.
Bone measurements.*

Measurement abbreviations

GB	greatest breadth	DPA	depth across processus anconeus
Bp	greatest breadth proximal	BPC	greatest breadth across coronoid
SD	smallest breadth of diaphysis		process
DLS	diagonal length of sole	GL1	greatest length, lateral side
Ld	length of dorsal surface	GLm	greatest length, medial side
MBS	middle breadth of sole	DM	greatest depth, medial side
L	length	DL	greatest depth, lateral side
W	width	Bd	greatest breadth, distal end
Lo	length of olecranon	Bt	greatest breadth, trochlea
SDo	smallest breadth of diaphysis	GL	greatest length

Cattle

   Foramen magnum GB: 45.3
   Metatarsal, proximal Bp: 40.7 SD: 22
   3rd phalanx, lateral DLS: 59 Ld: 19.6 MBS: 43.4

Pig

   Ulna, distal Lo: 38.6 SDo: 25.7 DPA: 32.4 BPC: 19.1
   Astragalus GL1: 38 GLm: 35 DM: 22.6 DL: 20 Bd: 20
   Astragalus GL1: 40 GLm: 36 DM: 22.6 DL: 21
   1st phalanx Bd: 11.7
   Maxilla, partial:

	P21	P31	P41	M11	M21	M31
L:	11	12	9	10	19	31
W:	9	10	13	13	16	18

   1st molar L: 19 W: 14.5
   1st molar L: 18.7 W: 11.2
   4th premolar L: 12 W: 9
   Upper male canine L: 45 W: 12

   Bronze Age occupation:
   Humerus Bt: 33 Bd: 37.3 W: 37

Sheep

   Metatarsal, distal Bd: 23.4 SD: 11.3
   3rd phalanx Ld: 20.7 DLS: 26.7 MBS: 8

Goat

   3rd phalanx Ld: 23.5 DLS: 28.5 MBS: 5.3
   3rd phalanx Ld: 25.6 DLS: 31 MBS: 5.7

Note: All measurements are in millimeters. Unless otherwise noted, specimens date from the main occupation of the site.

*See von den Driesch 1976.

Sheep or goat

  1st phalanx Glm: 20.6 Distal W: 7.8 Proximal W: 7
  Maxilla, partial:

	P41	P4r	M1l	M21
L:	8	8	11	14
W:	9	10	11	12

  2nd upper molar L: 11 W: 13.7
  1st upper molar L: 16 W: 11.8
  Mandible:

	P3	P4	M1	M2
L:	9	9	11	20
W:	6	7	8	8

  Mandible, right:

	P4	M1	M2	M3
L:	8	10	14	22
W:	6	7	9	9

  2nd lower right molar L: 15   W: 8
  3rd lower right molar L: 22   W: 8
  2nd lower molar L: 18.1 W: 12
  1st upper molar L: 13.4 W: 13

Deer

  Radius, proximal W: 37.5
  Metapodial, distal, female Bd: 41

Hare

  Calcaneum GL: 35.8 GB: 12

Dog

  Fibula, proximal L: 12 W: 7
  4th lower premolar L: 12.5 W: 6.2

Table 15 (continued).

Dog (continued)

Bronze Age:

	Maxilla		Mandible	
	L	W	L	W
M1r	12.6	15.8	21.3	8.4
M2r	7.4	10.8	8.7	6.5
P4r	17.6	9.9	10.9	5.8
P4l	17.6	9.8	11.4	6.4
M2l	7.4	10.5	8.9	6.6
P3l	12	5.3	10.5	5
Cr	6	10.4		
Cl	6.2	10.3		
P1r	6	4.2		
P1l	4.6	3.5		
P3r	10.7	4.5		
P3l	10.5	4.3	10.5	5
P2r	11.8	5		
P2l	10.5	5	9	5
I1l	4.5	5		
I2l	5.6	5.5		
M3l			5	4.5
I1r			2.6	
I2r			3.6	

Total length condyle-infradentale: 138.4
Length angular process-infradentale: 136
Length indentation of condyle and angular processes-infradentale: 135
Length indentation of condyle and angular processes-aboral border of canine alveolus: 113.2
Length M3 alveolus-canine alveolus: 76.8
Length M3-P1: 66.2
Length M3-P2: 62.5
Length P1-P4: 38
Length P2-P4: 33.5
Height of mandible behind M1: 24
Height of mandible between P2 and P3: 19

8

Pottery: An Examination of the Temper

by John D. Stubbs

This report presents the results of analysis of all pottery recovered from the settlement of Hascherkeller during the 1978, 1979, and 1980 field seasons. The study of the pottery and its temper was carried out in three parts, (1) classification of types, (2) petrological examination of samples taken from the types, and (3) testing of physical characteristics of the types.

The pottery at Hascherkeller was recovered primarily from the upper levels of the settlement pits. Smaller amounts were recovered from the fill of the ditches surrounding parts of the settlement. All of the pottery from the main occupation occurred in sherds. More than 95 percent of the sherds show no decoration, and no slips were used on the pottery. Surface color varied greatly, from light browns and oranges to reds and blacks. This color variation occurs even within individual sherds, suggesting inconsistent firing or differential weathering in the soil. Most vessels had been smoothed both on the interior and exterior, but even surfaces were not always achieved.

Cross sections of the pottery show more consistent patterns of variation. Different kinds of inclusions were used as temper. Tempering materials include quartz pebbles (fig. 80), sand, baked daub, crushed pottery, and organic substances. These different kinds of temper occur alone or in combination with others.

No applicable technological typology for Late Bronze/Early Iron Age settlement pottery in central Europe has been developed (but see Jaanusson 1981). Temper was chosen as the primary variable for classification at Hascherkeller because the addition of temper is an essential aspect of pottery production and because even the highly fragmented pottery from the site lent itself to study of the temper.

CLASSIFICATION AND ANALYSIS

Classification of the pottery was carried out during the 1979 and 1980 field seasons. All of the pottery

was examined, and several types were defined on the basis of the temper visible in cross sections. Once these types were defined, all of the pottery from the site was sorted and weighed according to type. These weights served to establish the frequency of each type at the site as a whole and within individual settlement features.

Thirty pottery samples representing each of the types (some represented by more than one sample) were drawn from the collection for further study during the winter of 1979 to 1980. A thin section was taken from the samples for petrological examination. The primary tempering materials were identified using a polarizing microscope (figs. 81, 82). Temper fragments were measured, and any evidence present concerning methods of production or firing temperatures was recorded.

In addition to the petrological examination, two physical tests were conducted on each sample. The average density and the apparent porosity of each sherd was determined in the laboratory. It was hoped that these tests would aid in identifying those pottery types that may have been brought into the

0   5

cm

Figure 80. Sherd with quartz pebble temper.

settlement from outside or types constructed of significantly different materials.

The average density of each sample was determined by the loss-of-weight method. The word average acknowledges the fact that these sherds are made up of many different materials. The weight of the sample in air was measured, then the sample was submerged in toluene and its weight again recorded. With each weighing the temperature was also measured. The average density of each sample was determined by using the following equation:

$$d_{sample} = \frac{m_1}{m_1 - m_2} \times d_{toluene}$$

$d_{toluene} = 0.8669 - (9 \times 10^{-4}(t - 20))$
d = density
m_1 = the weight of the sample in air
m_2 = the weight of the sample in toluene
t = temperature in degrees centigrade.

The primary source of error in the measurement is caused by sealed pore spaces, making the sample appear less dense than it really is. By measuring the apparent porosity of the sample, the influence of this factor can be estimated. Little is known about the range of variation of average density within a single pottery type (Shepard 1956, p. 137). The limited number of samples tested for each type did not allow for such a determination.

The apparent porosity of a sherd is a measure of the volume of open pore space expressed as a percentage of the total volume of the sherd. Three measurements are required: the volume of the sample, the weight of the sample in air, and the saturated weight of the sample. This last measurement is made by boiling the sample in water for one hour, then recording the weight of the still-saturated sample after removal from the water. The percent of apparent porosity is determined by the following equation (Shepard 1956, pp. 125–130):

$$P = \frac{Sf - Wf}{Vf} \times 100$$

P = percent apparent porosity
Sf = weight of saturated sample
Wf = weight of sample in air
Vf = volume of sample.

The error in this measurement lies in the saturated weight determination. Care must be taken to assure that the sample is saturated as fully as possible. Experiments by Matson have shown that the variation in apparent porosity measurements for a homogeneous collection of sherds is about 8 percent (1941, p. 471).

Results

In the field laboratory in 1979, 19 different pottery types were defined. Petrological examination led to the condensing of these 19 types to 12. The attributes of each of the 12 are shown in table 16. The components of the clay fabric, not including the primary tempering materials, were the same in every case. These are quartz, muscovite, and small amounts of hematite mixed in with the clay minerals. Under favorable conditions the geological and geographical origins of such materials can be determined using petrological examination, but the Hascherkeller area does not lend itself well to such tracing. Many of the

Figure 81. Microphotograph showing rounded quartz temper in thin section at 100 × magnification through crossed polars.

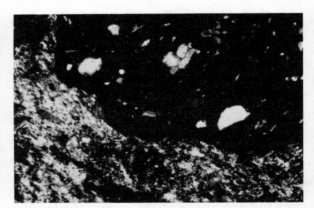

Figure 82. Microphotograph showing sherd temper in thin section at 100 × magnification through crossed polars.

sediments of the region consist of gravels and sands deposited by fluvial outwash from the Alpine glaciers (chapter 2); hence, minerals from different sources were available locally at Hascherkeller.

Some differences between the types that are not reflected in the table should be noted, particularly between Types VIII and X. Type VIII has considerably more temper than Type X. Sherds of Type VI are thinner and more delicate than those of the other types, are consistently black in color, and often have a graphite coating.

Only one type, V, stands out mineralogically from the rest. It has primarily plagioclase feldspar temper and has the largest quantity of temper of all the types.

The physical tests isolated two types from the general group. Types VII and XII both had average densities that were lower than the others, and both had the highest percentage of apparent porosity. Yet the petrological examination of these two types revealed nothing to indicate that they may have been imported or made from imported materials. One hypothesis that may explain this discrepancy is that the sample sherds tested may have been burned after they were fired. This hypothesis remains to be tested; the apparent porosity of a sherd can increase with a second firing, even at temperatures well below the original firing temperature (Shepard 1956, p. 223). Secondary burning could explain these deviations.

Overall the density and porosity measurements were found ineffective in determining exotic types; they are of relatively little use as classificatory traits.

Petrological examination provides evidence concerning temperature and conditions during firing (Hodges 1963). When temperatures exceed 850 degrees Celsius, some of the clay minerals break down and form spinels and glasses and therefore appear isotropic, or dark, when observed under the crossed nicols of the polarizing microscope. Since none of the samples exhibited this characteristic, a lower firing temperature was probably used. The atmospheric conditions of the kiln at the time of firing are difficult to determine. The amount of carbon left in the clay matrix suggests that most of the samples were fired in a reducing or semireducing atmosphere.

Conclusions

The potters at Hascherkeller were utilizing primarily local materials to produce their wares. Clay and rounded quartz sand and pebbles were available along the Isar River. Other tempers, such as crushed sherds, daub, and organic matter, were available within the settlement.

Two materials stand out as being significantly different: the feldspar temper in Type V pottery and the graphite used to decorate some of the Type VI vessels. The origin of the feldspar is not known; it may have been available in the local area. This type of pottery is not well represented at the settlement; it comprises less than 1 percent by weight of all the pottery recovered through the 1980 field season. The pottery, or its temper, may have been brought in from outside.

The graphite used to decorate some of the Type VI vessels must have been brought to the settlement from some distance away, perhaps from around Passau on the Danube to the east or from southern Bohemia (Kappel 1969; Kossack 1959, p. 71). Pottery decorated with graphite comprises less than 1 percent by weight of all the pottery recovered from the settlement.

POTTERY DISTRIBUTION ON THE SETTLEMENT

Two aspects of pottery distribution are of concern here: that of all the pottery recovered during the four seasons of excavation (1978 to 1981) and that of the 12 types discussed above. The distribution of all pottery shows that most was recovered from areas where there are significant settlement features (fig. 28). High concentrations of pottery occurred in Trenches BV, N, S, and AAI. Trench W had an exceptionally large amount of pottery, more than three times the amount from Trench N, which was the next greatest concentration. The patterns of concentration of pottery in the central part of the site compare closely with the distribution of bone but less so with that of daub (figs. 79, 83).

Distribution of pottery types by settlement feature is summarized in table 17. Two separate concentrations are apparent. Type I occurred in very high concentrations in the northern portions of Trenches N and S and was also represented in the pit in Trench DIII and the pit in Trench W. Type XII followed a similar pattern, mostly appearing in the northern parts of Trenches N and S. These types may have had a functional significance related to their locations on the site.

Type VII is concentrated in Trench BV. The only other area of the site where this type is represented in any quantity is in the borrow pit in Trench L.

Types II, IX, and XI are relatively evenly distributed over most parts of the site.

Conclusions

The potters at Hascherkeller relied almost exclusively on materials that were available in the vicinity of the settlement, a pattern similar to that ascertained for the slightly later settlement at Elchinger Kreuz near Ulm (Maggetti 1979, pp. 141–168).

The distribution of pottery types as defined here suggests that there may have been two special activity areas in the settlement where these particular kinds of pottery were especially used. Exotic types of pottery are poorly represented at Hascherkeller.

Table 16.
Attributes of pottery types.

Pottery type	Tempering materials						Average temper size (mm)	Largest dimension (mm)	Density (g/cm³)	Apparent porosity (%)	% occurrence (by wt.)
	Rounded quartz	Chunky quartz	Sherd	Daub	Feldspar	Organic					
I	x		x				2.7	5.5	2.2	37	23
II	x		x				1.4	6.0	2.2	39	28
III				x			4.0	7.8	2.2	47	<1
IV	x		x			x	3.8	8.5	2.2	36	11
V		x			x		1.4	8.8	2.3	29	<1
VI		x					<.2	0.2	2.2	29	<1
VII	x					x	1.0	1.5	1.8	51	10
VIII	x						2.0	3.7	2.1	41	7
IX	x					x	0.4	2.1	2.2	31	5
X	x						2.2	2.7	2.4	40	1
XI	x		x				2.0	2.7	2.1	27	10
XII						x			1.3	80	1

Table 17.
Distribution of pottery types, showing percentage of types in each pit.

Pit	Pottery type											
	I	II	III	IV	V	VI	VII	VIII	IX	X	XI	XII
BV	–	12	–	*	–	–	81	5	2	–	*	–
C	–	73	1	2	–	1	3	2	6	2	9	–
DIII	18	12	4	24	2	1	–	–	6	9	24	–
L	–	41	–	4	–	–	12	28	3	–	12	–
N, west extension	53	7	–	32	–	*	5	–	*	–	*	3
N, north end	88	9	–	1	–	–	–	*	*	–	1	–
S, north end	43	25	–	1	–	–	–	–	5	–	22	3
S, red	65	16	–	12	–	*	*	–	–	–	7	–
S, south end	1	58	–	7	–	1	3	9	8	–	13	–
W	15	14	–	14	–	*	1	5	3	–	27	1

9

The Daub

by Mary L. Hancock

Daub is clay used to plaster the wooden walls of structures, particularly houses. It is well represented ethnographically in rural parts of Europe (e.g., Bankoff and Winter 1979) and is well preserved on archaeological settlement sites throughout the continent. Fragments of daub were found scattered in small amounts over the entire excavated area at Hascherkeller, often on the surface above major pits, in the humus layers above and near the pits, and especially in the top levels of the pits (fig. 83). As a result of continual disturbance of the humus, especially from plowing, most daub pieces from the upper layers were small and rounded.

The daub at Hascherkeller consists of the local loess subsoil. Some of the daub contains small pebbles, perhaps intentionally added as temper. Some fragments of daub have whitewash on their surfaces, often in several layers, indicating that the walls were replastered and repainted several times (figs. 52, 53). A few pieces with whitewash also have brownish-red paint on their surfaces.

SORTING

In 1980 the daub sample from the first two seasons of excavation at Hascherkeller (1978 to 1979) was sorted into diagnostic and nondiagnostic groups. The diagnostic pieces were subdivided into four categories.

Wall Pieces

These specimens have a flattened or smoothed surface (fig. 84). The majority have only one flat surface; some have two flattened or smoothed sides. These latter pieces were probably either sandwiched between two flat structural beams or pressed against a flat beam on one side and exposed, and therefore intentionally smoothed, on an external surface of a building.

Structural Pieces

Several pieces have perpendicular or cornerlike impressions (fig. 85). These may have been packed against a corner or an edge of a split or flattened beam. Some have circular impressions suggesting a framework of unsplit branches or trunks of small trees (fig. 86). A series of cardboard disks ranging in diameter from 0.5 to 9.5 cm at intervals of 0.5 cm was prepared to measure the diameters of the impressions.

Structural Wall Pieces

Several fragments have both circular impressions and flattened edges. These were measured both with calipers and with the cardboard disks. The sum of the two measurements (the diameter of the circular impression plus the width of the specimen from the flattened outer edge to the circular impression) should be an indication of wall thickness.

Other

Many triangular or wedge-shaped pieces of daub are among the sample (fig. 87). They are probably remains of packing between logs, as Pertlwieser (1971, p. 69, fig. 6) illustrates from the slightly later settlement on the Waschenberg in Upper Austria. A small number of fragments have a continuous round edge with a flat base, perhaps from the finished edge of a structure such as a doorway.

MEASUREMENTS

All measurements taken from the daub specimens are listed in the tables below.

Wall Pieces

Specimens of this category were the most numerous,

with 165 pieces. Maximum widths varied from 0.61 to 9.11 cm. The mean maximum width was 1.86 cm. The minimum widths ranged from 0.39 to 5.85 cm. The mean minimum width was 1.33 cm, the median 1.20 cm. The most wall pieces came from the pit in Trench C; others were recovered in Trenches A, B, E, N, and S.

Structural Pieces

Structural pieces were also most abundant in the pit in Trench C. The 133 structural impressions measured ranged in size from 0.5 to 9.5 cm in diameter. The mean impression was 2.66 cm.

Structural Wall Pieces

Specimens of the structural wall category came principally from the pit in Trench C, from Trench N, and from the pit in Trench BV, with a single stray from Trench E. Twenty-seven pieces could be measured. Total width ranged from 2.16 to 11.35 cm. The mean was 6.79 cm.

The measurements of the diagnostic daub samples from Hascherkeller offer some insight into the structures that existed on the settlement. Trench C and the adjoining part of Trench BII yielded large amounts of daub associated with the long narrow pit. The wall specimens from that area averaged 1.76 cm in maximum width. It was originally hypothesized that the wall pieces might indicate the thickness of walls, but 1.76 cm is much too thin to represent a structure such as a dwelling. These specimens may have been situated between structural beams set close together, or they may have come from a smaller structure, perhaps a feature within a house such as an oven. The lack of larger pieces corresponding to the expected thickness of the wall of a dwelling may also be due to poor preservation resulting from fragmentation during and after deposition, and because the daub was not exposed to enough heat to fire it thoroughly. In any case, the abundance of daub pieces with two flat and parallel sides in Trench C suggests that the principal structure above the pit was constructed with flat beams.

Trench C also yielded the largest amount of

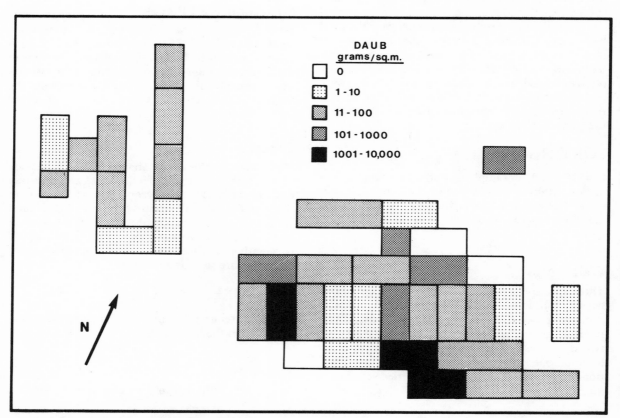

Figure 83. Plan showing quantities of daub recovered on different parts of the settlement (compare fig. 10).

Figure 84. Measuring a wall piece of daub.

structural pieces. Several have structural impressions between 9.0 and 9.5 cm in diameter, suggesting the size of timbers used in construction. Pieces with the smallest impressions of 0.5 cm may have come from the wattling interwoven between the larger structural beams. These fragments with small impressions may also have come from a small structure such as an animal pen or a storage bin.

Trench C yielded the highest amount of structural wall pieces. They averaged 6.21 cm in size. Because this measurement incorporates both the diameter of the structural timber and the thickness of the daub fragment from the impression to the exterior surface, it is perhaps the most informative concerning the actual thickness of the wall of a structure.

The pit in Trench BV yielded daub specimens similar to those from Trench C. They were fewer in number, perhaps because the pit was not as deep as that in Trench C and had been more severely disturbed by plows, but the average size was generally larger (see tables).

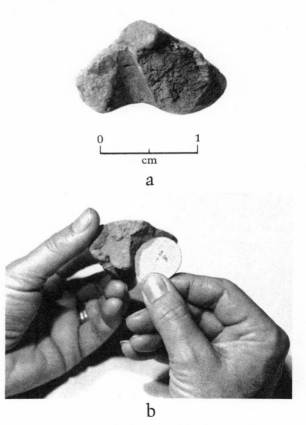

a

0   1
cm

b

Figure 85. Daub piece showing the impression of flat, right-angled boards.

0   3
cm

Figure 86. a. structural piece of daub. b. measuring the size of the impression with a cardboard disk.

The archaeological sample of daub at Hascher-keller is limited and can only begin to answer the principal questions concerning the structures on the site. Architecture during this period was characterized by a range of variation around the central theme of timber-frame construction with combinations of vertical timbers, sometimes sunken into the ground, horizontal timbers, and wattle-and-daub walls. The houses on the settlement of Wasserburg Buchau, where the preservation of wood was exceptionally good, illustrate some of the variations of construction within a single settlement (Reinerth 1936, pls. 30, 31). Daub was employed with wattle, and it was also packed between horizontal and vertical logs or planks. Both kinds of uses are suggested by the daub fragments preserved at Hascherkeller, to judge by the impressions preserved on them. Little can be said about the roofing on the buildings at Hascherkeller, since no apparent traces survive in the archaeological record. Thatched roofs would have been likely but cannot be demonstrated.

The daub fragments recovered at Hascherkeller compare closely with similar objects from other settlements of the Late Bronze and Early Iron Ages that have been published, for example, the Waschenberg in Upper Austria (Pertlwieser 1970) and Zug-Sumpf in Switzerland (Speck 1955).

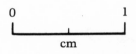

Figure 87. Triangular piece of daub.

Table 18.
Measurements (in cm) of wall pieces of daub, by provenience.

Provenience	Maximum	Minimum
Trench A, Cutting II	0.75	0.74
Trench B, stray	1.95	1.50
	1.26	0.99
	2.39	1.93
Average	1.87	1.47
Trench B, Cutting II	1.12	0.96
	2.30	2.00
	2.99	2.50
Average	2.14	1.82
Trench B, Cutting III	2.27	2.04
	9.11	5.85
Average	5.69	3.95
Trench B, Cutting IV	1.54	0.84
	2.98	1.85
Average	2.26	1.35
Trench B, Cutting V	2.45	2.42
	2.74	2.72
	0.76	0.56
	1.41	1.19
	3.36	1.36
Average	2.14	1.65
Trenches BII and C, balk between	2.95	1.04
	3.33	1.91
	2.32	1.57
	2.20	1.30
	2.44	2.15
	1.79	1.05
	1.49	1.02
	0.78	0.55
	2.44	2.15
	0.80	0.63
	0.89	0.69
	2.22	1.95
	1.49	1.29
	1.27	1.11
	1.68	1.43
	1.04	0.88
	1.00	0.63
	1.45	1.41
	1.88	1.32
	1.30	0.90
	1.39	1.12
	1.48	1.36

Table 18 (continued).

Provenience	Maximum	Minimum
Trenches BII and C, balk between (continued)	1.58	1.15
	2.32	1.28
	1.45	1.19
	1.44	0.77
	1.69	1.26
	1.39	0.91
	1.31	1.28
	1.34	1.15
	1.44	1.30
	0.61	0.55
	1.24	1.13
	0.69	0.65
	0.64	0.52
	2.08	1.18
	1.41	1.17
	0.80	0.67
	2.83	2.30
	2.54	2.00
	2.38	1.39
	2.91	1.99
	4.03	2.06
	3.68	2.14
	2.07	1.82
	2.18	1.92
	2.84	1.79
	1.46	1.24
	2.25	1.75
	1.75	1.06
	1.93	1.64
	2.08	1.30
	1.36	1.82
	2.89	2.38
	2.86	2.41
	2.54	2.10
	1.70	1.45
	1.89	1.11
Average	1.85	1.37
Trench C	0.71	0.69
	0.88	0.80
	0.91	0.71
	1.12	0.82
	0.69	0.62
	0.92	0.39
	4.33	1.39
	0.74	0.59
	1.49	0.84
	1.09	0.77
	0.76	0.57
	1.02	0.85
	1.14	0.94
	1.18	0.98
	2.67	1.20
	3.20	1.74
	1.84	1.27
	1.46	1.02
	0.95	0.92
	2.26	1.45
	2.62	1.72

Provenience	Maximum	Minimum
Trench C (continued)	0.88	0.82
	1.64	1.35
	1.11	0.91
	0.76	0.64
	1.58	1.36
	1.27	1.13
	0.91	0.73
	0.74	0.47
	1.22	0.69
	1.08	0.91
	0.79	0.65
	1.20	1.10
	1.15	1.02
	0.93	0.82
	2.99	1.20
	2.26	2.13
	2.72	1.41
	2.31	2.21
	2.22	1.94
	2.51	2.35
	2.64	0.96
	1.26	1.14
	1.26	0.74
	1.28	1.04
	2.27	1.50
	0.71	0.60
	2.80	1.95
	2.35	1.24
	1.84	1.65
	2.01	1.65
	1.69	1.28
	1.09	1.05
	1.40	1.15
	1.13	0.81
	0.86	0.75
	1.73	1.33
	0.80	0.68
	1.68	1.49
	1.31	1.21
	1.09	0.63
	0.77	0.62
	3.58	3.26
	3.05	1.68
	3.02	1.20
	2.93	1.19
	2.22	1.10
	1.50	1.08
	2.83	2.08
	1.43	1.33
	1.60	1.24
	1.68	1.49
	1.31	1.21
	2.52	1.16
	1.26	0.89
	1.33	1.06
	2.24	1.01
	3.92	3.10
	1.99	0.83
Average	1.68	1.17

Table 18 (continued).

Provenience	Maximum	Minimum
Trench E	2.35	1.05
Trench N	3.35	3.06
Trench S	1.60	1.30
	1.26	1.02
	1.15	0.96
	1.45	1.34
Average	1.37	1.16
Strays	3.94	1.20
	3.47	1.20
	2.00	1.28
	1.26	1.10
	1.29	0.90
	3.82	3.58
Overall average	1.86	1.33

Table 19.
Measurements (in cm) of structural pieces of daub, by provenience.

Provenience	1st dia.	2nd dia.	3rd dia.	Avg. dia.
Trench B, Cutting I	1.5	0.5		1.13
	1.5			
	1.0			
Trench B, Cutting II	2.5			
	2.0			
	1.0	1.0		1.63
Trench B, Cutting V	1.0	2.0		3.38
	7.0			
	1.5			
	3.5			
	2.0			
	4.5			
	5.5			
Trenches BII and C,	9.0			2.59
balk between	5.5			
	2.5	1.0		
	1.5			
	4.0			
	1.0			
	0.5			
	1.0			
	4.0			
	1.0			
	2.5			
	1.5			
	2.5			
	1.5			
	1.0			
	2.0			
	0.5			
	2.5			
	1.5			
	2.5			
	9.0			
	1.5			
Trench C	2.0			2.45
	4.5			
	2.5			
	5.0			
	2.0			
	1.5			
	1.0			
	1.0			
	3.5			
	1.0	1.5		
	1.5			
	2.0			
	0.5			
	1.0			
	1.5			
	0.5			
	5.5			
	2.0			
	1.5			
	3.5			
	2.0			
	1.5			
	2.0			
	3.5			
	2.5			

Table 19 (continued).

Provenience	1st dia.	2nd dia.	3rd dia.	Avg. dia.
Trench C (continued)	2.0	0.5	0.5	
	2.0			
	1.5	0.5		
	1.0			
	0.5			
	1.5			
	0.5			
	1.5			
	1.0			
	2.0			
	2.5			
	1.0	1.5		
	3.0			
	6.5			
	3.5			
	5.5			
	9.0			
	2.5			
	6.0			
	6.5			
	1.5			
	1.0			
	1.5			
	2.5			
	4.5			
	1.5			
	1.5			
	0.5			
	5.5			
	9.5			
	1.0			
Trench D, Cutting III	2.5			1.88
	1.5			
	1.5			
	2.0			
Trench E, Cutting II	3.0			2.08
	5.5			
	1.0			
	1.0			
	0.5			
	1.5	0.5		
Trench N	4.0			3.93
	5.5			
	3.0	0.5		
	3.0	0.5		
	5.0	0.5		
	2.0	0.5		
	1.0	0.5		
	8.5			
	6.5			
	9.5			
	6.0			
	4.0			
	6.0			
	7.0			
	4.0			
	4.5			
	4.5			
Overall average				2.66

Table 20.
Measurements (in cm) of structural wall pieces of daub, by provenience.

Provenience	Dia.*	Width**	Total
Trench B, Cutting V	1.0	1.16	2.16
	8.0	1.70	9.70
Average total			5.93
Trenches B & C, balk	2.5	1.38	3.88
	2.0	1.20	3.20
	1.0	1.20	2.20
Average total			3.09
Trench E	8.0	2.33	10.33
Trench C	2.0	1.20	3.20
	2.5	1.90	4.40
	6.0	1.90	7.90
	5.0	1.79	6.79
	5.5	1.93	7.43
	2.5	2.45	4.95
	4.0	1.20	5.20
	5.0	1.26	6.26
	4.5	2.27	6.77
	7.5	1.65	9.15
Average total			6.21
Trench N, Cutting I	6.0	1.55	7.55
	5.0	1.20	6.20
	4.5	1.15	5.65
	9.5	1.16	10.66
	5.5	1.34	6.84
	6.0	1.84	7.84
	8.5	2.85	11.35
	9.5	1.24	10.74
Average total			8.35
Trench N, west extention	3.5	1.10	4.60
	5.5	2.27	7.77
	8.5	2.10	10.60
Average total			7.66
Overall average of totals			6.79

*Diameter of circular impression.

**Width of specimen from flattened outer edge to circular impression.

10

The Iron Slag

by Michael Geselowitz

Five lumps of what appears to be iron slag have been recovered at Hascherkeller (see chapter 3), only one of them from a level below the modern plowsoil. This fragment (figures 60d, 88) was recovered in Trench E, Cutting II, in the top 20-cm level of the ditch fill below the level of the top of the loess subsoil. Since the piece was recovered below the level of the top of the subsoil in the humic fill of the prehistoric ditch, it is likely that it belongs to the prehistoric occupation of the site. But because it was found in the top 20-cm layer of the ditch fill and some movement of individual objects up and down through natural agencies (moles, worms) cannot be excluded, it cannot be said with certainty that the piece is prehistoric.

The object was examined and sampled at the Center for Archaeological Research and Development of the Peabody Museum of Harvard University. It is light gray to reddish-brown in color. Analysis indicates that the piece is definitely slag. It weighs 35 g, and its specific gravity is 3.5. The substance can be described as ropey and is porous only on the surface where weathered. Where not weathered, the surface contains inclusions that appear to be charcoal. The matrix is gray, blending to red where weathered. Observation by optical mineralogy revealed a thin section of the specimen to be large intergrown crystals of fayalite and less mafic silica, with some small magnetite dendrites interspersed. The object is not magnetic.

X-ray fluorescence was used to check the minor and trace constituent elements of the slag. Calcium was present in small amounts; the only other presence detected was that of very faint traces of nickel. There was no copper present.

This specimen is definitely an iron slag but could be a smelting furnace cinder from the original smelting or a smithing furnace bottom from subsequent hot-forging (see Tylecote 1980, p. 224 for explanation). The former seems more likely, given the charcoal inclusions. It was probably originally part of a larger slag flow, to judge by the evidence of slow cooling, and somehow later broken off and removed from the scene. No direct evidence for iron smelting has been found at Hascherkeller as yet.

It is interesting that the iron composition of the slag is so pure. Tylecote has noted (1980, p. 189) that there is no correlation between trace element content of the ores and metals, and the same is true for slags. Most of the elements present in the ore are likely to divide in a random, or at least not understood, fashion between the metal and the slag upon smelting.

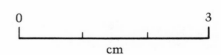

0   3

cm

Figure 88. Iron slag from the fill of the inner ditch of the western enclosure, Trench EII.

11

Depositional History of the Settlement

The interpretation of the archaeological remains recovered at Hascherkeller depends upon the depositional history of the site. Important issues include how the objects recovered came to be where they were found through excavation, what has happened to the archaeological remains since their original deposition at the time of occupation, how depressions in the settlement surface came to be filled by sediments, and the chronological relationships among the different features on the site (Schiffer 1976; Halstead et al. 1978). The main part of the settlement area at Hascherkeller was occupied during other periods of the past besides the time of the principal occupation of concern here. Five pits were found containing cultural materials of Early or Middle Bronze Age date, and one pit contained daub remains of a hut and associated pottery of the Roman period. Much glazed pottery of medieval date was recovered on the surface and in the plowsoil (similar to that described and illustrated in Dannheimer 1973), probably rubbish that was unintentionally scattered in the fields along with manure and kitchen refuse. In recent times the land on which the settlement is situated has been intensively farmed, and the local landscape has also been much altered by the construction of the modern highway cutting diagonally through the terrace from east to west just southwest of the settlement (figs. 4, 5).

The two main concerns of depositional history in a context such as that at Hascherkeller are (1) how the archaeological materials were originally deposited and (2) what has happened to them since the time of their deposition.

CHRONOLOGY OF SETTLEMENT FEATURES

Establishing chronological relationships among the structures of the main occupation phase of the settlement is difficult because the site offers very little stratigraphic evidence. The only clear case of stratigraphic superposition is the cutting of the pit in Trench S north end by the ditch (fig. 10; Wells et al. 1981, p. 290, fig. 2), indicating a later date for the ditch than for the pit. But even in this case, the cutting of the pit may have been by a late phase of the ditch, not necessarily the original ditch, since it is clear that the ditches were redug (fig. 13). On the eastern side of the field, where the team from the Bayerisches Landesamt für Denkmalpflege carried out rescue excavations in 1978, stratigraphic relationships are apparent. The posthole patterns of the houses overlap both the ditch of the easternmost enclosure (on its northeast corner) and the rectangular structure to the east of the enclosures (fig. 72). These structures on the eastern part of the field will be considered in detail in another context. For our purposes here it is important to note that the house foundations and the outer ditch of the eastern enclosure overlap; hence, they cannot have been contemporaneous.

Chronological techniques presently available do not permit the establishment of a chronological ordering of the individual pits on the settlement. The cultural materials recovered in all of the pits are very similar, and there is no reason to think that the pits were not all roughly contemporaneous, that is, in use within a few decades or at most a century of one another. Very similar sherds, perhaps often from the same broken pots, were found in many of the pits. In Trench N, for example, it is likely that the two pits excavated were open at the same time. Both contained similar pottery, and the two pits contained the only ceramic rings found on the site, five in the west extension and one in the pit in the north end.

The ditches around the western and central enclosures contained the same kinds of pottery and other material as the 11 principal pits; hence, the ditches were probably in use, and being redug, at the same time that the pits were accumulating their deposits of cultural debris. Thus the 11 principal pits and the enclosing ditches appear to have been contemporaneous.

DEPOSITION DURING THE OCCUPATION OF THE SETTLEMENT

In order to reconstruct the depositional history of the site, a general picture of life in the settlement must be conjectured (see chapter 12 for further elaboration). When occupied, the settlement was surrounded by a double palisade system or by an inner palisade and an outer ditch. Within each enclosure were one or more buildings, along with pits for the storage of grain and other foodstuffs and probably ancillary structures such as haystacks and fences. To judge by paintings and drawings of medieval farms and villages and by ethnographic examples, pottery, food remains, and other debris probably littered much of the settlement.

The principal tasks of daily life involved the production and consumption of food. Adults in the community probably spent most of the day working in the fields and tending the livestock. Much effort was also devoted to the preparation of food for consumption, grinding grains, cooking, baking, and otherwise processing foodstuffs for daily meals and for winter storage. Other tasks around the settlement included repairs on buildings, fences, palisades, and tools, occasional carving of bone to make useful items such as buttons, weaving of textiles; and probably seasonal activities such as pottery making and bronze casting.

All of these tasks are reflected, to a greater or lesser degree, in the archaeological materials recovered at the settlement. Comparison of the archaeological results of the research at Hascherkeller with evidence from medieval and early modern rural contexts in central Europe helps to fill out the picture and to suggest how the material remains relate to daily and seasonal activities of the community. The different kinds of cultural materials were deposited on the settlement surface in different ways, depending upon the nature of the materials and the uses to which they were put. The large ceramic vessels found in the supposed cellar holes in Trenches BV, C, and AAI, most of which are classified here as jars, are thought to have been placed intentionally in the pits from which they were recovered archaeologically. They held stores of grains and other foodstuffs for regular use, unlike grain storage pits that protected large quantities underground from dampness, cold, and animals and would not have been opened regularly (Reynolds 1974, p. 130).

Most of the pottery from Hascherkeller, with the principal exception of the large storage vessels in the cellars, is best classified as rubbish. Except for the pottery in the pit in Trench W, which was a special case associated with the kiln, most of the pottery in the rest of the pits was highly fragmented and scattered throughout the pit fill rather than concentrated in dense deposits and represented only one or a few sherds of a vessel rather than complete pots or even substantial portions of pots. In no case was evidence encountered for the presence of a whole ceramic vessel in a pit, except in the three supposed storage cellars. Thus the pottery in the seven other pits most probably represents rubbish, broken fragments of ceramics disposed of by the members of the community. The category of pottery best represented is that of intermediate thickness, the kind used for basic vessels employed in food preparation and consumption, which would be expected to break most frequently (Foster 1960; David 1972). The thin pottery, used for cups and beakers, would have been less abundant and less likely to break than the general kitchen ware, and it is correspondingly much less represented. In terms of numbers of sherds, the thick category of pottery is also little represented; storage vessels would tend to break least of all because they were kept safely underground and not carried about.

The animal bones recovered at Hascherkeller also belong to the category of rubbish. Late Bronze and Early Iron Age rubbish was very different from the modern varieties; most of it was biodegradable. Kitchen refuse was probably thrown onto a trash pile outside of the house to be carried to the fields or spread on the kitchen gardens as fertilizer. Vegetable scraps rotted and formed compost. Meat scraps were eaten by pigs and dogs; some of the bones recovered at Hascherkeller have such tooth marks on them. When pottery broke, it was simply tossed outside the door. Pottery was clean and made of the local soils, so it would quickly have blended in with the surrounding soil and only been preserved if it happened to fall into a hollow. Sometimes rubbish may have been consciously tossed into a convenient hollow on the settlement; other times sherds and animal bones were probably trodden into the ground or accidentally kicked into the hollows. The small amounts of debris in the ditches, relative to that in the pits, can be explained in the following way. When the palisade required renewal, the rotten logs were pulled or dug out, and the ditch was redug to make space for new posts. Once the new posts were in place, the dug-out soil was shoveled back in around the posts, along with any debris that happened to be lying about on the surface — pottery, daub, and bone fragments.

The carbonized plant remains also entered the settlement pits accidentally. The surviving plant parts represent only a minute proportion of the food plants that were in use at Hascherkeller. Plant seeds survived at the site only if they were carbonized, but did not burn up, during the occupation of the settlement and only if they happened to fall into one of the hollows on the site. Most of the foods that were eaten were, of course, not carbonized, and most of the seeds that were unintentionally carbonized remained on the surface of the settlement rather than fell into hollows. Thus the plant remains recovered represent only a very small, fortuitous sample of some of the foods used by the community.

The glass beads recovered in the two pits and the bronze fragments from different parts of the site were probably all lost accidentally. One of the four glass beads was fragmentary; it probably broke when it was lost or afterwards. The bronze fragments are unlikely to have been discarded and were probably lost. Bronze metal was valuable, and scraps were kept for reuse, as the hoards of this period make clear.

The collapse of buildings was the principal cause of the deposition of the daub on the site. In an environment such as that of central Europe, with greatly varying conditions of moisture and temperature, daub generally does not survive intact unless it has been fired (Schlichtherle 1977; Bankoff and Winter 1979), and many of the fragments of daub from Hascherkeller show clear signs of burning. Structures on the site are likely to have been burned both intentionally and unintentionally. Untreated wood remains strong and fresh only for about 30 years in central Europe before it rots and decays (Bakker et al. 1977, p. 223; Pauli 1980a, p. 311, n. 51). Hence, regular repairs were necessary on buildings, and it is likely that structures were erected anew every few decades, both because the wood rotted and because vermin (mice and insects) infested them. In order to destroy the vermin in an old house and prevent them from coming to a new one nearby, the inhabitants of the settlement are likely to have burned the old one once the new one was ready for occupancy. Buildings are also likely to have burned unintentionally. When the wood was dry, and particularly because of the probable thatched roofs, the structures could easily have been set on fire by a stray spark. Finally, even if a building did not end in a conflagration, parts of the walls that had been exposed to the heat of a hearth or oven could be preserved after an abandoned structure collapsed over time. In each case, the daub that had been sufficiently fired would end up on the ground. If there was a cellar hole beneath a structure, some of the daub would fall into that hole. At Hascherkeller and similar sites in central Europe where the actual settlement surface has been destroyed by plowing and erosion, the only daub that survives from the build-

ings is that which fell into hollows on the surface.

Daub entered the three cellar pits directly. A building stood over or next to them, and when it collapsed the daub from the walls landed in the pits. In Trench W, the daub probably came from the walls of the kiln. The daub in the pit in Trench N west extension also appears to have entered the pit directly from above, with a minimum of horizontal movement. Besides the large quantities of daub in the pit, the exceptional preservation of layers of whitewash and of red paint suggests that the daub was not moved about and fragmented on the settlement surface.

In the case of the other six pits, the small quantities of daub, the small average size of fragments, and the rounded, worn character of the pieces suggest that the daub did not enter the pits directly from above, but that the daub was subjected to considerable abrading before deposition in the hollows. Even more than in the case of fired pottery, disused daub that lay about on the surface of the settlement probably quickly reverted to loess through crushing underfoot and disintegration by rain. Only daub fragments that had been well fired and happened to land in hollows on the settlement surface survived.

Some of the cultural materials recovered at Hascherkeller must have been abandoned by the occupants of the settlement, for whatever reason. The sandstone mold was still in perfect casting condition, and there is no apparent reason why it would have been discarded. Similarly, the loom weights and spindle whorls were for the most part intact when deposited and hence still functional. The same is true of the quartzite hammerstone. None of these objects had been broken so that they could not have been used, nor are they small like the glass beads and bronze fragments that were probably lost accidentally. They were apparently left behind when the inhabitants moved to another settlement location. Ceramic loom weights and spindle whorls could have been quickly replaced with new objects, but the sandstone mold required both raw materials from distant and restricted sources and considerable skill and effort to manufacture. It may be that the settlement was abandoned in an emergency situation, such as an attack from outside, or that the inhabitants were killed as a result of attack or illness.

All of the pits except that in Trench W probably filled with silt naturally through erosion by rain and wind. None of the ten had any apparent layering that would suggest purposeful filling of the holes, nor were dense concentrations of cultural materials found in any that would indicate intensive one-time deposition. Only in the pit in Trench W, with the two distinct layers of waste pottery, daub, charcoal, and other debris, was there evidence that material was intentionally thrown into a pit. In that pit too, the soil above the two cultural layers was probably deposited by natural erosional agencies rather than by the hand of man.

POST-DEPOSITIONAL CHANGES ON THE SITE

The duration of the occupation of the settlement at Hascherkeller is unknown. The part of the settlement investigated by the Peabody Museum may have been occupied for several decades or for a century, but probably not for much longer. Nearby settlement remains, such as those on the terrace edge 250 m west of Hascherkeller, may represent the subsequent continuation of the settlement; future investigations will incorporate those remains and those of other settlements in the vicinity into a larger regional study.

When Hascherkeller was abandoned, a few buildings may have been left standing, and much settlement debris was probably left lying on the surface of the ground and in the open hollows. Probably within a decade, at most, no traces of the settlement were visible on the surface.

The greatest destruction of the settlement occurred when the land was plowed, probably by Roman times if not already during the Early or Late Iron Ages. There is little evidence of the disturbance of the archaeological features by natural agencies such as worms and moles. Although such animals are common in the soil at Hascherkeller, the state of preservation of the pits and ditches and location of cultural material in them suggest that disturbance of the materials was minimal. The situation of the Roman hut in Trench DI on the terrace edge suggests that the land around it was being cultivated. Iron plowshares were in use during the Late Iron Age and Roman period (Jacobi 1974, pp. 67–70), and plows so equipped probably destroyed the surface of the prehistoric settlement — including hearths, shallow

postholes and depressions, and house interiors — and displaced all cultural materials situated on or near the surface. During medieval times, deeper plows with iron shares, colters, and moldboards were introduced, and they cut still deeper into the soil (White 1962). The land on which Hascherkeller is situated was intensively cultivated during medieval and early modern times, as indicated by the quantities of medieval and early modern pottery and other debris recovered from the field.

Besides obliterating the surface features of the prehistoric settlement, the Roman and medieval plowing had the effect of removing the natural vegetation cover, regularly exposing fresh soil to the elements and thereby hastening erosion of the topsoil. As Modderman has demonstrated (1976), the loess soils of central Europe erode very rapidly when subjected to intensive cultivation. It was probably this erosion of materials from the field down the terrace edge into the Isar Valley, resulting from disruption of the ground surface by cultivation during medieval and early modern times, that was the principal factor in the loss of settlement features and cultural material from the site.

Later human activities on the field played a part in the disturbance of the site as well. When the highway from Landshut to Altdorf was constructed, a deep cut was made in the terrace from southeast to northwest along the southwestern boundary of the prehistoric settlement. This disturbance destroyed the edge of the settlement, and the change in the topography of the terrace resulted in increased erosion of topsoil from the western part of the site, as is evident in the light areas of loess subsoil showing up on the aerial photographs (figs. 4, 5).

The result of all of this topsoil erosion was the destruction and removal of the upper layers of the settlement pits, ditches, and postholes that had survived medieval plowing; only the lower portions of the deepest features remained intact for modern archaeological investigation.

12

The Community at Hascherkeller: Interpretations and Hypotheses

CHRONOLOGY

The principal occupation on the terrace at Hascherkeller took place sometime in the period 1000 to 800 B.C. The settlement can be dated by two independent means, through artifact typology and through radiocarbon determinations. The forms and decoration of the pottery vessels represented by sherds and the character of the bronze objects indicate a position in the relative chronological framework for central Europe in the period Hallstatt B. The glass beads, loom weights, spindle whorls, and other objects, though not as specifically datable as the pottery and bronze, are also consistent with such a position in the relative chronology. All of these objects compare closely with datable objects from other settlements and from cemeteries both in the region of Lower Bavaria and throughout central Europe.

The radiocarbon determinations agree with the evidence of artifact typology. Four of the dates obtained from the charcoal samples from three different pits indicate the period 1000 to 800 B.C., according to the recent calibration tables published by Suess (1979). Two other determinations are earlier, but both were obtained from charcoal from the same pit in Trench W that yielded two other dates corresponding closely with those from the other two pits, and hence the early determinations probably represent old wood in the pit.

This dating of the settlement within the years 1000 to 800 B.C. places the occupation in the latter half of the Late Bronze Age Urnfield Period just before the beginning of the Early Iron Age, or Hallstatt Period, of the traditional chronological sequence. This was the time during which iron was first coming into regular use, not yet for weapons and large tools but for ornaments and small tools used in the working of the softer metal bronze (Kimmig 1964, pp. 274–281; Bouzek 1978). Some investigators designate these centuries between 1000 and 800 B.C. as the end of the Bronze Age, others as the start of the

Iron Age. The issue concerns the applicability of the traditional period designations and is of little consequence in terms of the cultural changes of the time. There was no economic or other kind of break between the Bronze Age and Iron Age, but rather there was continuity and gradual change in material culture, economic practices, and social patterns.

It is not clear at present how long the settlement of Hascherkeller was occupied, and there is little evidence on the site that helps in making an estimate. The limited number of pits in the area excavated gives the impression that the occupation did not last a long time, at least on this spot. It is well to bear in mind the results of investigations at Elp in the Netherlands (Waterbolk 1964), where a farmstead was periodically relocated a slight distance from its previous situation. It is likely that the part of the settlement at Hascherkeller investigated by the Peabody Museum from 1978 to 1981 was occupied for several decades or at most a century. Further evidence bearing on this important issue will be collected in future investigations at the settlement and at others in the vicinity.

ENVIRONMENT

The terrace on which the settlement is situated was probably largely cleared of forest growth by the time the settlement was occupied around 1000 B.C., since the evidence of settlement activity nearby during Neolithic and Bronze Age times (e.g., Christlein 1981a, 1981b; Christlein and Engelhardt 1981; Engelhardt 1981) suggests that the original beech-oak forest had been cut down on the agriculturally useful lands in the area. The terrace may have been covered by light woods, including stands of larger trees and a ground flora of such species as hazel, hawthorn, elder, and bramble.

Sometime around 1000 B.C., this underbrush was cleared from the present settlement area, probably by people already living nearby. Indications of

Middle and Late Bronze Age settlement activity have been found throughout the area. Lands around the settlement were cleared for farmland and pasturage. The presence of hedgehog remains among the animal bones suggests grassy, shrubby vegetation in the vicinity, and the hazelnut shells also imply a light, open environment. The fields in which the cereal grains and garden crops were grown were most likely situated on the terrace next to the settlement. Small vegetable gardens may have been located within the enclosures close to the dwellings.

The broad valley of the Isar was probably marshy, with numerous streams of the river and small stagnant pools. This wet environment was rich in wildlife. The fish remains from the settlement attest to the exploitation of the aquatic fauna, and the deer bones may be those of animals that regularly came down to the valley to drink. The valley provided a limitless supply of water for the inhabitants of the settlement and also a transportation route for boats, perhaps dugouts similar to those found at the contemporaneous settlement at Buchau (Reinerth 1936, pl. 43).

SETTLEMENT STRUCTURE

Enclosures

The principal structural feature at Hascherkeller consisted of the three enclosures bounded by fences of vertical posts. Each enclosure was roughly square in shape and measured about 55 m across. The similarity of the three enclosures and the fact that the boundary ditches meet but do not overlap strongly suggest that the three were constructed at the same time and were in use contemporaneously.

Each enclosure probably encompassed a farmstead — including a dwelling for a family, byres and sheds for animals, and lighter structures such as drying racks and haystacks — perhaps like the enclosed farmstead of similar size at the Roman period settlement of Bennekom in the Netherlands, which had exceptionally well-preserved settlement structures (van Es 1973, p. 278, fig. 6). Domestic animals were probably kept inside the enclosures part of the time, at night and in the winter, when they required both shelter and stored food. During the daytime in the other seasons cattle, sheep, and goats probably pastured on the grassy and shrubby areas of the terrace around the settlement, including the fields in fallow, and the pigs routed in the same areas or in nearby woods. The palisade located in the inner ditch and perhaps in the outer one as well served to keep the animals in the enclosures at night

and to keep out predators such as wolves. The rectangular enclosure built at the reconstructed Iron Age farmstead at Butser in southern Britain is roughly the same size as those at Hascherkeller, and it has a wooden fence as the inner boundary and an open ditch as the outer (Reynolds 1979b).

Buildings

The evidence provided by the daub indicates the probable locations of some of the principal buildings on the settlement. The pits in Trenches BV, C, AAI, and N west extension contained daub that came from substantial structures with plastered walls. Three of these pits, those in Trenches BV, C, and AAI, were probably cellar holes beneath houses, which were used to store foodstuffs in large ceramic vessels that protected them from extremes of heat and cold and from animals. The pit in N west extension was associated with crafts production rather than cellar storage, but it too was located beneath a structure, indicated by the abundance of particularly large fragments of daub and delicate pieces preserving remains of paint. In the area investigated by the Peabody Museum from 1978 to 1981, only these four pits contained evidence of substantial plastered structures above them. Other structures with daubed walls may have existed on the site, but because no pits existed beneath them to protect daub fragments from plows (Reynolds 1980, p. 16) and erosion, no trace has survived. Other structures such as byres, sheds, and drying racks, which probably would not have had daubed walls, are not represented archaeologically at Hascherkeller, and we can only conjecture that they existed on the basis of better-preserved remains at other settlements and evidence from more recent farmsteads where documentary evidence is available (see discussions in Fél and Hofer 1972 and Reynolds 1979b and 1980).

No postholes from structures within the enclosures survived. Because all of the site experienced erosion since the prehistoric occupation, it is possible that shallow postholes were destroyed by plows. This possibility is particularly likely to the west of Trench C (see plan, fig. 10), where the field was especially badly eroded as a result of the large-scale earth removal connected with the construction of the highway south and southwest of the site. But it is unlikely that erosion played a big part in disturbing the upper layers of the subsoil east of Trench C. The scale of erosion on different parts of the site can be judged by the proportions of the ditches preserved. In Trench FII the ditch thinned out greatly toward the south, becoming a very shallow and narrow feature where surface erosion had been severe. Yet, elsewhere the ditches maintained consistent depths and widths, suggesting relatively little erosion. The fact that four distinct posthole-defined house foundations were found on the east side of the field (Christlein 1979, pl. 48,2) at a location where the boundary ditches survived to the same depth and thickness as on the western part of the field (Christlein 1979, pl. 47) suggests that the absence of such postholes on the western part may reflect a real absence of such structures there and may not be the result of subsequent erosion.

The daub structures were probably dwellings for the human inhabitants of the settlement. Daubing requires a great amount of effort and time (Reynolds 1979b; Percival 1980), and probably only the humans at the settlement needed such complete protection from the elements. Byres, sheds, and other ancillary structures were probably not daubed. On the basis of the number and character of the pits interpreted as cellar holes, it is likely that one dwelling existed at a time within each enclosure; those above Trenches BV and AAI may have been in use successively rather than contemporaneously. Each dwelling may have been in use an average of a generation before deterioration and infestation encouraged the building of a new one.

Only the daub from the pit in Trench N west extension preserved on it remains of white paint and, in a few cases, of red bands. The paint was probably preserved in that feature because the daub there was subjected to less fragmentation than that in the other pits. Hancock found that several categories of daub pieces from this pit were generally larger (hence less fragmented) than those in the other pits.

While the daub provides some helpful information about the structures on the site (chapter 9), there is not enough evidence available from Hascherkeller to enable us to ascertain the character of the buildings. One or both of two main structural types are likely to have existed at Hascherkeller, based on data from other contemporaneous settlements in central Europe. The walls may have been made of horizontal logs, such as buildings at Buchau (Reinerth 1936, pls. 31,1.2; 32; 33) and at Zug-Sumpf (Speck 1955), with daub packed into the spaces between the logs (for general discussion of this structural type see Pauli 1980, p. 98). The other principal type involved vertical timbers placed at intervals and resting on a horizontal sill on the ground, with wattling of branches covered with daub between them, also exemplified at Buchau (Reinerth 1936, pl. 30,2). Both techniques made use of daub, in the first case between the logs, in the second around the wattling.

The presence of both techniques at Buchau in the same chronological phase demonstrates that both were employed at the same time and in the same settlements.

Some of the daub fragments from Hascherkeller preserve impressions of flat structural members, apparently finished boards with smooth surfaces at right angles (fig. 85). This evidence, together with the presence of white and red paint, indicates that considerable skill and care went into the fashioning of the buildings at the settlement, and they must have been constructed and decorated to be aesthetically pleasing as well as protective against the elements. White paint has been identified on daub from a number of other settlements of the period (Gersbach 1961), and red painted bands have been identified from at least one other (Müller 1959). Reinerth's reconstructions of house interiors at Buchau (1936, pl. 34,1.2; pl. 35) with simple wooden furniture, and ceramic, wooden, and metal implements provide a good impression of the probable character of house interiors at Hascherkeller.

Workshop Areas

Just north of the settlement about 20 m from the central enclosure, the pottery kiln was situated in a large rectangular depression in the ground. The kiln probably had a domed structure of wattle and daub similar to that reconstructed on the basis of the well-preserved remains at Elchinger Kreuz (Pressmar 1979). Sherds of misfired pottery were thrown around the kiln, both outside the pit and on its floor. A supply of wood must have been kept near the kiln for the firings, collected from stands of trees near the settlement or from nearby forests, and perhaps may have been converted to charcoal before use.

A work area stood above or close to the pit in Trench N west extension. The pit contained objects representative of the casting of bronze objects and of the spinning and weaving of textiles, as well as the hammerstone and fragmentary grindstone which could have been used either in crafts activities or in food production. A building standing over this pit may have been used for manufacturing and may have contained a loom for weaving, a hearth for melting bronze, and perhaps other such structures not represented in the archaeological record. Because of the destruction of the settlement surface, all traces of such crafts furniture have been obliterated, and only the smaller objects that fell into the pit below the surface survived until the present day. The pit in Trench S, which contained pebbles and soil stained bright red by intense heat, was probably also associated with some manufacturing activity, perhaps the melting of bronze or the heating of iron, but the contents of the pit did not yield enough information to specify which.

Storage Pits

Storage pits for the preservation of cereal grains were situated within the settlement area. Three have been identified among the features excavated. Experimental studies by Reynolds (1974, 1979a) have shown that the underground storage of grain works very well if the pit is sealed at the top with a layer of clay. These storage pits probably provided both the food supply through the winter and spring for the inhabitants and the seed grain for the following planting season.

Borrow Pits

Open holes also existed on the settlement where the inhabitants had dug out loess subsoil for use in daubing houses, making pottery, building ovens for baking and the kiln for firing pottery, and for similar purposes. Two features investigated at the settlement have been interpreted as borrow pits. The other pits excavated by the inhabitants for storage or for the kiln also produced loess, of course, but only these two appear to have been dug principally to obtain the soil. The hollows would not have remained open on the settlement surface for long. After a couple of rainstorms they would have been nearly completely filled by sediments washed in.

Repair and Renewal

Evidence for the repair and renewal of the structures on the settlement shows that the the settlement was by no means a static combination of buildings, fences, and pits, but that wood in structures decayed, fences wore out, and pits filled through erosion. Natural forces of decay and erosion were constantly at work on the settlement and hence the appearance of the settlement was changing all of the time. Experiments by Reynolds in southern Britain, an environment not very different from that of Lower Bavaria, indicate that palisade timbers survived only some ten years before rotting away at their bases (Reynolds 1980, p. 16). Whether the timbers in the palisade at Hascherkeller lasted only ten years or two or three times as long, it is clear that they had to be replaced regularly in order to maintain the integrity of the palisade structure. At several different locations on the settlement where the ditch was sectioned, clear evidence was found for the redigging of the ditch,

probably done to renew the timbers of the palisade.

Traces of a palisade have been found only in the interior ditch at Hascherkeller. The outer ditch may also have contained a palisade, or it may have been open, as is the outer ditch in the reconstructed farmstead at Butser. An open ditch in the loess soil at Hascherkeller would have filled in very quickly through rain erosion and would have required regular redigging, at least annually.

The wood of the houses at Hascherkeller would also have required regular replacement as it rotted from dampness and insect activity. Individual beams may have been replaced as needed, or new houses may have been constructed every 10, 20, or 30 years as old ones fell into a state of decay. Since no wood survives at Hascherkeller, little can be said about the lengths of time that the buildings survived. Evidence for the repair of house walls does survive, however. The clearest evidence is in the daub from the pit in the west extension of Trench N. The daub from that pit was especially well preserved and hence shows many detailed features of the wall plaster that are missing from the daub in the other pits. A number of daub fragments from this pit show several distinct outer layers, indicating replastering of the walls as they deteriorated over time (fig. 52).

ECONOMIC ACTIVITY AT HASCHERKELLER

The evidence recovered from the settlement suggests that food production was the principal concern of the inhabitants of Hascherkeller. They also engaged in manufacturing in a variety of different materials and in some trade to bring in desired goods from other parts of central Europe.

Subsistence

The community utilized a wide range of domesticated plants and animals and also made some use of wild species available in the vicinity of the settlement. No single species of either plant or animal was so predominant as to suggest a strong reliance on a particular food resource; instead, several plants and animals were all well represented. The basis of subsistence was probably the cereals millet, wheat, and barley, which were cultivated in the rich and easily worked soils on the terrace next to the settlement. Wheat and barley are still cultivated on the same lands today, along with corn. Lentils were also grown. Gold of pleasure and poppy were probably raised for their oil. Hazelnuts, a popular food during the Bronze and Iron Ages as well as today in central

Europe, were harvested from trees in the vicinity, which were probably tended.

Principally because of the obliteration of the original settlement surface at Hascherkeller, the total sample of seeds from the settlement for analysis and interpretation is small. Those plants that are well represented in many of the pits on the site, such as millet, wheat, barley, and hazelnuts, probably played an important part in the diet. But it is impossible to judge how significant other plants, represented by small numbers of specimens, might have been. Many other food plants that have not yet been found at Hascherkeller have been identified at other settlements from this period in central Europe, especially at the lakeshore settlements of southwest Germany and Switzerland, where the ancient settlement surfaces survive and where conditions for preservation of organic remains are excellent. These include five different species of wheat, three species of barley, two of millet, two of oats, as well as horsebean, peas, flax, and cabbage. Apples and pears are well represented, and both kinds of trees were probably tended. Other fruits represented include plums, strawberries, raspberries, blackberries, grapes, cherries, beechnuts, and water nuts (Reinerth 1936, pp. 142–143; Lüdi 1955, p. 106; Wyss 1971a, p. 140; Körber-Grohne 1981).

Remains of prepared food were recovered in one cellar hole at Hascherkeller. The pit in Trench C contained plant remains fused with charcoal, apparently remains of porridge made from cereals. Such preparations were probably common forms of cereals for consumption, as they were through medieval into modern times.

The harvested and threshed cereals at Hascherkeller were probably stored in pits on the settlement to provide food for the winter and spring and seed grain for planting the following year. The only other artifacts recovered concerned with food production and preparation were a fragment of an apparent grindstone from the pit in Trench N west extension and possibly the quartzite hammerstone from the same pit.

Of the identified animal bones, 87 percent are from domestic species, 13 percent are from wild. Pigs are best represented, then cattle, sheep, goats, and dogs. Since the numbers are small, it is unsafe to draw any major conclusions from the sample, but the proportion of pig to other animals suggests that it was the principal meat source, as it still is in central Europe. The other animals all had important uses other than for meat. Sheep were raised mainly for wool, as their ages at death make apparent. Cattle were probably used to pull plows and produce dairy products, and for meat and leather after slaughter.

Goats provided dairy products as well as meat. Dogs were probably kept primarily as watchdogs and for helping with the animal herds.

Of the wild animals, only red deer and fish are represented in any appreciable quantity. It is possible that the deer were killed when they raided the crops rather than intentionally hunted (Uerpmann 1977), but in any case their meat was eaten. Shed antlers were collected from nearby woods and brought back to the settlement for carving.

The plants and animals represented on the site were parts of a complex of food production that was well developed by this time in central Europe. Cattle were used to plow the fields in preparation for the planting of cereal grains. Although no trace of plows survives at Hascherkeller, wooden ards are well documented from the bogs of Denmark and from rock carvings in Sweden, northern Italy, and southeastern France (Steensberg 1943; Glob 1951; Anati 1961). As the rock carvings indicate, the ards were generally pulled by two oxen. Bronze sickles are abundantly represented in the hoards of the Late Bronze Age (von Brunn 1958, 1968) and are common on many settlements, particularly the lakeshore sites (Primas 1977a, 1981). They were apparently in general use by 1000 B.C. and were most probably used by the inhabitants of Hascherkeller for harvesting cereal grains. After the harvest, the cattle, pigs, sheep, and goats were probably allowed to graze on the stubble of the fields, and they may have been put onto the fields when they were fallow. In such a way the livestock contributed to the production of plant foods by adding nutritive manure to the soil. It is likely that manure was carefully collected from the winter stalls on the settlement to be spread on the fields as well. Bouzek, Koutecký, and Neustupný (1966, p. 111) argue that by this time central Europeans had developed a sophisticated system of fallowing, manuring, and perhaps crop rotating as a means of preserving the fertility of the soil. There is every reason to think that the inhabitants of Hascherkeller were practicing such a well-managed and planned approach to their subsistence economy.

Manufacturing

Evidence of manufacturing in five different substances has been recovered at Hascherkeller — pottery, bone, textiles, bronze, and iron.

Pottery. The kiln at Hascherkeller was located at a slight distance away from the main settlement area (20 m to the north), a pattern also apparent at other sites (e.g., Pressmar 1979). The similarity of the waster sherds from the kiln debris to the pottery from the pits on the settlement makes clear that the kiln was being used to produce most, if not all, of the ceramics used by the occupants. Among the settlements of this period that have been partially excavated, a large proportion have yielded the remains of kilns — for example, Elchinger Kreuz in Bavarian Swabia (Pressmar 1979), Buchau in southern Württemberg (Pressmar 1979, p. 31), Breisach-Münsterberg in Baden (Bender et al. 1976, p. 217), the Hohlandsberg (Jehl and Bonnet 1968) and Cronenbourg (Hatt and Zumstein 1960) in Alsace, Sévrier in Haute-Savoie (Bocquet and Couren 1974), and several sites in the Saône Valley (Bonnamour 1976). The evidence suggests that most of the communities of the Late Bronze Age in central Europe were manufacturing their own pottery. Stubbs' thin-section study of the pottery from Hascherkeller indicates that almost all of the ceramics on the site were produced there, a finding similar to that of Maggetti (1979) for the settlement at Elchinger Kreuz.

The most important question raised by the kiln at Hascherkeller is that of the organization of pottery manufacture. In the context of a small settlement like Hascherkeller, it is unlikely that a full-time potter produced the ceramics needed by the community. Much more likely, to judge by studies of recent contexts of similar scale and economic development (e.g., David and David-Hennig 1971a, 1971b; David 1972; Fagg and Picton 1978; Papousek 1981), one or more individuals made pottery for the community during their spare time from the agricultural schedule. At this time in central Europe there is no evidence for any substantial trade in pottery; rather, the evidence suggests local production. Except in a few special instances, such as at the salt mine of Hallstatt in the Austrian Alps during the Early Iron Age (Köhler and Morton 1954), almost all pottery was produced by the individual communities for their own use.

In a context such as Hascherkeller where production was for local consumption, there was a fixed ceiling on the demand for new pots. The demand depended almost completely on breakage. (Since the pottery we are dealing with was all utilitarian ware and not the ornate pottery placed in graves, there is little likelihood that it would have been collected and hoarded.) As ethnographic studies in other parts of the world have shown (Foster 1960; David and David-Hennig 1971a, 1971b), pottery tends to have a relatively long life even with constant use — a year or two on the average for a cooking pot in regular use, slightly longer for vessels used in eating such as plates and cups, and longest for storage vessels, around ten years according to David's estimate. The ethnographic studies of David and Foster suggest

that a house might contain 20 to 70 pots at one time. If the Hascherkeller community had in it 15 to 30 persons, the demand for new pottery could not have been very high, surely not high enough to have kept a potter busy for more than a few weeks each year. We thus need to think of the kiln at Hascherkeller as having been used regularly at intervals, rather than frequently. Most of the time it was not in use, yet it had to be maintained so that it could be made ready for firing, perhaps each year during a regular period of pottery production.

Bone Carving. The working of bone is represented at Hascherkeller by fragments of red deer *(Cervus elaphus)* antler. The large base of an antler (fig. 60b) was recovered in the fill of the boundary ditch in Trench EII. The two tines had been sawn off, probably for use as raw material, and the base apparently discarded. Two finished objects of bone recovered, perhaps antler, are the button in figure 49j from the top of the pit in Trench N north end and the smooth, polished object in figure 70b from the plowsoil above the large pit in Trenches BII and C. Bone carving was probably a household industry at this time. The products of bone carving are well represented at all excavated settlements of the period, for example, at Buchau (Reinerth 1936, pl. 40,2) and Auvernier (Rychner 1979, vol. II, pl. 128). At some settlements, such as Auvernier, the bronze tools that were probably used in the processing of bone — saws, chisels, awls, and knives — have been recovered as well (Rychner 1979, vol. II, pls. 125, 126), and similar tools occur in some of the hoards (Müller-Karpe 1959a).

Textile Production. The 11 ceramic loom weights and 6 probable spindle whorls recovered attest to the production of textiles at the settlement. The concentrated distribution of the whorls in the pit in Trench N west extension suggests that spinning was carried out in the building above this pit. The loom weights are rather widely scattered over the settlement surface. A general concentration is suggested in the northern part of the central excavation area, perhaps indicating that they were used around Trenches N and S, where other crafts activities were also concentrated. The evidence for the spinning and weaving of textiles at the settlement fits well with that of the animal bones showing an age distribution for sheep indicating that they were raised primarily for wool production rather than for meat.

Loom weights and spindle whorls are relatively common at excavated settlements of this period, and it is apparent that most communities were producing their own textiles. At Hascherkeller the evidence of the sheep bones suggests that wool was being produced, but linen may have been made as well.

No textiles survive at Hascherkeller. Those textile fragments that have been preserved in the salt mines at Hallstatt (Hundt 1970; Mefford 1981) and in the bogs of Denmark (Hald 1950) provide a good view into the kinds of garments being made and worn at the time. The standard clothing items were tunics, shirts, dresses, and caps, often in plaid or with colorful patterns interwoven.

Bronzeworking. The presence of the sandstone mold at Hascherkeller suggests that bronze casting was carried out on the site, though no debris from the actual casting process, such as bronze droplets, was recovered. Sherds of small cup-shaped vessels with thick walls and with indications of intense secondary application of heat were found in the same pit as the mold. These vessels have not yet been analyzed for traces of metal; they may have been used as crucibles for melting bronze.

A number of small fragments of bronze objects were recovered at the settlement (fig. 64). Some of these may have been scrap that was collected for remelting and casting. Several were recovered close to the pit that contained the mold, and they may have formed part of a cache of scrap metal that was dispersed by plows after the abandonment of the settlement.

The evidence for on-site bronzeworking, the presence of the mold, does not suggest any activity beyond that of a part-time craftsman whose principal occupation was subsistence farming. As in the case of pottery, the demands of the community for bronze objects could not have been great, nor is it likely that members of the community possessed the surplus wealth with which to acquire substantial amounts of the metal. The person at Hascherkeller who did castings with the mold probably was not the same individual who made the mold. In the context of communities such as that at Hascherkeller, it is likely that part-time craftsmen cast bronze objects but that the molds were provided by specialists from outside the settlement (see Werner 1970 about such a situation in the early medieval period). Like the hypothetical potter at Hascherkeller, the bronze caster probably worked at occasional intervals when there was not more pressing work to be done.

Ironworking. The piece of slag from the ditch fill of Trench EII suggests that ironworking was carried out at the settlement. In his analysis of the object (chapter 10), Geselowitz concludes that it could be either smelting slag or forging slag. Since the only other indications of iron on the settlement are the small cylinder from Trench S south end and two small fragments from Trench AAI, little can be said about ironworking on the site. As yet, no actual workshop has been located at Hascherkeller. Iron ore is widely distributed throughout Bavaria, including the greater vicinity of Hascherkeller (Frei 1965–1966); hence, the ore did not have to be brought from far away.

Trade

Trade is indicated at Hascherkeller by the presence of bronze, graphite, and glass. Neither copper nor tin ores occur in the vicinity of Hascherkeller, and both had to be brought in from some distance away. Copper probably came from the mines to the south and southeast in the Tirol or near Salzburg, where the metal was actively being mined and smelted during this period (Pittioni 1951). Tin may have come from the Erzgebirge of modern East Germany or from a number of more distant sources (Piggott 1977).

The bronze recovered is only that which was lost — small bits and pieces, all but two of them fragmentary. To judge by the evidence at other settlements, the occupants of Hascherkeller probably had a range of bronze tools at their disposal, axes, sickles, hammers, chisels, and various forms of jewelry. These items were taken away when the inhabitants abandoned the settlement, leaving behind only those small items that had been lost.

The total amount of bronze metal that was being imported at Hascherkeller was probably not very large. If the population consisted of 15 to 30 individuals, we might hypothesize for the sake of discussion that they could have used 10 axes, 20 sickles, 5 saws, and 10 hammers, at the most. As the cemeteries of the region such as Kelheim (Müller-Karpe 1952a) and Altessing (Rochna 1965) demonstrate, little bronze was being placed in the graves at this time, and those objects that were put into graves were generally small ones such as pins, bracelets, pendants, and occasionally knives, not the tools that incorporated a lot of metal. Only a very few, exceptionally rich burials contained larger amounts of bronze metal, such as the slightly earlier one at Hart an der Alz (Müller-Karpe 1955). Hence, little bronze metal was being removed from circulation by the community at Hascherkeller. Broken and worn-out tools such as sickles and axes were most likely remelted and recast by the local bronzeworker or traded to a traveling metalsmith for new products.

Graphite was being brought to Hascherkeller for use as decoration on some of the pottery. As Stubbs notes (chapter 8), the pottery bearing graphite decoration comprises less than 1 percent by weight of all of the ceramics. Trade in graphite was thus not very substantial. Discovery of a lump of graphite at the slightly later settlement of Elchinger Kreuz near Ulm (Pressmar 1979, p. 41) suggests that the mineral itself was being traded, not pottery already decorated with it. Graphite sources primarily occur east of Passau along the north shore of the Danube, and they have been exploited there thoughout prehistoric and historic times (Paret 1929; Kappel 1969). Other possible sources of the mineral are situated in southern Bohemia and in the East Alpine region (Kossack 1959, p. 71).

The four dark blue glass beads were probably also imported to Hascherkeller. Glass beads first became abundant in prehistoric central Europe during the Late Bronze Age (Haevernick 1978), and they are widely distributed on settlements and in graves of the period. They may have been produced in the Tirol by an industry associated with copper smelting, as Neuninger and Pittioni suggest (1959), or they may have been produced in different regions. There is no direct evidence for the manufacture of glass beads during this period, however, and their origins must remain hypothetical pending further research.

Probably none of these substances — bronze, graphite, or glass — were being imported at Hascherkeller in large quantities, but their presence indicates that the community was in active contact with the outside world, and its members had sufficient surplus material to exchange for these imported items. By this period regular trade networks existed throughout central Europe. Central Europe was relatively densely settled, so it is unlikely that individuals from Hascherkeller traveled to ore bodies and obtained their own metals. The evidence at the copper mines indicates that established communities were mining the metal and were relying on the export trade for their livelihood, for example, the community represented in the cemetery at the Lebenberg at Kitzbühel in the Tirol (Pittioni 1952; Eibner et al. 1966). The widespread distribution of bronze metal throughout central Europe and the large quantities of it suggest that the transport and trade of the metal was in the hands of specialist traders. The same applies to graphite and glass beads, although the scale of trade in those substances was smaller than that in bronze metal. Salt may also have been imported at Hascherkeller, but no material evidence for its presence survives. The salt mines at Hallstatt were operating at the time of the occupation of Hascherkeller (Barth et al. 1975), and during the following centuries the evidence of the pottery and bronze objects in the graves at Hallstatt implies that the salt was being traded to southern Bavaria

(Wells 1978, pp. 86–88); salt may have been arriving at Hascherkeller and neighboring communities as well.

The transport of trade goods was probably carried out by individuals with packs on their backs and by merchants with packhorses. These modes of transport are well attested to in the earliest documentary evidence pertaining to transport in central Europe (Werner 1961; Pauli 1980, pp. 220–231). Wagons are known from this period and occur in some of the richest graves (e.g., Müller-Karpe 1955), but it is very unlikely that they were used to transport goods over distances.

Since the inhabitants of Hascherkeller were importing bronze metal, graphite, glass beads, and perhaps other products such as salt and exotic foodstuffs that do not survive in the archaeological record, they must have been producing something to exchange for the imports. One likely exchange product was wool. Sheep were raised at Hascherkeller, as the bones demonstrate, and the spindle whorls and loom weights attest to spinning and weaving on the site. Foodstuffs such as pork and beef may have been exchanged by the inhabitants of the settlement, especially if salt was available for preserving it. Another possible export product was leather. The communities mining and smelting copper and tin, such as those at the Lebenberg and slightly later at Uttendorf (Moosleitner 1977), resided in high mountainous regions of the Alps at the metal deposits, and they relied on importation of foodstuffs, clothing, and other essentials from outside. It is possible that communities such as Hascherkeller produced some of those essentials for the mining communities and in turn received the products of the mines. In order to further investigate this question we need many more floral and faunal samples, as well as other settlement debris, from more settlements of the period in order to obtain more data about possible surplus production.

Other settlements of the period in central Europe that have been excavated have yielded quantities of imported materials similar to those at Hascherkeller. By 1000 B.C. circulation of various materials was very active in central Europe, and the typical small hamlet communities were receiving a variety of materials from the outside, such as those represented at Hascherkeller.

SOCIAL ORGANIZATION

The archaeological evidence from the settlement of Hascherkeller offers little information about patterns of social organization, as is the case with most settlements in prehistoric Europe. For information about social organization we need to turn to the burial patterns. No cemetery associated with the settlement of Hascherkeller has been found. The best evidence for burial patterns in the region is that available 45 km north of Hascherkeller in the great cemetery at Kelheim, the largest cemetery of the period known in Bavaria. All aspects of the material culture at Kelheim and Hascherkeller are very similar, and the Kelheim cemetery and the Hascherkeller settlement were contemporaneous; Kelheim is dated in the relative chronological sequence from the end of Hallstatt A to the start of Hallstatt C (Müller-Karpe 1952a, pp. 16, 17). At Kelheim 263 graves were excavated, and others are likely to remain unexcavated on the edges of the cemetery. The population of the community that buried its dead in the Kelheim cemetery is likely to have been around 25 to 35, roughly the same size as what we imagine for Hascherkeller, or slightly larger. (For information about population estimates from cemetery data, see Wells 1981, pp. 97, 98, with earlier literature.)

The data from the cemetery at Kelheim can be used to suggest likely patterns in the distribution of the wealth of a central European community during this period, such as that at Hascherkeller. This reconstuction must remain very hypothetical until such time as a settlement and its associated cemetery are excavated. The principal grave goods at Kelheim were ceramic vessels; other common objects included in the burials were such small bronze items as pins, rings of different kinds, belt hooks, and arrowheads. Larger bronze objects, such as swords and axes, were lacking. Bronze occurred in 35.8 percent of the graves, a proportion close to the average for central European cemeteries of the period (Wells 1981, p. 110, table 9). The grave richest in bronze contained eight bronze objects; most of the graves containing bronze had just one (35 graves) or two (21 graves) bronze objects in them. Five graves contained one iron object each, a piece of wire, a small ring, an awl, a pin, and an unidentifiable fragment. One grave contained a small piece of sheet gold. Of the total 857 ceramic vessels in the graves, 32.4 percent were decorated with graphite, showing that graphite was used extensively at Kelheim for decorating burial pottery. Since graphite was generally used to ornament fine pottery rather than utilitarian ware, we would expect the cemetery of the Hascherkeller community to contain a much higher proportion of graphite-decorated pottery than the settlement deposits.

The distribution of grave wealth in the cemetery at Kelheim is shown in figure 89. The great majority of graves contained between 1 and 6 grave

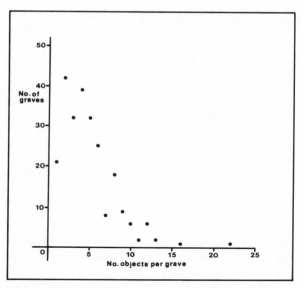

Figure 89. Graph showing the distribution of grave goods in the cemetery at Kelheim.

goods, and fewer contained between 7 and 22 objects. The distribution of wealth in graves is thus not equal, but there is a smooth curve on the graph from poorest to richest graves, without a distinct break in the continuum and without a bimodal distribution. The richest grave, which contained 22 objects, was not distinguished by the kinds of exceptional objects that occur in the richest burials of the period (swords, bronze vessels, and large gold ornaments), but rather by larger quantities of the same kinds of objects that occurred in the poorer graves. Hence, the cemetery at Kelheim suggests that there were not great disparities in wealth in the community. The archaeological evidence from the settlement of Hascherkeller would suggest a similar pattern. None of the materials recovered through excavation suggest exceptional workmanship or exotic materials such as gold. None of the pits excavated at the settlement contained objects indicative of any greater wealth or status than the others. The evidence from Hascherkeller and the comparable cemetery at Kelheim thus suggests that relatively little differentiation in wealth and status existed in the communities. A common material culture was shared by the members. Some individuals received more than others in their burials, perhaps because of individual achievements or because of position in age-grade systems. Müller-Karpe interprets the evidence from Kelheim to suggest that rough equality existed between the sexes in terms of burial wealth (1952a, p. 9).

The pattern of wealth distribution at Kelheim

is reflected at other contemporaneous cemeteries in Bavaria, for example, at Altessing (Rochna 1965), Manching (Rochna 1962), Gernlinden, Unterhaching, and Grünwald (Müller-Karpe 1957). Other excavated settlements, such as Künzing (Herrmann 1974–1975), show patterns of material culture and wealth similar to those at Hascherkeller. It is thus apparent that the distribution of wealth in the communities of the period, while not fully equal, did not show strong differences, certainly nothing like the differences apparent a few centuries later at the commercial centers of central Europe like the Heuneburg (Wells 1980b). A small number of graves have been found that were much more richly equipped than those in most cemeteries. The best example in the area of Hascherkeller is the slightly earlier grave at Hart an der Alz (Müller-Karpe 1955), in which a man was cremated on a wooden four-wheeled wagon with massive bronze fittings and buried with his sword, a gold wire ring, and three fine vessels of beaten bronze. The question of the connection between such richly outfitted individuals and agricultural communities such as Hascherkeller is considered in chapter 13.

Communities such as those represented at Hascherkeller, Kelheim, and other sites in central Europe during this period were probably made up of several (two to five) families living together in a settlement that can best be called a hamlet. The evidence from the settlements and the cemeteries suggests that the different members of the communities must have cooperated on agricultural and crafts activities, and accumulation and possession of material wealth was probably fairly equal. Perhaps as individuals aged they acquired more material accouterments in the form of bracelets, pins, weapons, and pottery, as reflected in the graves with somewhat larger amounts of material in them than others. Leadership in such communities was probably not strongly developed, to judge by the similarity in material culture represented in the settlement pits at Hascherkeller and in the graves at Kelheim. There are no outstanding signs of rank or status marking the special positions of certain individuals, as occur several centuries later. In such a context it is likely that one senior individual probably played a leadership role in settling disputes and representing the community in interactions with other communities.

DAILY LIFE

To judge from the evidence of the excavated settlement of Hascherkeller and from ethnographic information about the organization of peasant life in medieval and early modern Europe (e.g., Homans 1942; Bloch 1961; Fél and Hofer 1972; Hartley 1979), the lives of the inhabitants of Hascherkeller were probably dominated by the schedule of agriculture. Most of their time and energy was devoted to the tending of their fields and their livestock and maintaining the physical structure of the settlement. Life was probably organized around the agricultural seasons. Spring was occupied with preparing the ground for planting, planting the crops, and taking the livestock out to pasture. Summer was spent tending the crops and livestock, and fall was spent harvesting the crops, culling the herds, and very importantly arranging the preservation and storage of grains, vegetables, and meats for the long and barren winter months ahead. Probably the most critical aspect of peasant life in Europe before modern times was the preservation and storage of foods for the winter and early spring months, when no new foodstuffs were available and each family had to rely on what had been saved from the previous harvest. The leanest time of all was spring, when winter stocks were nearly exhausted, livestock were thin, hungry, and weak, and the new growth had not yet begun. The essential task of the farmer was to assure that his family could survive that difficult time through provision of adequate stores of food from each year's harvest.

Crafts industries and trade at Hascherkeller and at the similar communities throughout central Europe were probably carried out principally during the winter and early spring, when there was no agricultural work to do. Aside from tending the few animals that were not slaughtered in the fall or early winter, the farmer had little to do with respect to the production of food during the winter, and he and his family could spend time taking care of other necessary chores such as repairing the house and outbuildings, weaving textiles, carving needed implements from bone and wood, casting bronze tools and ornaments, and making pottery. Trade was also best carried on during the winter and early spring, when food production did not demand constant attention. Although the weather was cold and snow might cover the ground for long periods, it was still possible to travel throughout central Europe, and the snow cover and freezing of the rivers may even have aided transport of bulk goods.

Two principal aspects of life are thus reflected in the evidence at Hascherkeller: survival and procurement of luxuries. The most pressing concern for the inhabitants of Hascherkeller was the production of enough food to survive through the cold winter and barren early spring. Once this provision was taken care of, they were able, and apparently eager, to indulge in the production and procurement of luxury goods such as bronze ornaments and glass beads.

13

Hascherkeller and Central Europe: Formation of Commercial Towns in the Early Iron Age

The period of time between 1200 and 800 B.C. was one of great economic and cultural change in Europe, and during these centuries developments in metal production and trade took place that led to the formation, after 800 B.C., of the first large-scale industrial and commercial communities in non-Mediterranean Europe. Many investigators have designated these communities as the first European towns (Neustupný 1969; Hensel 1970). The results of the excavations at Hascherkeller provide a detailed view into the economy of one typical community of the period and thus contribute to our understanding of the major changes that were taking place. This chapter will explore the connection between settlements such as Hascherkeller and the major cultural changes taking place during this important period.

HASCHERKELLER AND OTHER COMMUNITIES

The Question of Population

McEvedy and Jones (1978, p. 19) suggest a population of about 10 million for all of Europe around 1000 B.C., with the highest densities in the Mediterranean lands of Greece and Italy. Comparison with the modern figure of 635 million gives a gross impression of the scale of the human habitation of Europe during the period that Hascherkeller was occupied. Exact figures are, of course, impossible to come by, and there was surely considerable regional variation then as there is now; but this estimate is probably on the right order of magnitude. Practically all settlements in non-Mediterranean Europe were farmsteads and hamlets, or very small villages, with populations under 50 persons. Larger estimates have been made on the basis of some excavated settlements; Reinerth suggests 200 for Wasserburg Buchau (1928, p. 38), Bersu proposes 400 at Wittnauer Horn (1946, p. 7), and Wyss suggests that 500 lived at Zürich-Alpen-

quai (1971b, p. 104). Settlements, particularly in an environment such as central Europe where conditions for wood preservation are generally poor, do not provide good evidence for making population estimates, as the example of Elp in the Netherlands well illustrates (Waterbolk 1964). Except in the rare instances in which foundations of structures on a settlement overlap one another, it is very difficult to ascertain which buildings were standing and in use at the same time, unless some independent means of dating such as radiocarbon or dendrochronology is available. Particularly in instances where settlements were occupied over several centuries, as at Elp and Buchau, we need to reckon with the abandonment of old and decaying structures and the erection of new ones, perhaps on the average as frequently as every 30 years (Bakker et al. 1977, p. 223; Pauli 1980, p. 311, n. 51). In central Europe cemeteries are a much better source of information than settlements for making population estimates.

Using the formula developed by Acsádi and Nemeskéri (1970) and employed extensively by Donat and Ullrich (1976), it is possible to calculate the probable approximate size of the community that used a cemetery (see discussion in Wells 1981, pp. 97, 98). Applied to cemeteries of the period 1200 to 800 B.C. that have been completely or nearly completely excavated — such as St. Andrä in Austria (C. Eibner 1974) and Kelheim (Müller-Karpe 1952a), Grünwald, Unterhaching, and Gernlinden (Müller-Karpe 1957) in southern Germany — this formula suggests that the great majority of communities were made up of between 5 and 35 persons. The excavated settlements indicate that these communities were organized as farmsteads and hamlets. No cemeteries of the period have been discovered that represent substantially larger communities (see discussions of settlement scale and character in Dehn 1972, p. 42; Herrmann 1974–1975, p. 79; Bakker et al. 1977, p. 223; Horst 1978; Kooi 1979, p. 5).

Other Settlements Contemporaneous with Hascherkeller

Settlements of the period are found in three principal types of locations in central Europe: on flat dry land like Hascherkeller, in boggy lakeshore areas (often underwater today), and on hilltops. Many settlements in all three situations have been partially excavated, and they yield evidence bearing on settlement size and structure and economic activity comparable to that observed at Hascherkeller.

Considerable variation exists in individual location of settlements, in areal extent and structure, and in the character of the settlement remains. Yet all of the features of the Hascherkeller settlement are represented in similar form at others. For example, Künzing and Elchinger Kreuz are also situated on river terraces covered with loess soil. Enclosures bounded by double ditches like those at Hascherkeller have been investigated at Aiterhofen (Christlein and Stork 1980) and Kelheim (Engelhardt 1980). Pits of form and character very much like those at Hascherkeller have been investigated at most flatland settlements of the period; at Künzing, for example, the same three morphological types were identified as at Hascherkeller — round pits with vertical sides and flat bottoms; broad, open amorphous pits; and long narrow ones (Herrmann 1974–1975, p. 76). The objects recovered from other contemporaneous settlements are also very similar to those at Hascherkeller.

This is not the place to discuss other settlements of the period in detail, but some of the most important and best excavated and published settlements can be cited. All show important similarities to Hascherkeller. In the same part of central Europe as Hascherkeller, the settlements of Künzing (Herrmann 1974–1975), Aiterhofen (Christlein and Stork 1980), Pliening and Kirchheim (Dannheimer 1976), and the hilltop site on the Bogenberg (Hundt 1955) are of roughly the same date as Hascherkeller. In greater central Europe, Elchinger Kreuz near Ulm (Pressmar 1979), Buchau in southern Württemberg (Reinerth 1928, 1936; Kimmig 1979), Lovčičky in southern Moravia (Říhovský 1972), and Dornholzhausen in Hessen (Janke 1971) all show important similarities. The Swiss lakeshore settlements of Auvernier (Rychner 1979), Auvernier-Nord (Arnold 1981), Zug-Sumpf (Speck 1955), and Zürich-Grosser Hafner (Primas and Ruoff 1981) yielded materials comparable to those at Hascherkeller, as well as many organic remains that do not survive in the flatland settlements. The hillforts of Wittnauer Horn (Bersu 1946) and Kestenberg (Laur-Belart 1955; Gersbach 1982) in Switzerland and Hohlandsberg in Alsace (Jehl and Bonnet 1968; Bonnet 1974) also yielded comparable materials. Further afield, on the North European Plain the settlements of Elp in the Netherlands (Waterbolk 1964), Berlin-Lichterfelde (von Müller 1964), Hallunda in Sweden (Jaanusson 1971, 1981), and Aldermaston Wharf in Britain (Bradley et al. 1980) are all contemporaneous and offer useful points of comparison with Hascherkeller.

Settlement Character and Economy, 1000 to 800 B.C.

The excavated settlements of the period 1000 to 800 B.C. all over Europe north of the Alps show a large number of important shared features. Most importantly, all are farmsteads or hamlets; none suggest populations of over 100 persons. All were inhabited by communities whose principal activities were those involved in food production. Some manufacturing was carried out at most of the settlements, including the production of pottery and casting of bronze objects, and trade is also apparent.

The areas of the settlements of this period range from under 1000 square meters to several hectares. Here again we face the problem of not knowing what parts of any settlement were in use at any one time. But where the foundations of buildings survive on settlement sites, either as postholes in the subsoil or as wooden timbers preserved in the boggy conditions of the lakeshore sites, approximate sizes of houses and other structures can be determined.

Small structures, probably sheds and drying racks, are often only a few square meters in size. Small buildings between 25 and 30 square meters, which were probably one-room huts, are well represented. Larger buildings, up to 100 square meters, are not uncommon. At Elp and other settlements on the North European Plain large structures around 200 square meters are common. These contained both residential quarters for humans and stalls for livestock, a pattern in use over much of northern Europe into modern times (Müller-Wille 1977). The mean size of the more substantial structures on settlements of the period is between 30 and 60 square meters, which may have been the average house size.

Construction of buildings in central Europe during this period varied somewhat; the raw materials used for buildings were logs, hewn boards, branches, and clay for daub. Some buildings employed stout vertical posts sunk into postholes in the ground as the main vertical supports. In general they had two, sometimes three, rows of vertical timbers, but most often six in total. Between these verticals were either horizontal beams — round logs or hewn boards — or else branchwork with daub packing. The post-

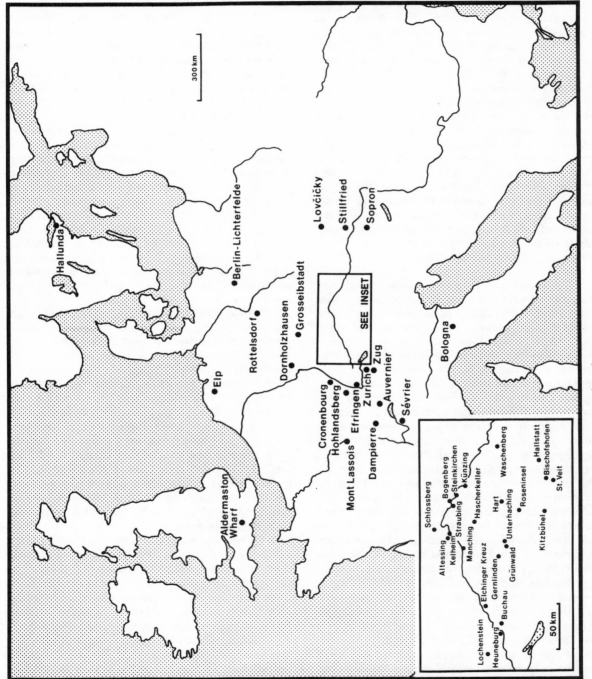

Figure 90. Map showing the principal sites mentioned in the text.

holes left by such structures, such as those on the eastern edge of the field at Hascherkeller (see fig. 72), constitute the type foundations for Late Bronze Age houses. The whole issue is best summarized in Herrmann 1974–1975 and Zippelius 1974–1975. As Herrmann notes (1974–1975, p. 68, n. 33), these foundations are very rarely dated by finds in the postholes; usually they are assumed to be contemporaneous with settlement pits in the vicinity.

Other buildings did not employ vertical timbers sunk into the ground, but instead horizontal beams placed on the ground surface with walls supported by this foundation. The favorable conditions of preservation in many of the lakeshore settlements have led to the survival of such structures, as for example, at Buchau and Zug-Sumpf. On flatland settlements, where the actual settlement surface has almost always been destroyed by plowing as at Hascherkeller, such a structural type would of course leave no detectable remains. Common use of this structural technique and the destruction of settlement surfaces by plows may be the reasons why the majority of Late Bronze Age settlements are known only from the settlement pits and not from identifiable posthole foundations (Coles and Harding 1979, p. 358).

The basic cereal grains, garden crops, and domestic animals that formed the subsistence base of the communities of this period were roughly similar throughout Europe, with some regional variations (see Jankuhn 1969; Bökönyi 1974; Körber-Grohne 1981 for general discussions). They had been introduced during the Neolithic Period; some variation occurred over time as well as over space. During the Late Bronze Age important changes took place in the technology of agricultural production. Most apparent was the general adoption of the bronze sickle for use in harvesting grains. Metal sickles appeared during the Middle Bronze Age but were not common until the Late Bronze Age. Bronze sickles are abundantly represented in many hoards of the period. That from Frankleben in central Germany contained over 230 sickles, and many others contain 25 or more (von Brunn 1958, 1968). Bronze sickles are also relatively common at lakeshore settlements of central Europe and even appear in a few burials. Molds for casting sickles are quite common in settlement deposits, and their wide distribution in small settlements throughout central Europe suggests that they were cast by persons in the communities rather than in specialized production centers (von Brunn 1968, pp. 240, 241). The widespread adoption of bronze sickles throughout central Europe at this time represents a new dependence on bronze metal for subsistence production. Before the Late

Bronze Age, bronze had been used primarily for ornaments and weaponry; tools were rare. In the Late Bronze Age a new relationship developed between metal production and subsistence.

Most agricultural implements were made of wood, as they were into modern times, and hence have rarely been preserved.

The evidence for manufacturing at Hascherkeller also corresponds closely with that from other settlements in central Europe. Most settlements that have been substantially excavated have yielded evidence for pottery production, bronze casting, weaving, and manufacture of tools from stone and bone. It is unlikely that full-time specialists were involved in any of these crafts. Even for potting and bronze casting it is more likely that one or more experienced persons worked in their spare time from the more pressing work of food production and preparation (Rowlands 1972; Papousek 1981). The existence of a single kiln so far discovered at Hascherkeller (and none other was indicated in the vicinity of the settlement by the magnetometer survey) suggests that this one facility was utilized to fill the whole community's need for pottery, a pattern also indicated for other excavated settlements. Probably one or two individuals in each community filled, on a part-time and probably seasonal schedule, the need for pottery and bronze.

The marked similarity of pottery and of bronze objects throughout central Europe implies considerable contact between potters and between bronzeworkers. This contact may have been maintained principally by a small number of specialists who traveled around particular regions, teaching local potters and smiths the techniques of working their materials and introducing new forms and motifs. In the case of pottery, such individuals may have been the same ones who transported and traded graphite for decoration. For bronze, they may have been the metal traders and those who made the molds for casting bronze objects. All of the evidence speaks for von Brunn's suggestion (1968, pp. 240, 241) that each community had its own bronzeworker to produce needed objects made of the metal. Casting, hammering, and finishing such relatively simple objects as sickles, rings, pins, and even axes are easier tasks than cutting the molds in which to cast them. With the information available at present we can do no more than hypothesize about this subject, but it seems likely that the molds were made by specialists and used by part-time community bronzesmiths.

The existence of at least a few full-time bronzesmiths is suggested by a small group of burials in central Europe containing tools used in working bronze and ingots of the metal. This group has been interpeted as graves of smiths (Jockenhövel 1973). The activity of such craft specialists is suggested by the regional distribution of many types of bronze objects (Wells forthcoming).

The evidence for trade from other central European settlements is also similar to that from Hascherkeller. Besides bronze, graphite, and glass, other traded substances include amber from the Baltic region, shells from the Mediterranean, and gold. It is likely that there was also trade in foodstuffs, wine, salt, textiles, and leather, though at present all evidence for such trade is indirect.

The trade in bronze metal is of particular importance. Bronze is well represented at most settlements of the period, and for the first time in the Late Bronze Age the metal became important not only for ornaments and occasional weapons, but also in the form of sickles for the production of food as well. The increase in quantity of bronze metal being traded at this time played an important part in the general intensification of production.

ECONOMIC CHANGE IN LATE BRONZE AGE CENTRAL EUROPE

During the Late Bronze Age important changes were taking place in the intensification of production and commerce that were to have profound effects on the future development of European society. Between 1200 and 800 B.C. was a major period of transition between the almost purely agricultural, small-scale settlement and economic systems of the Neolithic Period and the Early and Middle Bronze Ages and the more complex and larger-scale economic and social systems of the Iron Age, which led to the formation of the first towns and cities in Europe north of the Alps. The settlement of Hascherkeller was occupied during this time of change. The principal changes can be considered in three categories: settlement activity, production of metals and trade, and patterns in the accumulation of wealth.

The Settlement Evidence

Several important changes were taking place in settlement activity during the Late Bronze Age. Many more sites, including settlements, cemeteries, and hoards, are known from the period 1200 to 800 B.C. than from the preceding Early and Middle Bronze Ages (see Peroni 1979 and Otto 1978 for general discussion). There is good evidence for the clearing of forested lands in many different parts of Europe for agricultural use (Coles and Harding 1979), and for the first time in prehistoric Europe many settle-

ments were being occupied for several centuries rather than for only a few generations (Bouzek et al. 1966, p. 111). This last point suggests that during the Late Bronze Age new techniques were employed for preserving the fertility of agricultural soil, such as fallowing, manuring, and perhaps crop rotation, enabling communities to remain on one settlement site much longer than was previously possible. All of these changes suggest that population was increasing during the Late Bronze Age.

Increases in Metal Production

The quantity of bronze produced and worked increased greatly during this period. Much larger amounts of the metal have been recovered from hoards in the ground and from settlement deposits than during the preceding phases of the Bronze Age. Many different kinds of objects, such as swords, axes, and pins, were on the average much larger in the Late Bronze Age than previously and incorporated larger amounts of the metal in their manufacture (cf. objects shown in Müller-Karpe 1959a and Pirling 1980).

Whole new categories of bronze objects appeared for the first time or became common, including tools, weapons, and luxury goods. Among tools that first became common in the Late Bronze Age were sickles, hammers, anvils, chisels, gouges, and saws (Wyss 1967a, 1967b, 1971a). Swords and spearheads are more common from Late Bronze Age contexts than from earlier ones. Newly developed techniques of beating bronze into large sheets (Drescher 1958; 1980) were applied in the production of ornate luxury goods, especially bronze vessels and helmets, which have been found in the wealthiest burials and in hoards.

Finally, the evidence from the copper mines in Austria indicates that larger amounts of metal were being extracted than previously (Pauli 1980, p. 38). In the the mines around Bischofshofen in Land Salzburg and at Kitzbühel in the Tirol several hundred workers may have been involved in the various tasks of mining and smelting, according to estimates made by Pittioni and his colleagues (Pittioni 1951, 1976; Neuninger et al. 1969).

Greater amounts of bronze metal were being removed from circulation during the Late Bronze Age than during the preceding periods. Roughly a third of the graves of this period in central Europe contain some bronze (Wells 1981, p. 110, table 9), mostly small items such as pins, bracelets, and knives and usually only one or two such items in a grave. Richer burials, such as at Hart an der Alz at the beginning of the period and Villach at the end (Müller-Karpe 1952b), contain both larger numbers of bronze objects and objects of exceptional character such as vessels, swords, and helmets.

The greatest quantities of bronze metal occur in the tens of thousands of known hoards, which often contain 50 kilograms and more of bronze objects (Müller-Karpe 1959a; von Brunn 1968). Those that have been discovered in recent times surely constitute only a small proportion of the hoards that were buried. Most were probably recovered by the individuals who buried them, and the buried objects were used in production and trade. Those known today were not recovered by their owners for reasons having to do with the plans or health of the owners or with economic, political, or military changes of the time.

Besides the graves and the hoards that contain stored bronze, "votive offerings" constitute another kind of intentional deposition of bronze. Most of the "votive" finds are swords; other special objects such as vessels and helmets have also been found. These objects are found particularly in bodies of water such as rivers and swamps and are believed to have been offered to deities in much the same way offerings were made in Greek and Roman societies, about whose religious practices we are better informed (Torbrügge 1970–1971). Of more concern here than their religious purpose is the economic function of these offerings. Like the placing of bronze in graves, throwing them into rivers and ponds had the result of permanently removing them from circulation. Thus, at the same time that much scrap metal was being recycled in the hoards, much was also being disposed of. The economic function of this disposal may have been to keep the levels of production and trade of metal high. If objects were kept in use, passed on from generation to generation, and recycled when broken or worn out, then demand for new supplies of metal would have been low, just enough to satisfy desires for more wealth and provide equipment for a gradually increasing population. But if bronze was being systematically removed from circulation through deposition in graves and in votive offerings, a steady supply of new metal would have been required to maintain needed amounts of the metal.

Such removal of bronze also had the effect of keeping the value of metal high. If it were not removed and production went on at a high or increasing pace, enormous quantities of the metal would have accumulated, relative to needs of the time. The resulting drop in the value of bronze would have hurt individuals who had accumulated wealth in the metal. It has been proposed that some of the hoards were deposited by metalworkers or wealthy persons to get rid of excess metal temporarily in order to

keep the value high or to wait for it to increase (Primas 1977a). An individual who had accumulated wealth in bronze might have buried part of his wealth, both for safekeeping and to keep others unaware of how much was around. Such an interpretation would help explain the large number of hoards that were never recovered; persons who buried them waited for the value to increase, and after their deaths no one knew where the hoards were located. Perhaps the amounts of metal placed in graves and thrown into water were insufficient to offset the massive recycling going on and the stepped-up production at the mines, and hence the metal never became scarce or rose in value. At this time attention was being diverted to the new metal iron.

The earliest finds of iron objects in central Europe date from the latter half of the second millennium B.C. (Pleiner 1980, pp. 376–378). By the period 1000 to 800 B.C., iron had become relatively common in central Europe (see the distribution map in Pleiner 1981, p. 124, fig. 11), though these centuries are generally considered part of the Late Bronze Age rather than the Early Iron Age. The most common uses of iron in this period were as inlay in bronze objects such as pins, rings, and swords; as blades in composite tools with bronze handles, particularly swords and knives; and as small tools for working bronze (Rieth 1942, pp. 10–12; Vogt 1949–1950; Kimmig 1964, pp. 274–281; Bouzek 1978). Metallographic studies of some iron objects from this period have shown that some smiths had already mastered techniques of hardening iron for specific purposes (Pleiner 1968, p. 41).

The evidence of the slag lump from the ditch fill in Trench EII, as well as the four others recovered in the plowsoil above settlement pits, suggests that iron was being worked at Hascherkeller during the tenth and/or ninth centuries B.C. The iron objects recovered may have been manufactured on the site. Although slags and iron objects have been found at many central European settlements and cemeteries, no actual smithy sites have been identified from this period. The earliest well-documented ironworking site in central Europe is at the Waschenberg near Wels in Upper Austria, dating to the Early Iron Age (Pertlwieser 1970). There iron production was being carried out on a very small scale, involving the smelting of ores in small pits in the ground. It is probable that iron production was carried out on such a scale by residents of the small farmsteads and hamlet communities throughout central Europe, until the formation of the larger, commercially active communities of the Early Iron Age such as those in Slovenia (Wells 1981) and slightly later in west-central Europe. Since iron ores are widely distributed throughout Europe in easily workable form and often in rich surface deposits (Pleiner 1964, *Beilage* 1; Frei 1965–1966), once the technology of smelting and forging was learned individuals in the small communities could produce iron on a scale sufficient to fill their limited needs.

Increases in Trade

The expansion of trade activity in the period 1000 to 800 B.C. is most evident in the growing quantity of bronze throughout Europe. Since both copper and tin have very limited natural distributions in Europe, circulation of bronze implies trade. Many other goods were also being traded as well, to a much greater extent than during the preceding periods. Glass beads first became common during the Late Bronze Age (Haevernick 1978). Although a few beads have been found dating to earlier times, they were relatively common in settlement and burial contexts of the Late Bronze Age. Very little is known about the locations of bead production, but it is likely that production was limited to a small number of locations and that beads were circulated through trade (Haevernick 1978).

Graphite became a popular material for use in decorating pottery in central Europe during the Late Bronze Age, particularly during the phase Hallstatt B (1000 to 700 B.C.) (Herrmann 1974–1975, p. 86). Deposits of graphite are also restricted in nature, and this mineral, like the components of bronze, had to be transported and traded to the thousands of communities that used it to decorate their pottery.

Amber from the Baltic regions of northern Europe, perhaps exchanged for bronze metal (Hundt 1978), was also a popular trade item during the Late Bronze Age, and amber beads have been recovered from graves and settlements throughout central Europe (Bohnsack 1976). Other ornamental items, such as shells from the Mediterranean Sea, were also being traded in central Europe during the period (Wyss 1971a).

Accumulation of Wealth: New Possibilities in Late Bronze Age Europe

During the Palaeolithic, Mesolithic, and Neolithic periods in Europe there is little evidence for the accumulation of personal wealth. Ornaments of shell, bone, teeth, amber, and stone occur in a small proportion of burials, suggesting that some effort was expended in acquiring objects not directly involved in survival; but it was not until the very end of the Neolithic Period and the start of the Bronze Age that quantities of wealth were accumulated, and that spe-

cial objects were regularly produced for possession restricted to a few persons. The start of this trend is apparent in the occurrence of bronze and gold ornaments in some Bell Beaker graves (Harrison 1980) and in the exceptionally rich burials of the cemetery of Varna on the Black Sea coast of Bulgaria (Renfrew 1978). Bronze objects are common in graves of the Early Bronze Age, as for example, at Straubing in Lower Bavaria (Hundt 1958) and in the large cemetery at Gemeinlebarn in Lower Austria (Stein 1968). Hoards of copper and especially of bronze ingots found in large numbers in the lands north of the Alpine copper deposits (Reinecke 1930; Kleemann 1954; Hundt 1974) similarly attest to the accumulation of wealth in this period. A small number of exceptionally richly outfitted burials contained gold ornaments and ornate bronze objects, including weapons such as daggers. The grave at Leubingen in East Germany was situated under a large burial mound inside an oak chamber that was covered by a cairn of stones. The grave contained skeletal remains of a man and a child accompanied by three bronze daggers, a bronze halberd, two bronze axes, three bronze chisels, a serpentine axe, a gold bracelet, two gold pins, two small gold rings, and a gold wire ring (Grössler 1907). The grave at Leubingen and others similar to it in north-central Europe (Otto 1955) represent the beginning of a pattern that persisted throughout the rest of European prehistory and into historical times — the occurrence of a few graves much more richly outfitted than the majority, especially with weapons and gold ornaments.

These trends continued during the Middle Bronze Age, with substantial amounts of bronze metal often being placed in graves (e.g., see Pirling 1980; Stary 1980). Swords first appeared in central Europe during the Middle Bronze Age, incorporating much more bronze than the spearheads, halberds, and arrowheads of the earlier periods. Weapons and gold ornaments characterize the richest graves of the period.

In the Late Bronze Age, 1200 to 800 B.C., these trends toward the accumulation of material wealth reached a climax. The quantity of bronze metal in circulation was much greater than during any preceding period and is most apparent in the tens of thousands of hoards now known. Many new kinds of elite objects were produced, such as sheet bronze vessels and armor and large slashing swords. Many more tools, and many more kinds of tools, were in use than before.

As in the earlier phases of the Bronze Age, some individuals acquired much more wealth than others. The grave at Hart an der Alz (Müller-Karpe 1955), for example, contained such exceptional objects as a four-wheeled wagon with bronze fittings, a bronze sword, three vessels of fine beaten sheet bronze, and a gold bracelet. Such burials and the tens of thousands of hoards of bronze metal attest to the accumulation of substantial amounts of wealth by individuals and communities.

Accompanying these larger quantities of wealth being amassed were other related changes. During the Late Bronze Age a great many settlements in all parts of central Europe were established on hilltops and outfitted with substantial defensive walls (Herrmann 1969). This proliferation of hillforts reflects the need for the defense of accumulated wealth. Wealth in bronze and gold could easily have been captured by small raiding bands, and a principal way of protecting wealth was to build defenses around settlements.

The proliferation of weaponry can also be understood in relation to the new accumulation of wealth. The presence of weapons, particularly swords, in most of the richest graves implies a direct connection between the acquisition and protection of wealth and fighting. Wealth could be seized by force through the use of weapons, and weapons could be employed to protect wealth from seizure.

A more modest development in the protection of new wealth was that of keys. The earliest keys known in central Europe date from the Late Bronze Age, and their existence at settlements of this period suggests that for the first time people had enough valuables to make locking them up worth the trouble (Pauli 1978, pp. 261–263).

Finally, the proliferation of objects made of gold during the Late Bronze Age is another indication of the accumulation of new wealth. Gold vessels and ornaments are well represented all over Europe during this period for the first time (Drack 1980; Eogan 1981).

FORMATION OF COMMERCIAL TOWNS IN THE EARLY IRON AGE

The critical factor during the Late Bronze Age that led to the formation of the first larger, commercially oriented communities of Early Iron Age Europe was the new possibility to acquire and amass large stores of material wealth. From the time of the establishment of settled village life in Neolithic Europe, it had been possible to accumulate wealth in foodstuffs or in livestock herds. The principal advantage of bronze metal as a form of stored wealth was that, unlike food and cattle, it was practically nonperishable and needed no care. The growth of copper and tin mining operations and of the trade systems carrying the metals throughout Europe meant that the

quantity of bronze that could be produced, worked into finished goods, and accumulated as wealth was theoretically limitless. Once acquired, bronze metal could be buried in the ground for safekeeping and retrieved when needed. The development of this new form of wealth, available for the first time during the Late Bronze Age in large quantities, was one important factor that led to the changes during the first half of the final millennium B.C. resulting in the formation of Europe's first towns.

The new wealth was used for a variety of purposes. It was used to support specialized craftsmen who manufactured the many new exotic objects of the period, such as bronze vessels, helmets, shields, cuirasses, and gold beakers. It was used for commerce to exchange for a variety of desired goods including glass beads, graphite, Mediterranean shells, and among the wealthiest individuals, for such exotic products as wine from the Mediterranean region, implied by the bronze drinking equipment in rich graves like that at Hart an der Alz (Piggott 1959). Wealth was probably also expended by rich persons on public events such as festivals, feasts, and building projects, intended to enhance their status in the community and increase their power. Evidence consistent with these activities is apparent in the archaeological record.

Most important for the development of larger communities in the Early Iron Age was the use of wealth for investment in other profit-making ventures, specifically in the extraction of salt and iron for trade. Both substances were already being worked during the Late Bronze Age. Recent radiocarbon determinations obtained from wood in the galleries of the salt mines at Hallstatt in Upper Austria, 160 kilometers southeast of Hascherkeller, indicate substantial mining activity already in the period 1000 to 800 B.C. (Barth et al. 1975). Other central European communities may also have been involved in the production of salt for export trade at this time (Herrmann 1966, p. 8, n. 51).

The case of salt mining for trade at Hallstatt provides the best example of these changes, and it will be used to illustrate the processes involved. Similar developments took place in relation to the early working of iron (Wells 1981, pp. 122–128). Hallstatt is situated in the Austrian Alps. The modern town is located 511 meters above sea level; the valley where the mines and other prehistoric occupation remains are situated is 350 meters almost directly above the town. Very little evidence of prehistoric activity has been found in the lower areas in and around the modern town, and all of the evidence recovered to date, including that from the mine galleries and from the Early Iron Age cemeteries, has been recovered in the high valley. Hallstatt is an especially instructive case of early commercial development. The site is situated in a region of scanty and poor soil, and it receives little sunlight in the shade of the high surrounding mountains. The community that lived and mined and traded salt at Hallstatt had to import food and other essentials from outside.

There have been occasional finds of stone tools and pottery in the area around Hallstatt dating from the Neolithic and Bronze Ages (Reitinger 1968, pp. 126–128), but there is no indication of regular activity at the site until the Late Bronze Age. A large hoard of bronze objects of Late Bronze Age date, weighing over 50 kilograms, was found in the high mountain valley (Reinecke 1934; Reitinger 1968, pp. 128, 129), and the radiocarbon dating evidence now indicates that the entire north complex of galleries in the salt mountain date from the Late Bronze Age, specifically from the period 1000 to 800 B.C. (Barth et al. 1975). The site of Hallstatt and the surrounding lands have been systematically studied for nearly 150 years by many different investigators, and it is likely that the archaeological record at present is representative of prehistoric material at and around the site.

The evidence suggests that during the Late Bronze Age people came to the site for the first time and that they came specifically to mine salt for trade. There is no other plausible reason why people would have come to Hallstatt in the Late Bronze and Early Iron Ages; the environment is harsh and agriculturally unproductive, and until the development of the salt industry, no trade route ran near the site. Salt had been produced in Europe since at least Neolithic times, usually through evaporation rather than mining, and had been a significant item of trade (Nenquin 1961). Yet not until the Early Iron Age at the site of Hallstatt is there evidence that salt production for trade developed into a large commercial industry. Unlike Hallstatt, the majority of the earlier sites of salt production were located in agricultural regions, where persons who were raising their own food could in their spare time also produce salt for trade. The situation at Hallstatt was very different in that the salt miners could not support themselves but had to rely on imports of food and other necessities from outside. Once salt extraction and trade had developed in the Early Iron Age, the salt generated was surely the item traded for food and other necessities, as well as for the luxury goods abundantly represented in the graves (Kromer 1959). The important question here is, how were the first miners at Hallstatt supported before they had generated salt for trade and before the commercial systems had developed?

In experiments with replicas of the bronze picks recovered in the galleries at Hallstatt, Schauberger found that it took about 28 days for a pair of miners to extend a gallery one meter forward. The salt deposits at Hallstatt are covered with thick layers of heavily weathered salt and debris that had to be cut through before the miners reached the salt suitable for use; it probably took three to five years of mining before the miners even reached the salt (Jankuhn 1969, p. 85).

It is therefore clear that there was a period of time, perhaps three years, perhaps longer, when persons were beginning the mining operations at Hallstatt without producing any of the salt that could be traded for necessities or for luxury goods. These individuals had to be supported while they mined and presumably had to be rewarded sufficiently to be willing to devote their energies to that strenuous task. They were supported by enterprising individuals in possession of the surplus wealth being generated during the Late Bronze Age. One or more wealthy individuals invested in salt mining at Hallstatt with the expectation of profits when the mines became productive and the extracted salt could be traded. Salt mining began at Hallstatt during the period when vast quantities of disposable wealth in bronze metal first came into being.

The mining equipment recovered from the northern galleries at Hallstatt, which date from the Late Bronze Age, show that already during this early period of salt extraction the miners were making and using elegant leather knapsacks with wooden frames for carrying the mined salt to the surface, as well as a whole range of mining tools such as shovels and picks (Barth 1973). No graves of this early period of activity at Hallstatt have been discovered. The great cemetery of some 2,000 graves began around 800 B.C. During the period of use of the cemetery, roughly 800 to 400 B.C., an average of around 200 persons lived and worked at Hallstatt; Kromer suggests (1958) that the average during the period 800 to 600 B.C. was 150 and that the community grew in size over time to an average of 300 during the period 600 to 400 B.C. In any case, the community at Hallstatt was substantially larger than those at agricultural settlements throughout Europe, and it was a specialized community, devoting its energies to mining and trading salt.

Some time after the initial investment had been made at Hallstatt to support miners beginning work in the salt mountain and after salt had been extracted for trade, the operation became profitable. Perhaps when this happened a permanent community was established at Hallstatt and began burying its dead there. It is possible that the Late Bronze Age miners at Hallstatt worked only seasonally and returned to their permanent homes for the greater part of the year. When the operation became profitable, persons from agricultural communities in southern Bavaria and Upper Austria who had previously been working seasonally at Hallstatt may have settled at the site permanently. This change took place sometime around 800 B.C. when the great cemetery was begun. As it became evident that the salt trade was a source of great wealth, more individuals were attracted from farms and hamlets to participate in the mining operation, and the community at Hallstatt grew. (This same attraction to profitable industrial work in a dynamic and expanding commercial environment from rural agricultural life is apparent on a much larger scale throughout the West during the Industrial Revolution [e.g., see Landes 1969; Hareven and Langenbach 1978], as well as in other contexts throughout world history and ethnography.) It was this development of commercially profitable industries and the attraction they had for persons in the agricultural communities that led to the formation of the first larger communities of the period whose economies were oriented largely around production for trade instead of subsistence farming.

In summary, the critical factor in the formation of the larger, commercially oriented community at Hallstatt was the development of large stores of disposable wealth during the Late Bronze Age. This wealth could have been used to support the early stages of salt mining at Hallstatt before profits could be realized. And only when many persons living in different communities throughout central Europe had in their possession excess wealth available for trade could such an industry as the salt extraction at Hallstatt have developed. In order for the miners and investors at Hallstatt to have gained wealth through their production and trade, enough persons outside had to have had the wealth to exchange for salt. This wealth is readily apparent in the graves at Hallstatt, which were, as a whole, substantially wealthier than those in other cemeteries in central Europe. This wealth, which came into the Hallstatt community in the form of bronze jewelry, weapons, vessels, amber, gold, and such exotic luxuries as ivory ornaments, was the surplus disposable wealth accumulated by members of many different communities throughout central Europe who were trading for salt. Salt was principally a condiment at the time, though it also had practical uses for the preservation of meats and the processing of leather.

The pattern of the formation of larger and commercially oriented communities such as Hallstatt is also apparent elsewhere in Europe during the Early Iron Age — for example, at Stična, Magdalenska gora,

and Vače in Slovenia (Wells 1981) — and slightly later in west-central Europe at the Heuneburg, Mont Lassois, the Hohenasperg, and at other less fully investigated sites (Wells 1980b). In every case, the larger communities formed in response to the possibilities of profitable production for export trade (Wells forthcoming). Communities grew as people were attracted by the wealth becoming available through trade. The key feature in each of these cases was the initial investment, of material wealth or of effort, in beginning the productive activity for commercial purposes. Sizeable quantities of surplus wealth became available for such use for the first time in the Late Bronze Age, and at Hallstatt the first ramifications of this process of commercial development and town formation are apparent. Similar processes were at work between 150 and 50 B.C. when the oppida developed, the largest communities of pre-Roman central Europe (Alexander 1972; Břeň 1976; Nash 1976; Collis 1976, 1979).

THE EVIDENCE FROM HASCHERKELLER

The results of the excavations at Hascherkeller provide a detailed view into the economic and social contexts in which all of these changes took place. As comparison with other settlements of the period suggests, Hascherkeller was a typical community of the Late Bronze and Early Iron Ages. The floral and faunal evidence shows it to have had a rich and varied subsistence base; hence, the community would have had a good chance of weathering natural disasters such as severe storms, droughts, or plant and animal diseases with a minimum of hardship. The community was largely self-sufficient for its needs. It produced all of its own food and perhaps was able to export some in exchange for desired materials from outside. Most of the material culture of the community depended upon locally available resources such as wood, clay, bone, wool, and iron. Since copper and tin do not occur anywhere in the vicinity of Hascherkeller, bronze metal had to be brought in from outside, but the members of the community were able to fashion their own bronze jewelry, as the mold demonstrates. Since bronze was recycled regularly as the scrap hoards and scrap bronze fragments on this and other settlements suggest, the amount of the metal that had to be imported was probably very little. It is unclear whether or not bronze was used for tools at Hascherkeller, though it is likely on the basis of evidence elsewhere that bronze sickles were used for harvesting grain.

Import trade at Hascherkeller was principally in luxury goods. Bronze was used for jewelry, including the finger rings cast in the mold, the pins, and the small ring. Glass beads were luxury goods, and may have had apotropaic significance as well (see Pauli 1975). Graphite used to decorate pottery was also a luxury. The fact that bronze, glass beads, and graphite are well represented at Hascherkeller, as they are at other excavated settlements, implies that the community was producing a surplus for trade. Bronze is much less abundant at settlements of the Early and Middle Bronze Ages than at those of the Late Bronze Age; glass beads were very rare before this time but became common in the Late Bronze Age; and graphite first became widely used in central Europe during the latter part of the Late Bronze Age after 1000 B.C. This evidence all suggests that in the Late Bronze Age communities were producing regular surpluses for trade that were not being produced during the preceding periods. Some trade is apparent in all periods, but in the Late Bronze Age it was much more regular and of larger scale than previously. Production of surpluses for trade (foodstuffs, woolen textiles, and leather) by the farming communities throughout central Europe had the effect of stimulating commerce in general; at the same time, the general growth of commerce and the associated greater availability of desirable goods such as bronze,

glass beads, and graphite stimulated communities to produce greater surpluses. One process cannot be said to have caused the other; the two were mutually reinforcing. Unless specifically stimulated to do so, agricultural communities tend not to produce surpluses (Sahlins 1972, pp. 137–138); but when desirable goods are available through trade, communities are apt to produce the necessary surpluses for exchange for the desired goods.

The community at Hascherkeller lived in the latter part of the Late Bronze Age and beginning of the Early Iron Age when commerce throughout central Europe was growing rapidly and farming communities were being stimulated, by the growing availability of desirable luxury goods, to produce greater surpluses of tradable products. The archaeological evidence from the settlement shows the richness and diversity of the subsistence economy, the active, largely self-sufficient production of material goods, and the trade economy dependent upon the community's production of exchangeable surpluses. Such farming communities and the surpluses they generated formed the basis of the intensification of production and trade that led to the development of the first commercial towns north of the Alps.

References Cited

Acsádi, G. and J. Nemeskéri
    1970 *History of Human Life Span and Mortality*. Akadémiai Kiadó, Budapest.

Aitken, M. J.
    1974 *Physics and Archaeology*. 2nd ed. Clarendon, Oxford.

Alexander, J.
    1972 "The Beginnings of Urban Life in Europe," in P. J. Ucko, R. Tringham, G. W. Dimbleby (eds.), *Man, Settlement and Urbanism*, pp. 843–850. Duckworth, London.

Anati, E.
    1961 *Camonica Valley*. Knopf, New York.

Arnold, B.
    1981 "Strukturanalyse der spätbronzezeitlichen Seeufersiedlung Auvernier-Nord," *Archäologisches Korrespondenzblatt*, vol. 11, pp. 37–50. Mainz.

Bakker, J. A., R. W. Brandt, B. van Geel, M. J. Jansma, W. J. Kuijper, P. J. A. van Mensch, J. P. Pals, and G. F. Ijzereef
    1977 "Hoogkarspel-Watertoren: Towards a Reconstruction of Ecology and Archaeology of an Agrarian Settlement of 1000 B.C.," in B. L. van Beels, R. W. Brandt, and W. Groenman-van Waatringe (eds.), *Ex Horreo IPP 1951–1976*, pp. 187–225. University of Amsterdam.

Bankoff, A. and F. Winter
    1979 "A House-Burning in Serbia," *Archaeology*, vol. 32, no. 5, pp. 8–12. New York.

Barth, F. E.
    1973 "Versuch einer typologischen Gliederung der prähistorischen Funde aus dem Hallstätter Salzberg," *Mitteilungen der Anthropologischen Gesellschaft in Wien*, vol. 102, pp. 26–30. Vienna.

Barth, F. E., H. Felber, and O. Schauberger
    1975 "Radiokohlenstoffdatierung der prähistorischen Baue in den Salzbergwerken Hallstatt und Dürrnberg-Hallein," *Mitteilungen der Anthropologischen Gesellschaft in Wien*, vol. 105, pp. 45–52. Vienna.

Becker, H.
    1978 "Archäomagnetismus und magnetische Datierung," in B. Hrouda (ed.), *Methoden der Archäologie*, pp. 139–150. Beck, Munich.

    1979 "Magnetische Prospektion im allgemeinen und im Bereich der hallstattzeitlichen Siedlung Landshut-Hascherkeller im besonderem," in H. Becker, R. Christlein, P. S. Wells, "Die hallstattzeitliche Siedlung von Landshut-Hascherkeller, Niederbayern," *Archäologisches Korrespondenzblatt*, vol. 9, pp. 291–297. Mainz.

Beer, J., V. Giertz, M. Möll, H. Oeschger, T. Riesen, and C. Strahm
    1979 "The Contribution of the Swiss Lake-Dwellings to the Calibration of Radiocarbon Dates," in R. Berger and H. E. Suess (eds.), *Radiocarbon Dating*, pp. 566–584. University of California Press, Berkeley and Los Angeles.

Bender, H., R. Dehn, and I. Stork
    1976 "Neuere Untersuchungen auf dem Münsterberg in Breisach (1966-1975): 1: Die vorrömische Zeit," *Archäologisches Korrespondenzblatt*, vol. 6, pp. 213–224. Mainz.

Bersu, G.
    1940 "Excavations at Little Woodbury, Wiltshire," *Proceedings of the Prehistoric Society*, vol. 6, pp. 30–111. London.

    1946 "A Hill-fort in Switzerland," *Antiquity*, vol. 20, pp. 4–8. Cambridge.

Bersu, G. and P. Goessler
    1924 "Der Lochenstein bei Balingen," *Fundberichte aus Schwaben*, n.s., vol. 2, pp. 73–103. Stuttgart.

Bittel, K. and A. Rieth
1951   *Die Heuneburg an der oberen Donau: Ein frühkeltischer Fürstensitz.* Kohlhammer, Stuttgart.

Bloch, M.
1961   *Feudal Society.* Translation by L. A. Manyon. University of Chicago Press.

Bocquet, A.
1979   "Lake-Bottom Archaeology," *Scientific American,* vol. 240, no. 2, pp. 56–64. New York.

Bocquet, A. and J.-P. Couren
1974   "Le four de potier de Sévrier, Haute-Savoie (Age du Bronze Final)," *Etudes Préhistoriques,* vol. 9, pp. 1–6. Lyon.

Böhner, K.
1958   *Die fränkischen Altertümer des Trierer Landes.* Mann, Berlin.

Bökönyi, S.
1974   *History of Domestic Mammals in Central and Eastern Europe.* Akadémiai Kiadó, Budapest.

Bohnsack, D.
1976   "Bernstein und Bernsteinhandel," in J. Hoops (ed.), *Reallexikon der Germanischen Altertumskunde,* 2nd ed., vol. 2, pp. 290–292. Walter de Gruyter, Berlin.

Bonnamour, L.
1976   "Siedlungen der Spätbronzezeit (Bronze Final III) im Saône-Tal südlich von Chalon-sur-Saône," *Archäologisches Korrespondenzblatt,* vol. 6, pp. 123–130. Mainz.

Bonnet, C.
1973   "Une station d'altitude de l'époque des champs d'Urnes au sommet du Hohlandsberg," *Bulletin de la Société Préhistorique Française,* vol. 70, pp. 455–478. Paris.

1974   "Un nouvel aperçu sur la station d'altitude de Hohlandsberg, Wintzenheim (Haut-Rhin)," *Cahiers alsaciens d'archéologie, d'art et d'histoire,* vol. 18, pp. 33–50. Strasbourg.

Bouzek, J.
1978   "Zu den Anfängen der Eisenzeit in Mitteleuropa," *Zeitschrift für Archäologie,* vol. 12, pp. 9–14. East Berlin.

Bouzek, J. and D. Koutecký
1964   "Knovízské zásobní jámy [Knovízer Vorratsgruben]," *Archeologické Rozhledy,* vol. 16, pp. 28–43. Prague.

Bouzek, J., D. Koutecký, and E. Neustupný
1966   *The Knovíz Settlement of North-West Bohemia.* National Museum, Prague.

Bowen, H. C. and D. Wood
1967   "The Experimental Storage of Corn Underground and Its Implications for Iron Age Settlements," *Institute of Archaeology Bulletin,* vol. 7, pp. 1–14. London.

Bradley, R. and M. Fulford
1980   "Sherd Size and the Analysis of Occupation Debris," *Institute of Archaeology Bulletin,* vol. 17, pp. 85–94. London.

Bradley, R., S. Lobb, J. Richards, and M. Robinson
1980   "Two Late Bronze Age Settlements on the Kennet Gravels: Excavations at Aldermaston Wharf and Knight's Farm, Burghfield, Berkshire," *Proceedings of the Prehistoric Society,* vol. 46, pp. 217–295. London.

Břeň, J.
1976   "Earliest Settlements with Urban Character in Central Europe," in B. Cunliffe and T. Rowley (eds.), *Oppida: The Beginnings of Urbanisation in Barbarian Europe,* pp. 81–94. British Archaeological Reports, Supplementary Series, vol. 11. Oxford.

von Brunn, W. A.
1958   "Der Schatz von Frankleben und die mitteldeutschen Sichelfunde," *Praehistorische Zeitschrift,* vol. 36, pp. 1–70. Berlin.

1968   *Mitteldeutsche Hortfunde der jüngeren Bronzezeit.* Walter de Gruyter, Berlin.

Bulleid, A.
1924   *The Lake Villages of Somerset.* Folk Press, London.

Butler, J. J.
1976   "An Iron Find of the Middle Bronze Age," *Summaries, Ninth Congress UISPP,* p. 431. Nice.

Christlein, R.
1973   "Besitzabstufungen zur Merowingerzeit im Spiegel reicher Grabfunde aus West- und Südwestdeutschland," *Jahrbuch des Römisch-Germanischen Zentralmuseums Mainz,* vol. 20, pp. 147–180. Mainz.

1974   "Ausgrabungen und Funde in Niederbayern," *Verhandlungen des Historischen Vereins für Niederbayern,* vol. 100, pp. 53–107. Landshut.

1975 "Ausgrabungen und Funde in Niederbayern," *Verhandlungen des Historischen Vereins für Niederbayern,* vol. 101, pp. 5–96. Landshut.

1976 "Ausgrabungen und Funde in Niederbayern," *Verhandlungen des Historischen Vereins für Niederbayern,* vol. 102, pp. 5–104. Landshut.

1979 "Die Untersuchung im Ostteil des Siedlungsgeländes," in H. Becker, R. Christlein, P. S. Wells, "Die hallstattzeitliche Siedlung von Landshut-Hascherkeller, Niederbayern," *Archäologisches Korrespondenzblatt,*vol. 9, pp. 289–291. Mainz.

1981a "Neues aus Altheim, Gemeinde Essenbach, Landkreis Landshut, Niederbayern," in R. Christlein (ed.), *Das archäologische Jahr in Bayern,*pp. 64–65. Theiss, Stuttgart.

1981b "Ein Friedhof der kupferzeitlichen Glockenbecherkultur von Altdorf, Landkreis Landshut, Niederbayern," in R. Christlein (ed.), *Das archäologische Jahr in Bayern,* pp. 66–67. Theiss, Stuttgart.

Christlein, R. and B. Engelhardt
1981 "Keramik vom Ende der frühen Bronzezeit aus Siedlungen bei Altdorf, Landkreis Landshut, Niederbayern," in R. Christlein (ed.), *Das archäologische Jahr in Bayern,* pp. 70–71. Theiss, Stuttgart.

Christlein, R. and S. Stork
1980 "Der hallstattzeitliche Tempelbezirk von Aiterhofen, Landkreis Straubing-Bogen, Niederbayern," *Jahresbericht der Bayerischen Bodendenkmalpflege,*vol. 21, pp. 43–55. Munich.

Clark, R. M.
1975 "A Calibration Curve for Radiocarbon Dates," *Antiquity,* vol. 49, pp. 251–266. Cambridge.

Clarke, D. L.
1976 "The Beaker Network — Social and Economic Models," in J. N. Lanting and J. D. van der Waals (eds.), *Glockenbecher Symposium,* pp. 459–477. Fibula-Van Dishoeck, Bussum.

Coles, J. M.
1979 *Experimental Archaeology.* Academic Press, London.

Coles, J. M. and A. Harding
1979 *The Bronze Age in Europe.* St. Martin's Press, New York.

Collis, J.
1976 "Town and Market in Iron Age Europe," in B. Cunliffe and T. Rowley (eds.), *Oppida: The Beginnings of Urbanisation in Barbarian Europe,*pp. 3–23. British Archaeological Reports, Supplementary Series, vol. 11. Oxford.

1979 "Urban Structure in the Pre-Roman Iron Age," in B. C. Burnham and J. Kingsley (eds.), *Space, Hierarchy and Society,* pp. 129–136. British Archaeological Reports, International Series, vol. 59, Oxford.

Courtain, J., J. Guilaine, and J.-P. Mohen
1976 "Les débuts de l'agriculture en France: les documents archéologiques," in J. Guilaine (ed.), *La Préhistoire Française,* vol. 2, pp. 172–179. CNRS, Paris.

Cunliffe, B. and T. Rowley (eds.)
1976 *Oppida: The Beginnings of Urbanisation in Barbarian Europe.* British Archaeological Reports, Supplementary Series, vol. 11. Oxford.

Dannheimer, H.
1973 *Keramik des Mittelalters aus Bayern.* Prähistorische Staatssammlung, Munich.

1976 "Siedlungsgeschichtliche Beobachtungen im Osten der Münchener Schotterebene," *Bayerische Vorgeschichtsblätter,* vol. 41, pp. 107–120. Munich.

David, N.
1972 "On the Life Span of Pottery, Type Frequencies, and Archaeological Inference," *American Antiquity,* vol. 37, pp. 141–142. Washington.

David, N. and H. David-Hennig
1971a "Zur Herstellung und Lebensdauer von Keramik: Untersuchungen zu den sozialen, kulturellen und ökonomischen Strukturen am Beispiel der Ful aus der Sicht der Prähistoriker," *Bayerische Vorgeschichtblätter,*vol. 36, pp. 289–317. Munich.

David, N. and H. Hennig
1971b "The Ethnography of Pottery: A Fulani Case Seen in Archaeological Perspective," *McCaleb Module in Anthropology,* vol. 21, pp. 1–29. Reading, Mass.

Dehn, R.
1967 "Eine Siedlungsgrube der Urnenfelderkultur bei Efringen-Kirchen, Ldkrs. Lörrach," *Badische Fundberichte,* vol. 23, pp. 47–71. Freiburg.

1972 *Die Urnenfelderkultur in Nord-württemberg.* Müller and Gräff, Stuttgart.

Dennell, R. W.
1976 "The Economic Importance of Plant Resources Represented on Archaeological Sites," *Journal of Archaeological Science,* vol. 3, no. 3, pp. 229–247. London.

Dickinson, R. E.
1953 *Germany: A General and Regional Geography.* Dutton, New York.

Dimbleby, G.
1978 *Plants and Archaeology.* 2nd ed. John Baker, London.

Donat, P. and H. Ullrich
1976 "Bevölkerungszahlen: Archäologie," in J. Hoops (ed.), *Reallexikon der Germanischen Altertumskunde,* 2nd ed., vol. 2, pp. 349–353. Walter de Gruyter, Berlin.

Drack, W.
1980 "Gold," in E. Lessing (ed.), *Hallstatt: Bilder aus der Frühzeit Europas,* pp. 64–71. Jugend und Volk, Vienna.

Drescher, H.
1958 *Der Überfangguss.* Römisch-Germanisches Zentralmuseum, Mainz.
1980 "Zur Technik der Hallstattzeit," *Die Hallstattkultur,* pp. 54–66. Oberösterreichischer Landesverlag, Linz.

Drexler, H.
n.d. "Landeskundliche Betrachtungen über das Kartengebiet," in T. Bosch, G. Spitzlberger, and K. Weber (eds.), *Führer zur Umgebungskarte Landshut,* pp. 33–40. Verkehrsverein, Landshut.

von den Driesch, A.
1976 *A Guide to the Measurement of Animal Bones from Archaeological Sites.* Bulletin 1. Peabody Museum, Harvard University, Cambridge, Mass.

Eggert, M. K. H.
1976 *Die Urnenfelderkultur in Rheinhessen.* Steiner, Wiesbaden.

Egloff, M.
1981 "Versunkene Dörfer der Urnenfelderzeit im Neuenburgersee: Forschungen der Luftbildarchäologie," *Archäologisches Korrespondenzblatt,*vol. 11, pp. 55–63. Mainz.

Eibner, A.
1974 "Zum Befund einer hallstattzeitlichen Webgrube aus Stillfried," *Veröffentlichungen der Österreichischen Arbeitsgemeinschaft für Ur- und Frühgeschichte,*vol. 6, pp. 76–84. Vienna.

Eibner, C.
1974 *Das spaturnenfelderzeitliche Gräberfeld von St. Andrä v. d. Hgt. P. B. Tulln, NÖ.* Archaeologia Austriaca, Supplement, vol. 12, Vienna.

Eibner, C., L. Plank, and R. Pittioni
1966 "Die Urnengräber vom Lebenberg bei Kitzbühel, Tirol," *Archaeologia Austriaca,* vol. 40, pp. 215–248. Vienna.

Ellison, A. and P. Drewett
1971 "Pits and Post-Holes in the British Early Iron Age: Some Alternative Explanations," *Proceedings of the Prehistoric Society,* vol. 37, pt. 1, pp. 183–194. London.

Engelhardt, B.
1980 "Ergebnisse der archäologischen Ausgrabungen 1976–1980 im Zuge der Altmühl-Mündungsstrecke des Main-Donau-Kanals," *Baubericht 1980 der Rhein-Main-Donau AG,* pp. 3–11. Munich.
1981 "Zwei neue Fundstellen des Jungneolithikums von Teugn, Landkreis Kelheim und Altdorf, Landkreis Landshut, Niederbayern," in R. Christlein (ed.), *Das archäologische Jahr in Bayern,* pp. 62–63. Theiss, Stuttgart.

Eogan, G.
1981 "The Gold Vessels of the Bronze Age in Ireland and Beyond," *Proceedings of the Royal Irish Academy,* vol. 81, C, no. 14, pp. 345–382. Dublin.

van Es, W. A.
1973 "Roman-period Settlement on the 'Free Germanic' Sandy Soil of Drenthe, Overijssel, and Gelderland," *Berichten van de Rijksdienst voor het Oudheidkundig Bodemonderzoek,* vol. 23, pp. 273–280. Amersdorf.

Evans, J. D.
1973 "Sherd Weights and Sherd Counts: A Contribution to the Problem of Quantifying Pottery Studies," in D. Strong (ed.), *Archaeological Theory and Practice,* pp. 131–149. Seminar Press, London.

Fagg, W. and J. Picton
1978 *The Potter's Art in Africa.* 2nd ed. British Museum, London.

Fél, E. and T. Hofer
1972   *Bäuerliche Denkweise in Wirtschaft und Haushalt.* Schwarz, Göttingen.

Foster, G. M.
1960   "Life-Expectancy of Utilitarian Pottery in Tzintzuntan, Michoacan, Mexico," *American Antiquity,* vol. 25, pp. 606–609. Washington.

Frei, H.
1965–1966   "Der frühe Eisenerzbergbau im nördlichen Alpenvorland," *Jahresbericht der Bayerischen Bodendenkmalpflege,* vols. 6/7, pp. 67–137. Munich.

Frey, O.-H.
1976   "Bemerkungen zur figürlichen Darstellungen des Osthallstattkreises," *Festschrift Richard Pittioni,* Archaeologica Austriaca, supplement 13, vol. 1, pp. 578–587. Vienna.

Gersbach, E.
1951   "Ein Beitrag zur Untergliederung der jüngeren Urnenfelderzeit (Hallstatt B) im Raume der südwestdeutsch-schweizerischen Gruppe," *Jahrbuch der Schweizerischen Gesellschaft für Urgeschichte,* vol. 41, pp. 175–191. Zurich.

1961   "Siedlungserzeugnisse der Urnenfelderkultur aus dem Limburger Becken und ihre Bedeutung für die Untergliederung der jüngeren Urnenfelderzeit in Südwestdeutschland," *Fundberichte aus Hessen,* vol. 1, pp. 45–62. Bonn.

1982   "Die urnenfelderzeitliche Höhensiedlung auf dem Kestenberg ob Mörigen, Kanton Aargau/Schweiz," *Archäologisches Korrespondenzblatt,* vol. 12, pp. 179–186. Mainz.

Glob, P. V.
1951   *Ard og plov in Nordens oldtid.* Universitetsforlaget, Aarhus.

Goldmann, K.
1981   "Guss in verlorener Sandform — das Hauptverfahren alteuropäischer Bronzegiesser?" *Archäologisches Korrespondenzblatt,* vol. 11, pp. 109–116. Mainz.

Gradmann, R.
1964   *Süddeutschland,* vol. 2. H. Gentner, Bad Homburg vor der Höhe.

Grant, A.
1975   "The Use of Tooth Wear as a Guide to the Age of Domestic Animals," in B. Cunliffe (ed.), *Excavations at Portchester Castle I: Roman,* pp. 437–450. Society of Antiquaries, London.

Grierson, P.
1959   "Commerce in the Dark Ages," *Transactions of the Royal Historical Society,* ser. 5, vol. 9, pp. 123–140. London.

Grössler, H.
1907   "Das Fürstengrab im grossen Galgenhügel am Paulusschachte bei Helmsdorf (im Mansfelder Seekreise)," *Jahresschrift für die Vorgeschichte der sächsisch-thüringischen Länder,* vol. 6, pp. 1–87. Halle.

Haevernick, T. E.
1974   "Zu gen Glasperlen in Slowenien," *Situla,* vols. 14–15, pp. 61–65. Ljubljana.

1978   "Urnenfelderzeitliche Glasperlen," *Zeitschrift für Schweizerische Archäologie und Kunstgeschichte,* vol. 35, pp. 145–157. Basel.

Haffner, A.
1971   "Kriegergräber mit Schleuderkugeln aus Luxemburg und dem Trierer Land," *Hémecht,* vol. 23, pp. 206–214. Luxembourg.

1973   "Zur Schleuderwaffe im vorrömischen Gallien," *Kurtrierisches Jahrbuch,* vol. 13, pp. 170–176. Trier.

Hald, M.
1950   *Olddanske Tekstiler.* Nordisk Forlag, Copenhagen.

Halstead, P., I. Hodder, and G. Jones
1978   "Behavioral Archaeology and Refuse Patterns: A Case Study," *Norwegian Archaeological Review,* vol. 11, pp. 118–131. Oslo.

Harding, A. F.
1980   "Radiocarbon Calibration and the Chronology of the European Bronze Age," *Archeologické Rozhledy,* vol. 32, pp. 178–186. Prague.

Hareven, T. K. and R. Langenbach
1978   *Amoskeag: Life and Work in an American Factory-City.* Pantheon, New York.

Harrison, R. J.
1980   *The Beaker Folk.* Thames and Hudson, London.

Hartley, D.
1979   *Lost Country Life.* Pantheon, New York.

Hatt, J.-J. and H. Zumstein
1960   "Découverte d'un four de potier de l'âge

de bronze final à Cronenbourg," *Cahiers alsaciens d'archéologie, d'art et d'histoire*, vol. 4, pp. 17–26. Strasbourg.

Helbaek, H.
1955 "The Botany of the Vallhagar Iron Age Field," in M. Stenberger (ed.), *Vallhagar: A Migration Period Settlement on Gotland/Sweden*, pp. 653–699. Ejnar Munksgaards Forlag, Copenhagen.
1970 "The Plant Husbandry of Hacilar," in J. M. Mellaart (ed.), *Excavations at Hacilar*, pp. 189–244. Edinburgh University Press, Edinburgh.

Hell, M.
1971 "St. Veit im Pongau als Siedlungsraum der Urnenfelderzeit," *Archaeologia Austriaca*, vol. 49, pp. 36–47. Vienna.

Hencken, H.
1971 *The Earliest European Helmets*. American School of Prehistoric Research, Bulletin 28. Peabody Museum, Harvard University, Cambridge, Mass.

Hennig, H.
1970 *Die Grab- und Hortfunde der Urnenfelderkultur aus Ober- und Mittelfranken*. Lassleben, Kallmünz.

Hensel, W.
1970 "Remarques sur les origines des villes en Europe centrale," *Atti del convegno di studi sulla città etrusca e italica preromana*, vol. 1, pp. 323–328. Istituto per la Storia di Bologna, Bologna.

Herrmann, F.-R.
1966 *Die Funde der Urnenfelderkultur in Mittel- und Südhessen*. Walter de Gruyter, Berlin.
1974–1975 "Die urnenfelderzeitliche Siedlung von Künzing," *Jahresbericht der Bayerischen Bodendenkmalpflege*, vols. 15–16, pp. 58–106. Munich.

Herrmann, J.
1969 "Burgen und befestigte Siedlungen der jüngeren Bronze- und frühen Eisenzeit in Mitteleuropa," in K.-H. Otto and J. Herrmann (eds.), *Siedlung, Burg und Stadt*, pp. 56–94. Akademie-Verlag, East Berlin.

Hinton, D. A.
1977 "'Rudely Made Earthen Vessels' of the Twelfth to Fifteenth Centuries A.D.," in D. P. S. Peacock (ed.), *Pottery and Early Commerce: Characterization and Trade in Roman and Later Ceramics*, pp. 221–238. Academic Press, London.

Hodges, H. W. M.
1963 "The Examination of Ceramic Materials in Thin Section," in E. Pyddoke (ed.), *The Scientist and Archaeology*, pp. 101–110. Roy Publishers, New York.

Hodges, R.
1982 *Dark Age Economics: The Origins of Towns and Trade A.D. 600–1000*. Duckworth, London.

Homans, G. C.
1942 *English Villagers of the Thirteenth Century*. Harvard University Press, Cambridge, Mass.

Hopf, M.
1955 "Formveränderung von Getreidekörnern beim Verkohlen," *Bericht der Deutschen Botanischen Gesellschaft*, vol. 68, pp. 191–193. Stuttgart.

Horst, F.
1978 "Zum Stand der Erforschung des jungbronzezeitlichen Siedlungswesens auf dem Gebiet der DDR," in W. Coblenz and F. Horst (eds.), *Mitteleuropäische Bronzezeit*, pp. 231–238. Akademie-Verlag, East Berlin.

Hundt, H.-J.
1955 "Der Bogenberg bei Bogen (Niederbayern) in vor- und frühgeschichtlicher Zeit," *Bayerische Vorgeschichtsblätter*, vol. 21, pp. 31–46. Munich.
1958 *Katalog Straubing I*. Lassleben, Kallmünz.
1964 *Katalog Straubing II*. Lassleben, Kallmünz.
1970 "Gewebefunde aus Hallstatt: Webkunst und Tracht der Hallstattzeit," in *Krieger und Salzherren: Hallstattkultur im Ostalpenraum*, pp. 53–71. Römisch-Germanisches Zentralmuseum, Mainz.
1974 "Donauländische Einflüsse in der frühen Bronzezeit Norditaliens," *Preistoria Alpina*, vol. 10, pp. 143–178. Trento.
1978 "Die Rohstoffquellen des europäischen Nordens und ihr Einfluss auf die Entwicklung des nordischen Stils," *Bonner Jahrbücher*, vol. 178, pp. 125–162. Bonn.

Ihmig, M.
1971 "Ein bandkeramischer Graben mit Einbau bei Langweiler, Kr. Jülich, und die zeitiche Stellung bandkeramischer Gräben im westlichen Verbreitungsge-

biet," *Archäologisches Korrespondenz-blatt,*vol. 1, pp. 23–30. Mainz.

Jaanusson, H.
1971 "Bronsålderboplatsen vid Hallunda," *Fornvännen,* vol. 66, pp. 173–185. Stockholm.

1981 *Hallunda: A Study of Pottery from a Late Bronze Age Settlement in Central Sweden.* Statens Historiska Museum, Stockholm.

Jacobi, G.
1974 *Werkzeug und Gerät aus dem Oppidum von Manching.* Steiner, Wiesbaden.

Janke, H.
1971 "Eine Siedlungsstelle der Urnenfelderzeit bei Dornholzhausen, Kreis Wetzlar," *Fundberichte aus Hessen,* vol. 11, pp. 12–31. Bonn.

Jankuhn, H.
1969 *Vor- und Frühgeschichte vom Neolithikum bis zur Völkerwanderungszeit.* Ulmer, Stuttgart.

Janssen, W.
1976 "Some Major Aspects of Frankish and Medieval Settlement in the Rhineland," in P. H. Sawyer (ed.), *Medieval Settlement,*pp. 41–60. Edward Arnold, London.

Jehl, M. and C. Bonnet
1968 "Un potier de l'époque champs d'urnes au sommet du Hohlandsberg," *Cahiers alsaciens d'archéologie, d'art et d'histoire,* vol. 12, pp. 5–30. Strasbourg.

1971 "La station d'altitude de Linsenbrunnen-Wintzenheim-Hohlandsberg," *Cahiers alsaciens d'archéologie, d'art et d'histoire,* vol. 15, pp. 23–48. Strasbourg.

Joachim, H.-E.
1980 "Jüngerlatènezeitliche Siedlungen bei Eschweiler, Kr. Aachen," *Bonner Jahrbücher,* vol. 180, pp. 355–441. Bonn.

Jockenhövel, A.
1973 "Urnenfelderzeitliche Barren als Grabbeigaben," *Archäologisches Korrespondenzblatt,* vol. 3, pp. 23–28. Mainz.

1975 "Zu befestigten Siedlungen der Urnenfelderzeit aus Süddeutschland," *Fundberichte aus Hessen,* vol. 14, pp. 19–62. Bonn.

Joffroy, R.
1976 "Les civilisations de l'Age du Fer en Bourgogne," in J. Guilaine (ed.), *La*

Préhistoire Française, vol. 2, pp. 816–825. CNRS, Paris.

Jones, M. U. and D. Bond
1980 "Later Bronze Age Settlement at Mucking, Essex," in J. Barrett and R. Bradley (eds.), *Settlement and Society in the British Later Bronze Age,* pp. 471–482. British Archaeological Reports, British Series, vol. 83 (i), Oxford.

Kappel, I.
1969 *Die Graphittonkeramik von Manching.* Steiner, Wiesbaden.

Kastelic, J
1965 *Situla Art.* McGraw-Hill, New York.

Kimmig, W.
1940 *Die Urnenfelderkultur in Baden.* Walter de Gruyter, Berlin.

1964 "Seevölkerbewegung und Urnenfelderkultur," in R. von Uslar and K. J. Narr (eds.), *Studien aus Alteuropa,* vol. 1, pp. 220–283. Böhlau, Cologne.

1975 "Early Celts on the Upper Danube: Excavations at the Heuneburg," in R. Bruce-Mitford (ed.), *Recent Archaeological Excavations in Europe,* pp. 32–64. Routledge and Kegan Paul, London.

1979 "Buchau," in J. Hoops (ed.), *Reallexikon der Germanischen Altertumskunde,*2nd ed., vol. 4, pp. 37–55. Walter de Gruyter, Berlin.

Kleemann, O.
1954 "Eine neue Verbreitungskarte der Spangenbarren," *Archaeologia Austriaca,* vol. 14, pp. 68–77. Vienna.

Knörzer, K.-H.
1971 "Eisenzeitliche Pflanzenreste im Rheinland," *Bonner Jahrbücher,* vol. 171, pp. 40–58. Bonn.

1978 "Entwicklung und Ausbreitung des Leindotters *(Camelina sativa* sl.)," *Bericht der Deutschen Botanischen Gesellschaft,* vol. 91, pp. 187–195. Stuttgart.

Köhler, A. and F. Morton
1954 "Mineralogische   Untersuchung prähistorischer Keramik aus Hallstatt im Zusammenhang mit der Frage nach ihrer Herkunft," *Germania,* vol. 32, pp. 66–72. Berlin.

Körber-Grohne, U.
1981 "Pflanzliche Abdrücke in eisenzeitlicher Keramik — Spiegelbild damaliger Nutzpflanzen?" *Fundberichte aus Bad-*

en-Württemberg, vol. 6, pp. 165–211. Stuttgart.

Kollmann, H.
n.d.   "Zur Geologie der weiteren Umgebung von Landshut," in T. Bosch, G. Spitzlberger, K. Weber (eds.), *Führer zur Umgebungskarte Landshut,* pp. 41–43. Verkehrsverein, Landshut.

Kooi, P.B.
1979   *Pre-Roman Urnfields in the North of the Netherlands.*Wolters-Nordhoff, Groningen.

Kossack, G.
1959   *Südbayern während der Hallstattzeit.* Walter de Gruyter, Berlin.

1964   "Trinkgeschirr als Kultgerät der Hallstattzeit," in P. Grimm (ed.), *Varia Archaeologica,* pp. 96–105. Deutsche Akademie der Wissenschaft, East Berlin.

1970   *Gräberfelder der Hallstattzeit an Main und Fränkischer Saale.* Lassleben, Kallmünz.

Kostelníková, M.
1980   "Nové poznatky o přeslenech a Mikulčic" [Neue Erkenntnisse über Spinnwirtel aus Mikulčice], *Archeologické Rozhledy,* vol. 32, pp. 78–82. Prague.

Kromer, K.
1958   "Gedanken über den sozialen Aufbau der Bevölkerung auf dem Salzberg bei Hallstatt, Oberösterreich," *Archaeologia Austriaca,* vol. 24, pp. 39–58. Vienna.

1959   *Das Gräberfeld von Hallstatt.* Sansoni, Florence.

Kruyff, L. and P. J. R. Modderman
1979   "Urnenfelderzeitliche Siedlungsspuren am Weinberg, Gde. Hienheim, Ldkr. Kelheim," *Bayerische Vorgschichtsblätter,* vol. 44, pp. 1–11. Munich.

La Baume, W.
1955   *Die Entwicklung des Textilhandwerks in Alteuropa.* Rudolf Habelt, Bonn.

Lamberg-Karlovsky, C. C. and J. A. Sabloff
1979   *Ancient Civilizations: The Near East and Mesoamerica.* Cummings, Menlo Park, Calif.

Landes, D. S.
1969   *The Unbound Prometheus: Technological Change and Industrial Development in Western Europe from 1750 to the Present.* Cambridge University Press, Cambridge.

Lanting, J. N.
1976   "Zwei C14-datierte Funde von spätbronzezeitlicher Keramik mit Kerbschnittverzierung," *Helinium,* vol. 16, pp. 55–61. Wetteren.

Laur-Belart, R.
1955   "Kestenberg III 1953," *Ur-Schweiz,* vol. 19, no. 1, pp. 1–28. Basel.

Lüdi, W.
1955   "Beiträge zur Kenntnis der Vegetationsverhältnisse im schweizerischen Alpenvorland während der Bronzezeit," in W. U. Guyan (ed.), *Das Pfahlbauproblem,* pp. 89–109. Birkhäuser, Basel.

Lüning, J.
1972   "Zur quantitativen Untersuchung neolithischer Scherben," *Praehistorische Zeitschrift,* vol. 47, pp. 213–222. Berlin.

Maggetti, M.
1979   "Mineralogisch-petrographische Untersuchung des Scherbenmaterials der urnenfelderzeitlichen Siedlung Elchinger Kreuz, Ldkr. Neu-Ulm," in E. Pressmar, *Elchinger Kreuz, Ldkr. Neu-Ulm: Siedlungsgrabung mit urnenfelderzeitlichem Töpferofen,* pp. 141–168. Lassleben, Kallmünz.

Maier, R. A.
1979   "Tönerne Schleudergeschosse vom Kastell Pförring an der Oberen Donau," *Germania,* vol. 57, pp. 166–168. Berlin.

Matson, F.
1941   "Porosity Studies of Ancient Pottery," *Michigan Academy of Science, Arts, and Letters, Papers,* vol. 26, pp. 469–477. Ann Arbor.

McEvedy, C. and R. Jones
1978   *Atlas of World Population History.* Penguin, Harmondsworth.

Mefford, J.
1981   "The Textile Fragment," in P. S. Wells, *The Emergence of an Iron Age Economy: The Mecklenburg Grave Groups from Hallstatt and Stična,* American School of Prehistoric Research, Bulletin 33, pp. 39–43. Peabody Museum, Harvard University, Cambridge, Mass.

Menke, M.
1977   "Zur Struktur und Chronologie der spätkeltischen und frührömischen Siedlungen im Reichenhaller Becken," in B. Chropovský (ed.), *Symposium: Ausklang der Latène-Zivilisation und Anfänge der*

germanischen Besiedlung im mittleren Donaugebiet, pp. 223–238. Slovakian Academy of Sciences, Bratislava.

von Merhart, G.
1952 "Studien über einige Gattungen von Bronzegefässen," *Festschrift der Römisch-Germanischen Zentralmuseums Mainz,* vol. 2, pp. 1–71. Mainz.

1954 "Panzer-Studie," *Origines: Raccolta di Scritti in Honore di Mons. Giovanni Baserga,* pp. 33–61. Como.

Milisauskas, S.
1978 *European Prehistory.* Academic Press, New York.

Modderman, P. J. R.
1976 "Abschwemmung und neolithische Siedlungsplätze in Niederbayern," *Archäologische Korrespondenzblatt,* vol. 6, pp. 105–108. Mainz.

Moosleitner, F.
1977 "Hallstattzeitliche Grabfunde aus Uttendorf im Pinzgau (Österreich)," *Archäologisches Korrespondenzblatt,* vol. 7, pp. 115–119. Mainz.

Motyková, K.
1973 "Sídliště lidu popelnicových polí u Sobčic" [Die Siedlung der Urnenfelderkultur von Sobčice], *Památky Archeologické,* vol. 64, pp. 235–271. Prague.

von Müller, A.
1964 *Die jungbronzezeitliche Siedlung von Berlin-Lichterfelde.* Hessling, Berlin.

Müller, H. H.
1959 "Bemalter Wandverputz aus einer Siedlungsgrube der späten Bronzezeit von Rottelsdorf," *Ausgrabungen und Funde,* vol. 4, pp. 15–18. East Berlin.

Müller-Karpe, H.
1948 *Die Urnenfelderkultur im Hanauer Land.* Elwert-Gräfe and Unzer, Marburg.

1952a *Das Urnenfeld von Kelheim.* Lassleben, Kallmünz.

1952b "Das Kriegergrab von Villach," *Festschrift Rudolf Egger,* vol. 1, pp. 104–113. Geschichtsverein für Kärnten, Klagenfurt.

1955 "Das urnenfelderzeitliche Wagengrab von Hart a.d. Alz, Oberbayern," *Bayerische Vorgeschichtsblätter,* vol. 21, pp. 46–75. Munich.

1957 *Münchener Urnenfelder.* Lassleben, Kallmünz.

1959a *Beiträge zur Chronologie der Urnenfelderkultur nördlich und südlich der Alpen.* Walter de Gruyter, Berlin.

1959b *Funde von Bayerischen Höhensiedlungen.* Prähistorische Staatssammlung, Munich.

1962 "Zur spätbronzezeitlichen Bewaffnung in Mitteleuropa und Griechenland," *Germania,* vol. 40, pp. 255–286. Berlin.

1969 "Das urnenfelderzeitliche Toreutengrab von Steinkirchen, Niederbayern," *Germania,* vol. 47, pp. 86–91. Berlin.

1975 "Zur urnenfelderzeitlichen Besiedlung der Gegend von Steinkirchen, Niederbayern," *Ausgrabungen in Deutschland 1950–1975,* vol. 1, pp. 171–186. Römisch-Germanisches Zentralmuseum, Mainz.

Müller-Wille, M.
1977 "Bäuerliche Siedlungen der Bronze- und Eisenzeit in der Nordseegebieten," in H. Jankuhn, R. Schützeichel, F. Schwind (eds.), *Das Dorf der Eisenzeit und des frühen Mittelalters,* pp. 153–218. Vandenhoeck and Ruprecht, Göttingen.

Mutton, A. F. A.
1961 *Central Europe: A Regional and Human Geography.* Longman, London.

Nash, D.
1976 "The Growth of Urban Society in France," in B. Cunliffe and T. Rowley (eds.), *Oppida: The Beginnings of Urbanisation in Barbarian Europe,* pp. 95–113. British Archaeological Reports, Supplementary Series, vol. 4, Oxford.

Needham, S. and D. Longley
1980 "Runnymede Bridge, Egham: A Late Bronze Age Riverside Settlement," in J. Barrett and R. Bradley (eds.), *Settlement and Society in the British Later Bronze Age,* pp. 397–436. British Archaeological Reports, British Series, vol. 83 (i), Oxford.

Nenquin, J.
1961 *Salt: A Study in Economic Prehistory.* De Tempel, Brugge.

Neuninger, H. and R. Pittioni
1959 "Woher stammen die blauen Glasperlen der Urnenfelderkultur?" *Archaeologia Austriaca,* vol. 26, pp. 52–66. Vienna.

1961 "Nachtrag zu den blauen Glasperlen der Urnenfelderkultur," *Archaeologia Austriaca,* vol. 30, pp. 150–151. Vienna.

Neuninger, H., R. Pittioni, and E. Preuschen
1969   *Salzburgs Kupfererzlagerstätten und Bronzefunde aus dem Lande Salzburg: Ein weiterer Beitrag zur Frage der Relation Lagerstätte — Fertigobjekt.*Deuticke, Vienna.

Neustupný, J.
1969   "Urgeschichtliche Vorformen des Städtewesens," in K.-H. Otto and J. Herrmann (eds.), *Siedlung, Burg und Stadt,* pp. 26–41. Akademie-Verlag, East Berlin.

Orton, C. R.
1975   "Quantitative Pottery Studies: Some Progress, Problems and Prospects," *Science and Archaeology,* vol. 16, pp. 30–35. Stafford.

Otto, K.-H.
1955   *Die sozialökonomischen Verhältnisse bei den Stämmen der Leubinger Kultur in Mitteldeutschland.* Ethnographisch-Archäologische Forschungen, vol. 3, pt. 1, East Berlin.
1978   "Die historische Bedeutung der mittleren und jüngeren Bronzezeit," in W. Coblenz and F. Horst (eds.), *Mitteleuropäische Bronzezeit: Beiträge zur Archäologie und Geschichte,* pp. 57–69. Akademie-Verlag, East Berlin.

Pahič, S.
1972   *Pobrežje.* Narodni muzej, Ljubljana.

Papousek, D. A.
1981   *The Peasant-Potters of Los Pueblos.* Von Gorcum, Assen.

Paret, O.
1929   "Der Graphit im vorgeschichtlichen Europa," *Sudeta,* vol. 5, pp. 30–53. Reichenberg.

Pauli, L.
1975   *Keltische Volksglaube: Amulette und Sonderbestattungen am Dürrnberg bei Hallein und im eisenzeitlichen Mitteleuropa.* Beck, Munich.
1978   *Der Dürrnberg bei Hallein III.* Beck, Munich.
1980   *Die Alpen in Frühzeit und Mittelalter.* Beck, Munich.

Pauli, L. (ed.)
1980   *Die Kelten in Mitteleuropa.* Salzburger Landesregierung, Salzburg.

Payne, S.
1973   "Kill-Off Patterns in Sheep and Goats: The Mandibles from Asvan Kale," *Ana-tolian Studies,* vol. 23, pp. 281–303. London.

Percival, J.
1980   *Living in the Past.* British Broadcasting Corporation, London.

Peroni, R.
1979   "From Bronze Age to Iron Age: Economic, Historical, and Social Considerations," in D. and F. R. Ridgway (eds.), *Italy Before the Romans,* pp. 7–30. Academic Press, New York.

Pertlwieser, M.
1970   "Die hallstattzeitliche Höhensiedlung auf dem Waschenberg bei Bad Wimsbach/Neydharting, Politischer Bezirk Wels, Oberösterreich: Die Objekte," *Jahrbuch des Oberösterreichischen Musealvereins,*vol. 115, pp. 37–70. Linz.
1971   "Die hallstattzeitliche Höhensiedlung auf dem Waschenberg bei Bad Wimsbach/Neydharting, Politischer Bezirk Wels, Oberösterreich: Die Funde," *Jahrbuch des Oberösterreichischen Musealvereins,*vol. 116, pp. 51–80. Linz.

Pétrequin, P., J.-P. Urlacher, and D. Vuaillat
1969   "Habitat et sépultures de l'age du bronze final a Dampierre-sur-le Doubs (Doubs)," *Gallia Préhistoire,* vol. 12, pp. 1–35. Paris.

Piggott, S.
1959   "A Late Bronze Age Wine Trade?" *Antiquity,* vol. 33, pp. 122–123. Cambridge.
1977   "A Glance at Cornish Tin," in V. Markotic (ed.), *Ancient Europe and the Mediterranean,* pp. 141–145. Aris and Phillips, Warminster.

Pirling, R.
1980   *Die mittlere Bronzezeit auf der Schwäbischen Alb.* Beck, Munich.

Pittioni, R.
1951   "Prehistoric Copper-mining in Austria," *Institute of Archaeology Annual Report,* no. 7, pp. 16–43. London.
1952   "Das Brandgrab vom Lebenberg bei Kitzbühel, Tirol," *Archaeologia Austriaca,* vol. 10, pp. 53–60. Vienna.
1976   "Bergbau: Kupfererz," in J. Hoops (ed.), *Reallexikon der Germanischen Altertumskunde,* 2nd ed., vol. 2, pp. 251–256. Walter de Gruyter, Berlin.

Pleiner, R.
1964   "Die Eisenverhüttung in der 'Germania

Magna' zur römischen Kaiserzeit," *Berichte der Römisch-Germanischen Kommission*, vol. 45, pp. 11–86. Berlin.

1968   "Schmiedetechnik der Hallstattzeit im Lichte der Untersuchung des Hortfundes von Schlöben," *Archeologické Rozhledy*, vol. 20, pp. 33–42. Prague.

1977   "Neue Grabungen frühgeschichtlicher Eisenhüttenplätze in der Tschechoslowakei und die Bedeutung des Schachtofens für die Entwicklung des Schmelzvorganges," in A. Ohrenberger and K. Kaus (eds.), *Archäologische Eisenforschung in Europa*, pp. 107–117. Burgenländisches Landesmuseum, Eisenstadt.

1980   "Early Iron Metallurgy in Europe," in T. A. Wertime and J. D. Muhly (eds.), *The Coming of the Age of Iron*, pp. 375–415. Yale University Press, New Haven.

1981   "Die Wege des Eisens nach Europa," in R. Pleiner (ed.), *Frühes Eisen in Europa*, pp. 115–128. Peter Meili, Schaffenhausen.

Pleiner, R. (ed.)
1981   *Frühes Eisen in Europa*. Peter Meili, Schaffhausen.

Pressmar, E.
1979   *Elchinger Kreuz, Ldkr. Neu-Ulm: Siedlungsgrabung mit urnenfelderzeitlichem Töpferofen*. Lassleben, Kallmünz.

Primas, M.
1977a   "Beobachtungen zu den spätbronzezeitlichen Siedlungs- und Depotfunden der Schweiz," in K. Stüber and A. Zürcher (eds.), *Festschrift Walter Drack*, pp. 44–55. Gut and Co., Stäfa (Zurich).

1977b   "Zur Informationsausbreitung im südlichen Mitteleuropa," *Jahresschrift des Instituts für Vorgeschichte der Universität Frankfurt am Main*, 1977, pp. 164–184. Frankfurt.

1981   "Erntemesser der jüngeren und späten Bronzezeit," in H. Lorenz (ed.), *Studien zur Bronzezeit*, pp. 363–374. Philipp von Zabern, Mainz.

Primas, M. and U. Ruoff
1981   "Die urnenfelderzeitliche Inselsiedlung 'Grosser Hafner' im Zürichsee (Schweiz)," *Germania*, vol. 59, pp. 31–50. Berlin.

Ralph, E. K., H. N. Michael, and M. C. Han
1973   "Radiocarbon Dates and Reality," *MASCA Newsletter*, vol. 9, no. 1, pp. 1–20. Philadelphia.

Redman, C. L.
1978   *The Rise of Civilization*. Freeman, San Francisco.

Reinecke, P.
1930   "Die Bedeutung der Kupferbergwerke der Ostalpen für die Bronzezeit Mitteleuropas," in *Schumacher-Festschrift*, pp. 107–115. Wilckens, Mainz.

1934   "Der Bronzedepotfund von Hallstatt in Oberösterreich," *Wiener Prähistorische Zeitschrift*, vol. 21, pp. 1–11. Vienna.

Reinerth, H.
1928   *Die Wasserburg Buchau*. Filser, Augsburg.

1936   *Das Federseemoor*. Kabitzsch, Leipzig.

Reitinger, J.
1968   *Die ur- und frühgeschichtlichen Funde in Oberösterreich*. Oberösterreichischer Landesverlag, Linz.

Renfrew, C.
1973   *Before Civilization: The Radiocarbon Revolution and Prehistoric Europe*. Jonathan Cape, London.

1978   "Varna and the Social Context of Early Metallurgy," *Antiquity*, vol. 52, pp. 199–203. Cambridge.

Renfrew, J.
1973   *Palaeoethnobotany*. Columbia University Press, New York.

Reynolds, P. J.
1974   "Experimental Iron Age Storage Pits," *Proceedings of the Prehistoric Society*, vol. 40, pp. 118–131. London.

1979a   "A General Report of Underground Grain Storage Experiments at the Butser Ancient Farm Research Project," in M. Gast and F. Sigaut (eds.), *Les techniques de conservation des graines à long terme, leur role dans la dynamique des systemes de cultures et des sociétés*, pp. 70–80. CNRS, Paris.

1979b   *Iron-Age Farm: The Butser Experiment*. British Museum, London.

1980   *Butser Ancient Farm: Impressions*. Archaeological Research, Petersfield, Hampshire.

Riek, G.
1962   *Der Hohmichele*. Walter de Gruyter, Berlin.

Rieth, A.
1942   *Die Eisentechnik der Hallstattzeit*. Barth, Leipzig.

Říhovský, J.
1972 "Dosavadní výsledky výzkumu velatikého sídliště v Lovčičkách na Slavkovsku" [Die bisherigen Ergebnisse der Ausgrabungen in der Velativer Siedlung von Lovčičky in Slavkov], *Archeologické Rozhledy*, vol. 24, pp. 173–181. Prague.

Rochna, O.
1962 "Ein Gräberfeld der jüngeren Urnenfelderkultur (Hallstatt B) von Manching, Ldkr. Ingolstadt," *Bayerische Vorgeschichtsblätter*, vol. 27, pp. 61–81. Munich.

1965 "Ein Gräberfeld der jüngeren Urnenfelderzeit (HaB) von Altessing, Ldkr. Kelheim," *Bayerische Vorgeschichtsblätter*, vol. 30, pp. 105–134. Munich.

Rowlands, M. J.
1972 "The Archaeological Interpretation of Prehistoric Metalworking," *World Archaeology*, vol. 3, pp. 210–223. London.

Rutte, E.
1981 *Bayerns Erdgeschichte*. Ehrenwirth, Munich.

Rychner, V.
1979 *L'age du bronze final a Auvernier*. Bibliothèque historique vaudoise, Lausanne.

Sahlins, M.
1972 *Stone Age Economics*. Tavistock, London.

Šaldová, V.
1981 "Rovinná sídliště pozdní doby bronzové v západních Čechách" [Die Flachlandsiedlungen der Spätbronzezeit in Westböhmen], *Památky Archeologické*, vol. 72, pp. 93–152. Prague.

Schauer, P.
1971 *Die Schwerter in Süddeutschland, Österreich und der Schweiz*. Beck, Munich.

Schiffer, M.
1976 *Behavioral Archaeology*. Academic Press, New York.

Schlichtherle, H.
1977 "Abdrücke in Hüttenlehm aus Michelsberger Gruben bei Ammerbuch-Reusten, Kreis Tübingen," *Fundberichte aus Baden-Württemberg*, vol. 3, pp. 107–114. Stuttgart.

Schröter, P.
1975 "Zur Besiedlung des Goldberges im Nördlinger Ries," *Ausgrabungen in Deutschland 1950–1975*, vol. 1, pp. 98–114. Römisch-Germanisches Zentralmuseum, Mainz.

Schwabedissen, H.
1978 "Konventionelle oder kalibrierte C14-Daten?" *Archäologische Informationen*, vol. 4, pp. 110–117. Cologne.

Schwellnus, W. and J. Hermanns
1979 "Eine spätbronzezeitliche Siedlung im Tagebau Zukunft-West," *Ausgrabungen im Rheinland '78*, pp. 49–51. Rheinland-Verlag, Bonn.

Scollar, I.
1975 "Wissenschaftliche Methoden bei der Prospektion archäologischer Fundstätten," *Ausgrabungen in Deutschland 1950–1975*, vol. 3, pp. 158–165. Römisch-Germanisches Zentralmuseum, Mainz.

Shepard, A. O.
1956 *Ceramics for the Archaeologist*. Carnegie Institution, Washington D. C.

Snodgrass, A.
1975 "Mycenae, Northern Europe and Radiocarbon Dates," *Archaeologia Atlantica*, vol. 1, pt. 1, pp. 33–48. Hamburg.

Solheim, W. G.
1960 "The Use of Sherd Weights and Counts in the Handling of Archaeological Data," *Current Anthropology*, vol. 1, pp. 325–329. Chicago.

Speck, J.
1955 "Die Ausgrabungen in der spätbronzezeitlichen Ufersiedlung Zug-'Sumpf'," in W. U. Guyan (ed.), *Das Pfahlbauproblem*, pp. 275–334. Birkhäuser, Basel.

Starè, F.
1975 *Dobova*. Posavski muzej, Brežice.

Stary, P. F.
1980 "Das spätbronzezeitliche Häuptlingsgrab von Hagenau, Kr. Regensburg," in K. Spindler (ed.), *Vorzeit zwischen Main und Donau*, pp. 46–97. Universitätsbund Erlangen-Nürnberg, Erlangen.

Steensberg, A.
1936 "North West European Plough-Types of Prehistoric Times and the Middle Ages," *Acta Archaeologica*, vol. 7, pp. 244–280. Copenhagen.

1943 *Ancient Harvesting Implements*. Nordiske Forlag, Copenhagen.

Stein, F.
1968   "Beobachtungen zu Tracht- und Bestattungssitten der frühbronzezeitlichen Bevölkerung von Gemeinlebarn," _Berichte der Römisch-Germanischen Kommission_, vol. 49, pp. 1–40. Berlin.

Stuart, W. F.
1972   "Earth's Field Magnetometry," _Reports on Progress in Physics_, vol. 35, pp. 803–881. London.

Suess, H. E.
1979   "A Calibration Table for Conventional Radiocarbon Dates," in R. Berger and H. E. Suess (eds.), _Radiocarbon Dating_, pp. 777–784. University of California Press, Berkeley and Los Angeles.

Torbrügge, W.
1970–1971 "Vor- und frühgeschichtliche Flussfunde," _Berichte der Römisch-Germanischen Kommission_, vol. 51–52, pp. 1–145. Berlin.

Tylecote, R.
1980   "Furnaces, Crucibles, and Slags," in T. A. Wertime and J. D. Muhly (eds.), _The Coming of the Age of Iron_, pp. 183–228. Yale University Press, New Haven.

Uerpmann, H.-P.
1977   "Betrachtungen zur Wirtschaftsformen neolithischer Gruppen in Südwestdeutschland," _Fundberichte aus Baden-Württemberg_, vol. 3, pp. 144–161. Stuttgart.

Unz, C.
1973   "Die spätbronzezeitliche Keramik in Südwestdeutschland, in der Schweiz und in Ostfrankreich," _Praehistorische Zeitschrift_, vol. 48, pp. 1–124. Berlin.

Vermeersch, P. M. and R. Walter
1978   "Die Palisadengräben des Michelsberger Fundplatzes in Thieusies (Belgien)," _Archäologisches Korrespondenzblatt_, vol. 8, pp. 169–176. Mainz.

Vince, A. G.
1977   "Some Aspects of Pottery Quantification," _Medieval Ceramics_, vol. 1, pp. 63–74. Sheffield.

Vogt, E.
1949–1950 "Der Beginn der Hallstattzeit in der Schweiz," _Jahrbuch der Schweizerischen Gesellschaft für Urgeschichte_, vol. 40, pp. 209–231. Zurich.

Wagner, F.
1949–1950 "Zwei Urnengrabfelder bei Regensburg," _Praehistorische Zeitschrift_, vols. 34/35, pp. 195–202. Berlin.

Waterbolk, H. T.
1964   "The Bronze Age Settlement of Elp," _Helinium_, vol. 4, pp. 97–131. Wetteren.

Wells, P. S.
1978   "Twenty-Six Graves from Hallstatt Excavated by the Duchess of Mecklenburg," _Germania_, vol. 56, pp. 66–88. Berlin.

1979   "The Early Iron Age Settlement of Hascherkeller in Bavaria: Preliminary Report on the 1979 Excavations," _Journal of Field Archaeology_, vol. 6, pp. 17–28. Boston.

1980a   "The Early Iron Age Settlement of Hascherkeller in Bavaria: Preliminary Report on the 1979 Excavations," _Journal of Field Archaeology_, vol. 7, pp. 313–328. Boston.

1980b   _Culture Contact and Culture Change: Early Iron Age Central Europe and the Mediterranean World_. Cambridge University Press, Cambridge.

1981   _The Emergence of an Iron Age Economy: The Mecklenburg Grave Groups from Hallstatt and Stična_. American School of Prehistoric Research, Bulletin 33, Peabody Museum, Harvard University, Cambridge, Mass.

1982   "C14-Bestimmungen von der Siedlung Landshut-Hascherkeller in Niederbayern," _Archäologisches Korrespondenzblatt_, vol. 12, pp. 357–362. Mainz.

forthcoming   _From Villages to Cities: Economic and Social Change in Late Prehistoric Europe_. Cornell University Press, Ithaca.

Wells, P. S., B. Benefit, C. C. Quillian, and J. D. Stubbs, Jr.
1981   "Excavations at Hascherkeller in Bavaria: Field Research into the Economy of a Late Bronze/Early Iron Age Village," _Journal of Field Archaeology_, vol. 8, pp. 289–302. Boston.

Werner, J.
1961   "Bemerkungen zu norischen Trachtzubehör und zu Fernhandelsbeziehungen der Spätlatènezeit im Salzburger Land," _Mitteilungen der Gesellschaft für Salzburger Landeskunde_, vol. 101, pp. 143–160. Salzburg.

1970   "Zur Verbreitung frühgeschichtlicher Metallarbeiten (Werkstatt — Wander-

handwerk — Handel — Familienverbin-
dung)," *Early Medieval Studies*, vol. 1,
pp. 65–81. Stockholm.

Wheeler, R. E. M.
1943   *Maiden Castle, Dorset.* Oxford University Press, Oxford.

White, L.
1962   *Medieval Technology and Social Change.*
Oxford University Press, Oxford.

Willerding, U.
1966   "Urgeschichtliche Siedlungsreste in
Rosdorf," *Neue Ausgrabungen und Forschungen in Niedersachsen*, vol. 3, pp.
49–62. Hildesheim.

Wyss, R.
1967a *Bronzezeitliche Gusstechnik.* Paul Haupt,
Bern.
1967b *Bronzezeitliches Metallhandwerk.* Paul

Haupt, Bern.
1971a "Technik, Wirtschaft und Handel," in
W. Drack (ed.), *Ur- und frühgeschichtliche
Archäologie der Schweiz, II: Die Bron-
zezeit*, pp. 123–144. Schweizerische
Gesellschaft für Ur- und Frühgeschichte,
Basel.
1971b "Siedlungswesen und Verkehrswege," in
W. Drack (ed.), *Ur- und frühgeschichtliche
Archäologie der Schweiz, II: Die Bron-
zezeit*, pp. 103–122. Schweizerische
Gesellschaft für Ur- und Frühgeschichte,
Basel.

Zippelius, A.
1974–1975 "Zur Rekonstruktion der urnenfelderzeitlichen Holzbauten von
Künzing," *Jahresbericht der Bayerischen
Bodendenkmalpflege*, vols. 15–16, pp.
71–76. Munich.

Concordance for Figures

Since many of the figures in this bulletin have been published previously, this concordance lists the journals in which they originally appeared. *JFA* is the *Journal of Field Archaeology* (Boston), and *AK* is the *Archäologisches Korrespondenzblatt* (Mainz).

Figure 3. *JFA* vol. 6, 1979, p. 18, fig. 2.
Figure 4. *JFA* vol. 6, 1979, p. 20, fig. 4.
Figure 12. *JFA* vol. 6, 1979, p. 23, fig. 7.
Figure 13. *JFA* vol. 6, 1979, p. 23, fig. 8.
Figure 15. *JFA* vol. 7, 1980, p. 317, fig. 6.
Figure 16. *JFA* vol. 7, 1980, p. 318, fig. 7.
Figure 25c. *JFA* vol. 8, 1981, p. 291, fig. 4.
Figure 36f. *AK* vol. 12, 1982, p. 359, fig. 2,9.
Figure 37c. *AK* vol. 12, 1982, p. 359, fig. 2,6.
Figure 38c. *AK* vol. 12, 1982, p. 359, fig. 2,9.
Figure 38m. *AK* vol. 12, 1982, p. 359, fig. 2,10.
Figure 39a. *AK* vol. 12, 1982, p. 359, fig. 2,8.
Figure 39d. *JFA* vol. 8, 1981, p. 292, fig. 5a.
Figure 39f, g. *JFA* vol. 8, 1981, p. 292, figs. 5d, e.
Figure 41a. *JFA* vol. 6, 1979, p. 26, fig. 10,4.
Figure 41b. *JFA* vol. 6, 1979, fig. 10,6.
Figure 41c. *JFA* vol. 6, 1979, p. 25, fig. 9,4.
Figure 41d. *JFA* vol. 6, 1979, p. 25, fig. 9,6.
Figure 42a. *JFA* vol. 6, 1979, p. 25, fig. 9,1.
Figure 42c. *JFA* vol. 6, 1979, p. 25, fig. 9,3.
Figure 42d. *JFA* vol. 7, 1980, p. 319, fig. 10,5.
Figure 43f. *JFA* vol. 6, 1979, p. 25, fig. 9,8.
Figure 43g. *JFA* vol. 6, 1979, p. 25, fig. 9,10.
Figure 43h. *JFA* vol. 6, 1979, p. 26, fig. 10,7.
Figure 44d. *JFA* vol. 6, 1979, p. 26, fig. 10,2.
Figure 44f. *JFA* vol. 6, 1979, p. 25, fig. 9,9.
Figure 44g. *JFA* vol. 6, 1979, p. 25, fig. 9,7.
Figure 44i. *JFA* vol. 6, 1979, p. 26, fig. 10,8.
Figure 46. *JFA* vol. 7, 1980, p. 318, fig. 8.
Figure 47. *JFA* vol. 7, 1980, p. 318, fig. 9.
Figure 48a. *JFA* vol. 7, 1980, p. 323, fig. 17,8.
Figure 48d. *JFA* vol. 7, 1980, p. 323, fig. 17,2.
Figure 48e. *JFA* vol. 7, 1980, p. 322, fig. 16,7.

Figure 48f. *JFA* vol. 7, 1980, p. 322, fig. 16,2.
Figure 49b. *JFA* vol. 7, 1980, p. 322, fig. 16,8.
Figure 49d. *JFA* vol. 7, 1980, p. 322, fig. 16,5.
Figure 49f. *JFA* vol. 7, 1980, p. 322, fig. 16,3.
Figure 49h. *JFA* vol. 7, 1980, p. 322, fig. 16,1.
Figure 49j. *JFA* vol. 7, 1980, p. 319, fig. 10,4.
Figure 49k. *JFA* vol. 7, 1980, p. 319, fig. 10,1.
Figure 51. *JFA* vol. 7, 1980, p. 321, fig. 13.
Figure 52. *JFA* vol. 7, 1980, p. 321, fig. 14.
Figure 54a. *JFA* vol. 7, 1980, p. 323, fig. 17,1.
Figure 54h. *JFA* vol. 7, 1980, p. 323, fig. 17,6.
Figure 54i. *JFA* vol. 7, 1980, p. 323, fig. 17,4.
Figure 55b. *JFA* vol. 7, 1980, p. 321, fig. 15,6.
Figure 55f. *JFA* vol. 7, 1980, p. 323, fig. 17,3.
Figure 55g. *JFA* vol. 7, 1980, p. 319, fig. 10,6.
Figure 55i. *JFA* vol. 7, 1980, p. 319, fig. 10,7.
Figure 55k. *JFA* vol. 7, 1980, p. 320, fig. 11.
Figure 56a. *JFA* vol. 8, 1981, p. 292, fig. 5c.
Figure 56f. *JFA* vol. 7, 1980, p. 319, fig. 10,2.
Figure 56j. *JFA* vol. 7, 1980, p. 321, fig. 15,5.
Figure 56l. *AK* vol. 12, 1982, p. 359, fig. 2,1.
Figure 56o. *JFA* vol. 7, 1980, p. 322, fig. 16,6.
Figure 57b. *JFA* vol. 7, 1980, p. 321, fig. 15,1.
Figure 56e. *JFA* vol. 7, 1980, p. 321, fig. 15,4.
Figure 56g. *JFA* vol. 7, 1980, p. 321, fig. 15,3.
Figure 60a. *JFA* vol. 7, 1980, p. 319, fig. 10,8.
Figure 60b. *JFA* vol. 7, 1980, p. 319, fig. 10,3.
Figure 60e. *JFA* vol. 6, 1979, p. 26, fig. 10,1.
Figure 60f. *JFA* vol. 7, 1980, p. 323, fig. 17,5.
Figure 60g. *JFA* vol. 7, 1980, p. 321, fig. 15,2.
Figure 61a. *JFA* vol. 6, 1979, p. 26, fig. 10,3.
Figure 61b. *JFA* vol. 6, 1979, p. 26, fig. 10,5.
Figure 66. *JFA* vol. 7, 1980, p. 320, fig. 12.
Figure 71. *AK* vol. 12, 1982, p. 360, fig. 3.
Figure 72. *AK* vol. 9, 1979, p. 290, fig. 4.
Figure 73. *JFA* vol. 8, 1981, p. 295, fig. 7.
Figure 76. *JFA* vol. 8, 1981, p. 295, fig. 8.
Figure 77. *JFA* vol. 8, 1981, p. 297, fig. 9.
Figure 81. *JFA* vol. 8, 1981, p. 300, fig. 11.
Figure 82. *JFA* vol. 8, 1981, p. 300, fig. 12.